SPIRITUAL SURVIVAL
—IN THE—
LAST DAYS

BLAINE AND BRENTON
YORGASON

Deseret Book Company
Salt Lake City, Utah

Library of Congress Cataloging-in-Publication Data

Yorgason, Blaine M., 1942–
    Spiritual survival in the last days / by Blaine M. Yorgason and Brenton G. Yorgason.
        p.   cm.
    Includes index.
    ISBN 0-87579-409-2 (hard)
    1. Eschatology.   2. Bible—Prophecies—Eschatology.   3. Prophets (Mormon theology)   4. Church of Jesus Christ of Latter-day Saints—Doctrines.   5. Mormon Church—Doctrines.   6. Survivalism.
    7. United States—Forecasting.   I. Yorgason, Brenton G.   II. Title.
    BX8643.E83Y67   1990
    236'.9—dc20   90-44379
                                                                        CIP

Printed in the United States of America

10   9   8   7   6   5   4   3

Contents

Contents

Part 3:
Belonging to the Family of Jesus Christ

Preface

As we have researched the prophetic material that now comprises this book, we have discovered that as far as the future of the land of America is concerned, a great deal of confusion exists. To help alleviate that confusion, let us state that prophecies concerning America, both scriptural and modern, seem to deal with at least three separate entities. Our own definitions of these entities are:

1. The *land* of America.
2. The *nation* of the United States of America.
3. The *government* of the United States of America.

As we see it, the land of America deals with the scriptural land of promise, which apparently includes all of North and South America, where the righteous are promised at least spiritual peace and freedom as long as they serve the God of the Land, who is Jesus Christ.

The nation of the United States of America deals with the Constitution of the United States, which President Benson refers to as an inspired, heavenly banner. Prophetically, this Constitution, or the principles of freedom it embodies, will be seriously jeopardized in our day, and, if preserved at all, will be preserved by faithful Latter-day Saints.

According to prophetic statements, the government of the United States of America, which comprises all the branches of U.S. government and their political (mostly self-serving) appendages, has become basically corrupted, and at some point in the future will be absolutely destroyed or overthrown. This, of course, is in harmony with the Lord's promise to bring to a full end, before his coming, all nations. (See D&C 87:6.)

If we can keep in mind these three divisions, what follows will be easier to understand.

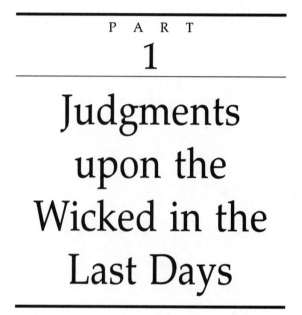

PART

1

Judgments upon the Wicked in the Last Days

1

The Wrath and Indignation of God

During the fall of 1989, while most of the world watched in amazement and perhaps horror, the lives of thousands of citizens of the United States were affected and even ended by a series of startlingly severe disasters. First, Hurricane Hugo slammed into the southeastern coast of the United States, the seas heaving themselves beyond their bounds as many drowned, thousands of others were rendered homeless, and millions of dollars in property was lost. Scarcely had the country stopped reeling when the San Francisco area of California was jolted by an earthquake that grew increasingly "major" as reports continued filtering in. Again there were numerous deaths, again thousands were left homeless, and again millions of dollars in destroyed property was chalked up to a natural disaster. Only days later, an oil refinery in Texas exploded, killing several and causing great property damage. Shortly thereafter another major earthquake was reported, this time near Japan. And while these things were going on, there were also wars and counter-wars being waged in Central and South America, the Middle East, China, and the Eastern Bloc countries of Europe.

As we conversed about these great calamities and speculated upon their possible meanings as "signs of the times," we decided to conduct an unofficial survey of what was happening throughout the world. For the next thirty days, we counted articles on just the front page of our local daily newspaper, listing only those that dealt with war, disaster, local crime, and crime on the national or international scene.

Perhaps not surprisingly, not a day went by without at least one front-page article about war. Further, at the end of the thirty days, we calculated that there had been fifty-seven articles dealing with war in one form or another, in one place or another. In the same thirty days, twenty-five articles dealt with disasters, both natural and manmade; seventeen articles dealt with local crime; and eleven articles dealt with crime outside of Utah, either nationally or internationally. (*Deseret News,* November 1–30, 1989.)

Again we pondered these things, and our discussions grew into a determination to understand better, through the scriptures and through the words of our latter-day prophets, why such calamities were happening around us, what additional calamities we could expect in the near future, and what we could do to alleviate the effects of these disasters upon us as individuals.

What we found was both intriguing and sobering. But surprisingly, we came away from our study with a great deal of hope and even a certain amount of confidence. Mostly, however, we felt — and still feel — deep gratitude, for God our Father has not left us to make our way through this troubled time alone.

Turmoil in the Last Days

As we should be aware, we are living during the time period referred to scripturally as the last days. Significantly, in the Doctrine and Covenants, the Lord often refers to them as "these" last days. So far as we can learn, that means the last days of wickedness before the ushering in of the millennium and the earth's renewal to its paradisiacal state. Further, these last days comprise the dispensation of the fulness of times. These are the days when the Lord will hasten his work in its time (D&C 88:73; Isaiah 60:22), when the weak of the earth will be prepared for the Lord's errand (D&C 133:57–58), and when he shall perform his strange act and do his strange work (D&C 101:95; Isaiah 28:21). Finally, these are the days when all the signs of Christ's second coming will be made manifest. It is to a certain few of these signs that we now turn.

To his apostles prior to his crucifixion, Christ declared that before his second coming "nation shall rise against nation, and kingdom against kingdom: and there shall be famines, and pestilences, and earthquakes, in divers places. All these things are the beginning of sorrows." (Matthew 24:7–8.) We wonder why such events are to occur. The answers that come from the prophets confirm that the Lord allows such calamities because of the wickedness of the people. Paul describes these people of the last days as "lovers of their own selves, covetous, boasters, proud, blasphemers, disobedient to parents, unthankful, unholy, without natural affection, truce-breakers, false accusers, incontinent, fierce, despisers of those that are good, traitors, heady, high-minded, lovers of pleasure more than lovers of God; Having a form of Godliness, but denying the power thereof: from such turn away." (2 Timothy 3:2–4.) Nephi adds: "But, behold, in the last days, or in the days of the Gentiles — yea, behold all the nations of the Gentiles and also the Jews, both those who shall come upon this

5

land and those who shall be upon other lands, yea, even upon all the lands of the earth, behold, they will be drunken with iniquity and all manner of abominations — and when that day shall come they shall be visited of the Lord of Hosts, with thunder and with earthquake, and with a great noise, and with storm, and with tempest, and with the flame of devouring fire." (2 Nephi 27:1–2.)

To Joseph Smith the Lord declared, further clarifying what we should expect in these last days: "Before this great day shall come the sun shall be darkened, and the moon shall be turned into blood, and the stars shall fall from heaven, and there shall be greater signs in heaven above and in the earth beneath; and there shall be weeping and wailing among the hosts of men; and there shall be a great hailstorm sent forth to destroy the crops of the earth. And it shall come to pass, because of the wickedness of the world, that I will take vengeance upon the wicked, for they will not repent; for the cup of mine indignation is full; for behold, my blood shall not cleanse them if they hear me not." (D&C 29:14–17.)

The Wrath and Indignation of God

The 25th verse of the 14th chapter of Ether is a commentary by Moroni on the final destruction of the Jaredite nation: "And thus we see that the Lord did visit them in the fulness of his wrath, and their wickedness and abominations had prepared a way for their everlasting destruction."

As we ponder this verse, two phrases strike us with great force. They are: "In the fulness of his wrath" and "their wickedness and abominations had prepared a way for their . . . destruction."

God's Wrath Is Not Uncontrolled Emotional Response

The word *wrath,* which is frequently used in connection with and is occasionally a synonym for *indignation,* does not refer to God's temper. Nor does it refer to his anger, at least as we define the uncontrolled emotion we sometimes see in ourselves and others. God is a God of law and order – all kingdoms are ruled by law, and there is no space in which there is no kingdom. (See D&C 88:37; Blaine and Brenton Yorgason, *Binding the Lord* [Orem UT: Keepsake BookCards, 1989], pp. 10–12.) Therefore, law exists in all things and in all places. For God to remain God, he must abide by every law in existence in all of his kingdoms, and he must do so completely and totally. With such perfect exactness of purpose and will, there is obviously no room left for uncontrolled temper or anger. (See D&C 88:34–50.) God's wrath and indignation, therefore, must refer to perfectly controlled responses, by God, to particular sins of his children. Stated more plainly, wrath and indignation refer to God's judgments, his just punishments upon the wicked for the deeds they have chosen to commit.

God's Wrath and Indignation Usually Accomplished through War

Throughout history we see an interesting pattern wherein wickedness is slowed down or terminated altogether through warfare – which at times seems to be the tool that God allows his wicked children to use to inflict his wrath. For example, we read concerning Nephi's brothers: "I have feared lest for the hardness of your hearts the Lord your God should come out in the fulness of his wrath upon you, that ye be cut off and destroyed forever. Or, that a cursing should come upon you for the space of many generations; and ye are visited by sword and by famine, and are hated, and are led according to the will and captivity of the devil." (2 Nephi 1:17–18.)

The behavioral pattern the Lord dislikes is hardness of heart (refusing to repent), the consequences of which might be to be cut off and destroyed forever or to be visited by sword and famine (invasion, warfare, and subsequent food shortages, we would probably call it) and being led according to the will of the devil for many generations. As we now know, both occurred in Nephite history.

Concerning the posterity of his brothers, Nephi stated that God's wrath would be upon their seed (1 Nephi 13:11) because they had dwindled in unbelief, being full of idleness and all manner of abominations (1 Nephi 12:20–23), thus allowing the Gentiles to scatter and smite them (1 Nephi 13:14). Again, the negative behavior pattern was idleness and all manner of abominations, while the wrath that God allowed to come upon them took the form of the onrushing Europeans destroying and pushing aside the native Americans.

God's wrath is also upon the great and abominable church, whose founder is the devil, and whose desires are gold, silver, silks, scarlets, fine-twined linen, precious clothing, and harlots—God's wrath allowing wars and rumors of wars among all the nations and kindreds of the earth, which wars and rumors of wars will signal the commencing of the work of the Father in the last days, in preparing the way for the fulfilling of his covenants which he has made with Israel. (See 1 Nephi 14:15–17.)

Finally, God's wrath was upon all who gathered to fight the Gentiles who had scattered and smitten the seed of Nephi's brethren. (1 Nephi 13:18.) Again, war was the method God allowed to be used, and consequently both Canada and the United States of America were born.

Not Enemies but Wickedness That Brings Wrath

Interestingly, it was neither the enemies of the Nephites nor the enemies of the Gentiles (Colonial Americans), nor will it be the enemies of the great and abominable church, that bring destruction upon them or her. Rather, as Moroni explained, it is the wickedness and abominations of the people themselves that prepare a way for their own destruction. (Ether 14:25.) Once they have fully ripened in iniquity, then war is allowed to come upon them as a consequence of their own behavior.

Fulness versus Incompleteness

If there is a fulness of God's wrath and indignation, then there must also be an "incompleteness" of it, or, in other words, lesser levels of perfectly controlled judgments by God (wrath and indignation) according to mankind's different levels of wickedness and abomination. That is why, before wrath and indignation are at a fulness, there is room for repentance and hope for us as individuals and as a society. Destruction has not been assured.

For example, Amulek says to the people of Ammonihah, "Ye are laying plans to pervert the ways of the righteous, and to bring down the wrath of God upon your heads, even to the utter destruction of this people." (Alma 10:18.) The people of Ammonihah hadn't done it yet, but they were indeed laying plans to commit enough wickedness to ensure their destruction, individually and as a people. However, Amulek was still holding out to them the opportunity to repent. Alma the younger says in verification of this, "And now, my brethren, seeing we know these things, and they are true, let us repent, and harden not our hearts, that we provoke not the Lord our God to pull down his wrath upon us . . . but let us enter into the rest of God, which is prepared according to his word." (Alma 12:37.)

Then and now, the Lord esteems all flesh as one; nevertheless he favors the righteous. If, as individuals or as a people, we are still striving to obtain the Spirit, still making sincere effort at repentance and a closer walk with God, then the fulness of God's wrath will not fall upon us. On the other hand, if we do not care about the things of God, if we rejoice

9

and glory in our own iniquity and reject every word of God as it is presented to us, then we have become ripened in iniquity. (See 1 Nephi 17:35–38.) In other words, God can give only so many chances and warnings to a specific person or people—as his cup of wrath fills and as the individual or group ripens toward rottenness—then he must abide by the eternal law of wrath and indignation, which judgment brings to pass ultimate destruction.

2

The Chastening Hand of God

The first two verses of the 95th section of the Doctrine and Covenants read: "Verily, thus saith the Lord unto you whom I love, and whom I love I also chasten that their sins may be forgiven, for with the chastisement I prepare a way for their deliverance in all things out of temptation, and I have loved you—wherefore, ye must needs be chastened and stand rebuked before my face." (D&C 95:1–2.)

A few pages later, we read: "I, the Lord, have suffered the affliction to come upon them [the Saints in Missouri], wherewith they have been afflicted, in consequence of their transgressions; yet I will own them, and they shall be mine in that day when I shall come to make up my jewels. Therefore, they must needs be chastened and tried, even as Abraham, who was commanded to offer up his only son. For all those who will not endure chastening, but deny me, cannot be sanctified." (D&C 101:2–5.)

Chastening—a New Word for the Same Troubles

In these last days, we are seeing the wrath of God upon the wicked in the form of wars, invasions, and natural disasters. The word *chastening* seems to describe more of the same sort of turmoil but with a new focus—deliverance.

The difference is obvious in the two scriptures we quoted above. Whereas wrath and indignation are directed against the wicked and ungodly and always result in destruction, both temporal and eternal, chastisement is directed toward the righteous, and has, as its purpose, their deliverance, either temporal or spiritual.

Chastisement to Be Appreciated

Where prophets warn mankind to fear wrath and indignation and to avoid the judgments of God at all costs, they tell the Saints to rejoice in chastisement and to grow from it. As Eliphaz counseled Job: "Behold, happy is the man whom God correcteth: therefore despise not thou the chastening of the Almighty." (Job 5:17.) The proverbs say: "My son, despise not the chastening of the Lord, neither be weary of his correction: for whom the Lord loveth he correcteth; even as a father the son in whom he delighteth." (Proverbs 3:11–12.) The Apostle Paul expands the thought further when he says: "My son, despise not thou the chastening of the Lord, nor faint when thou art rebuked of him. . . . If ye endure chastening, God dealeth with you as sons; for what son is he whom the father chasteneth not? Now no chastening for the present seemeth to be joyous, but grievous: nevertheless afterward it yieldeth the peaceable fruit of righteousness unto them which are exercised thereby." (Hebrews 12:5, 7, 11.) To John the Revelator the Lord said, "As many as I love, I rebuke and chasten: be zealous, therefore, and repent." (Revelation 3:19.) And the great King Benjamin declared: "The natural man is an enemy to God, and has been from the fall of Adam, and will be forever and ever, unless he yields to the enticings of the Holy Spirit, which putteth off the natural man and becometh a saint through the atonement of Christ the Lord, and becometh as a child, submissive, meek, humble, patient, full of love, willing to submit to all things which the Lord seeth fit to inflict upon him, even as a child doth submit to his father." (Mosiah 3:19.)

In other words, the entire point of chastening seems to be a bringing about of humility and repentance in the Lord's people—those who have made covenants, through baptism and other sacred ordinances, to obey and serve him by building up his kingdom.

Chastening Is the Result of Our Iniquity

It should not be supposed that God capriciously chastens the pure and innocent. He does not. In fact, other than Christ and little children, there are no totally pure and innocent in this world. (See Moroni 8:8, 11, 19–20; D&C 45:4; 109:34; Hebrews 4:14–15; 1 Peter 2:21–22; Romans 3:23; 5:12. See also Bruce R. McConkie, *Mormon Doctrine* [Salt Lake City: Book-craft, 1966], p. 736.) Each of the rest of us, to one degree or another, can be classed as a sinner. And the scriptures declare emphatically that chastening comes as a result of such sinning. Remember what the Lord says: "Whom I love I also chasten that their sins may be forgiven." (D&C 95:1.) And how will such sins be forgiven? Through faith and trust in the Lord Jesus Christ, who forgives all sins through repentance. This faith, trust, and repentance is often brought forth through what we suppose should be called enforced humility—humility from the chastening of the Lord: "And inasmuch as they sinned they might be chastened, that they might repent." (D&C 1:27.)

Chastening, therefore, is the result of our own unrighteous choices and activities, however small they might seem to us.

13

For instance, the Lord says, "My disciples, in days of old, sought occasion against one another and forgave not one another in their hearts; and for this evil were they afflicted and sorely chastened." (D&C 64:8.) To us such a sin might seem insignificant, but apparently it was not insignificant to the Lord. Again: "And that those who call themselves after my name might be chastened for a little season with a sore and grievous chastisement, because they did not hearken altogether unto the precepts and commandments which I gave unto them . . . but . . . inasmuch as they hearken from this very hour unto the counsel which I, the Lord their God, shall give unto them . . . they shall never cease to prevail. . . . For after much tribulation . . . cometh the blessing." (D&C 103:4–5, 7, 12.)

Further, God informs us that unless he uses chastisement as a constant reminder, he will lose us to sin anyway. As Mormon declared: "Except the Lord doth chasten his people with many afflictions, yea, except he doth visit them with death and with terror, and with famine and with all manner of pestilence, they will not remember him. O how foolish, and how vain, and how evil, and devilish, and how quick to do iniquity, and how slow to do good, are the children of men; yea, how quick to hearken unto the words of the evil one, and to set their hearts upon the vain things of the world! Yea, how quick to be lifted up in pride; yea, how quick to boast, and do all manner of that which is iniquity; and how slow are they to remember the Lord their God, and to give ear unto his counsels; yea, how slow to walk in wisdom's paths. Behold, they do not desire that the Lord their God, who hath created them, should rule and reign over them; notwithstanding his great goodness and his mercy towards them, they do set at naught his counsels, and they will not that he should be their guide." (Helaman 12:3–6.)

Only the Clean May Dwell with God

God's people are chastened so that they might humble themselves enough to repent of their iniquities, thus bringing to pass, through Christ's atonement, a cleansing of their souls. And this cleansing must occur for them to dwell in the presence of the Lord. "No unclean thing can dwell with God," Nephi declares. (1 Nephi 10:21.) Therefore "the people of Nephi hath [the Lord] loved, and also hath he chastened them; yea, in the days of their iniquities hath he chastened them because he loveth them." (Helaman 15:3.) "I, the Lord, will contend with Zion, and plead with her strong ones, and chasten her until she overcomes and is clean before me." (D&C 90:36.)

This does not seem an overly pleasant doctrine, but the scriptural admonitions and explanations are plain and specific. Because the Lord loves his people, and because the nature of those people seems to lean toward unrighteousness, they are going to experience chastisement that they might repent and be ready for the second coming of Christ.

Chastening Brings Humility

We often find it easy, as a people, to become negligent in our daily prayers when all is going well in our lives. More often than not, we fall to our knees in humble prayer, pleading for guidance, only when our needs are great. But the Lord knows this as well as we do, and so he chastens us so that we will be humble enough to kneel before him.

To the Zoramites, the prophet Alma declared: "I say unto you, it is well that ye are [chastened], that ye may be humble, and that ye may learn wisdom; for it is necessary that ye should learn wisdom; for it is because that ye are [chastened], that ye are despised of your brethren because of your exceeding poverty, that ye are brought to a lowliness of heart; for ye are necessarily brought to be humble. And now, because ye are compelled to be humble blessed are ye; for a man sometimes, if he is compelled to be humble, seeketh repentance; and now surely, whosoever repenteth shall find mercy; and he that findeth mercy and endureth to the end the same shall be saved." (Alma 32:12–13.)

Chastening Brings Rewards

Thus, chastening remains a positive experience with great rewards promised to those who endure it well. As we learn again from the Book of Mormon: "The Lord seeth fit to chasten his people; yea, he trieth their patience and their faith. Nevertheless—whosoever putteth his trust in him the same shall be lifted up at the last day." (Mosiah 23:21–22.) And finally: "My people must be tried in all things, that they may be prepared to receive the glory that I have for them, even the glory of Zion; and he that will not bear chastisement is not worthy of my kingdom." (D&C 136:31.)

3

Chastisement and Wrath
the Same Events

Intriguingly, the chastisements of the Saints of God, those miseries that will be poured out upon those whom God loves, seem to be tied hand-in-glove with the judgments of destruction heaped upon the wicked through the Lord's wrath and indignation. Apparently God uses the same events to bring about destruction on the one hand or deliverance on the other—the one for the wicked and the other for his people.

In fact, the Lord even links the two together. To Joseph Smith he said: "It shall come to pass, after many days, slaves shall rise up against their masters, who shall be marshalled and disciplined for war. And it shall come to pass also that the remnants who are left of the land will marshal themselves, and shall become exceedingly angry, and shall vex the Gentiles with a sore vexation. *And thus, with the sword and by bloodshed the inhabitants of the earth shall mourn; and with famine, and plague, and earthquake, and the thunder of heaven, and the fierce and vivid lightning also, shall the inhabitants of the earth be made to feel the wrath, and indignation, and chastening hand of an Almighty God,* until the consumption decreed hath made an end of all nations. Wherefore, stand ye in holy places, and be not moved, until the day of the Lord come; for behold, it cometh quickly, saith the Lord." (D&C 87:4–6, 8; italics added.)

All those horrid but vividly described events are declared to be either the wrath of God or else the chastisements of God, poured out upon his children in the last days. To us, it seems apparent that the Lord wants us to learn, through these difficult experiences, whether we will stand on his right hand or his left. Depending upon our choices, we will then be experiencing wrath and indignation unto destruction, or chastisement unto deliverance.

Again, who or what determines whether we are experiencing wrath and indignation unto destruction, or are being chastised unto deliverance? We do! By our attitudes, by our desires, by our willingness to submit ourselves to the mind and will of God without murmuring, by our eagerness to forsake all of our sins, even the little ones, and thereafter strive diligently to live by every word of God. These determine whether we are being destroyed or being delivered. In the Lord's words, by our choosing to "stand in holy places" by being holy ourselves, we decide our destiny. Once again the agency we fought for so valiantly in the premortal sphere is brought into play, and we alone are given the privilege of determining our ultimate fate or reward during the calamitous events of these last days.

4

Judgments to Begin
upon the House of God

Both through the scriptures and by the mouths of his holy prophets, God has declared that he will begin pouring out his wrath, indignation, and chastisements by first visiting them upon his own house, the Church and kingdom of God. He says, "Upon my house shall it begin, and from my house shall it go forth, saith the Lord. First among you, saith the Lord, who have professed to know my name and have not known me, and have blasphemed against me in the midst of my house, saith the Lord." (D&C 112:25–26.) "Behold, I say unto you, there were jarrings, and contentions, and envyings, and strifes, and lustful and covetous desires among them; therefore, by these things they polluted their inheritances. They were slow to hearken unto the voice of the Lord their God; therefore, the Lord their God is slow to hearken unto their prayers, to answer them in the day of their trouble." (D&C 101:6–7.) "Nevertheless, Zion [the pure in heart] shall escape if she observe to do all things whatsoever I have commanded her. But if she observe not to do whatsoever I have commanded her, I will visit her according to all her works, with sore affliction, with pestilence, with plague, with sword, with vengeance, with devouring fire." (D&C 97:25–26.)

But there is a purpose even in this. President Joseph F. Smith stated: "We believe that [God's] judgments are poured out to bring mankind to a sense of his power and purposes, that they may repent of their sins, and prepare themselves for the second coming of Christ to reign in righteousness here upon the earth. . . . We firmly believe that Zion—which is the pure in heart—shall escape, if she observes to do all things whatsoever God has commanded; but in the opposite event, even Zion shall be visited 'with sore affliction, with pestilence, with plague, with sword, with vengeance, with devouring fire.' All this that her people may be taught to walk in the light of truth, and in the way of the God of their salvation." (*Improvement Era*, June 1906, p. 653.)

He also said: "Judgement is not an end in itself. Calamities are only permitted by a merciful Father, in order to bring about redemption. Behind the fearful storms of judgement, which often strike the just and the unjust alike, overwhelming the wicked and the righteous, there arises bright and clear the dawn of the day of salvation. . . . What he permitted to occur seems clearly to have been for the purpose of calling attention, by the finger of his power, to the wickedness and sins of men—not alone to the sins of the people of the stricken city, for there are many elsewhere who are just as evil minded, but to the transgressions of all mankind, that all may take warning and repent. Men who stand in the way of God's wise purposes, whether they be good or evil, must suffer in the turmoil. Thus it is that often the righteous suffer for the unrighteous; and it is not satisfactory to the thinking mind to say that therefore God is unjust. The perfect Christ suffered, the just for the unjust." (Ibid., p. 650.)

Wilford Woodruff adds: "Zion is not going to be moved out of her place. The Lord will plead with her strong ones, and if she sins he will chastise her until she is purified before the Lord. I do not pretend to tell how much sorrow you or I are going to meet with before the coming of the Son of Man. That will depend upon our conduct." (*Millennial Star*, 51:547.) And: "It matters not what the mind and feelings of men are, the Lord is determined to raise up a people that will worship Him; and if he has to whip, and scourge, and drive us through a whole generation, He will chastise us until we are willing to submit to righteousness and truth, or until we are like clay in the hands of the potter. The chastisements we have had from time to time have been for our good, and are essential to learn wisdom, and carry us through a school of experience we never could have passed through without. I hope, then, that we may learn from the experience we have had to be faithful, and humble, and be passive in the hands of God, and do His commandments." (*Journal of Discourses*, 26 vols. [London: Latter-day Saints' Book Depot, 1854–86], 2:198.)

We Must Not Fear

If we can become the people that the Lord needs as his Saints of the latter days, we need not fear. As President John Taylor declared: "The judgments of God will begin at the house of God. We have to pass through some of these things, but it will be only a very little compared with the terrible destruction, the misery and suffering that will overtake the world who are doomed to suffer the wrath of God. It behooves us, as the Saints of God, to stand firm and faithful in the observance of His laws, that we may be worthy of his preserving care and blessing." (*Journal of Discourses*, 21:100.)

Thus, even in the midst of this approaching turmoil, we should have hope and peace. As one gospel scholar puts it: "Although the righteous have no guarantee of escape, the wicked have no hope. It is true that some of the righteous will suffer, but all of the wicked will, and without the assurance of an eternal reward which the righteous have." (Gerald N. Lund, *The Coming of the Lord* [Salt Lake City: Bookcraft, 1971], p. 80.)

For each of us, that should be a statement of great hope.

5

Warfare in America

From what we have examined thus far, we are forced to conclude that as God's wrath and indignation reaches a fulness, we will most likely experience warfare upon this land of America, as well as upon the rest of the earth. This is because many people in our nation are ripening in iniquity, being filled with all manner of abominations. Because of this gross wickedness, the Lord has declared that He needs to remove the wicked. (D&C 29:17.) In fact, in 1831 Joseph Smith prophesied that the Lord would soon say: "Behold, the day has come, when the cup of the wrath of mine indignation is full." (D&C 43:26.)

As indicators of our ripeness in iniquity, look at what our modern movies or television programs portray, or what fills the headlines of our newspapers, or what sorts of ungodly conversations usually occur in the hallways and locker rooms of our schools. Even our humorists recognize and mirror the degradation in our world. In a recently printed comic strip, one character asks another: "Well, what do you predict for the coming decade?" The second character answers: "I see corruption, decadence, immorality, perversion, wars, famine, pestilence and disease, vandalism, drugs, street gangs, terrorists, bad schools, potholes, toxic waste, acid rain, fraud, embezzlement, government waste . . . " And the first character interrupts: "What about the downside?" (Parker and Hart, "The Wizard of Id," *Deseret News*, Sunday, February 25, 1990.) Truly the majority of us do not serve the God of this land, who is Jesus Christ. Rather He is mocked and His commandments are scorned.

Sadly, this is true in some ways even within The Church of Jesus Christ of Latter-day Saints, where activity levels rarely rise above 50 percent. As Elder Bruce R. McConkie put it: "We weep for those in the true Church who are weak and wayward and worldly and who fall by the wayside. . . . As the Saints prepare to meet their God, so those who are carnal and sensual and devilish prepare to face their doom. As the meek among men make their calling and election sure, so those who worship the God of this world sink ever lower and lower into the depths of depravity and despair. . . . The wicked and ungodly shall be swept from the Church." ("The Coming Tests and Trials and Glory," *Ensign*, May 1980, pp. 72–73.)

In modern revelation concerning such "active" but sadly uncommitted Latter-day Saints, the Lord says: "Hearken, O ye people who profess my name, saith the Lord your God; for behold, mine anger is kindled against the rebellious, and they shall know mine arm and mine indignation, in the day of visitation and wrath upon the nations." (D&C 56:1.) "Behold, I, the Lord, am not well pleased with many who are in the church. . . . For they do not forsake their sins, and their wicked ways, the pride of their hearts, and their covetousness, and all their detestable things, and observe the words of wisdom and eternal life which I have given them. Verily, I say unto you, that I, the Lord, will chasten them and will do whatsoever I list, if they do not repent and do all things whatsoever I have said unto them. And again I say unto you, if ye observe to do whatsoever I command you, I, the Lord, will turn away my wrath and indignation from you, and the gates of hell shall not prevail against you." (D&C 98:19–22.)

But if we don't repent? Then "instead of blessings, ye, by your own works, bring cursings, wrath, indignation, and judgments upon your own heads, by your follies, and by all your abominations, which you practice before me, saith the Lord. And I will answer judgment, wrath, and indignation, wailing, and anguish, and gnashing of teeth upon [your] heads, unto the third and fourth generation, so long as [you] repent not, and hate me, saith the Lord your God." (D&C 124:48, 52.)

According to God's word, it is the desolation of abomination that awaits the wicked of this generation, whether they be Latter-day Saints or otherwise. (D&C 84:117; 88:85.) And despite the Lord's infinite patience with us if we are striving to overcome our wickedness, it seems apparent that the cup of the wrath of his indignation is about to overflow, and our nation as well as the rest of the world is about to reap the whirlwind.

We Yet Face Warfare

Why do we believe that warfare will be the result of our society's wickedness? Because in all ages past, the fulness of God's wrath has meant destruction by the forces of war. Further, since God is unchangeable and his course is one eternal round, and since in modern revelation to Joseph Smith he declared that the Gentiles (us; see D&C 109:60) would be vexed with a "sore vexation . . . *with the sword and bloodshed* . . . and be made to feel the wrath and indignation . . . of God . . . until the full end of all nations" (D&C 87:5–6; italics added), it can be seen why we have come to this conclusion.

Hugh Nibley has written: "We rightly cite the prophecy on war (D&C 87) as clear evidence for the prophetic guidance of the Church—without ever bothering to take to heart its message for us. It still comes through loud and clear with a prophetic message: the consummation of the whole thing [the Lord's wrath and indignation] is to be 'a *full end* of *all* nations' (D&C 87:6), not a full end of some or a partial end of all, but a *full end* of *all*; and that by *war*, not as a possibility or contingency, but as a 'consumption decreed'—it *must happen.*" (Hugh Nibley, *Approaching Zion* [Salt Lake City: Deseret Book Company, 1989], p. 155.) In other words, according to the Lord's words expressed in the Doctrine and Covenants, as well as the perception of Brother Nibley, through war this nation and all others must ultimately come to an end.

As a further clarification and witness to these events, let us turn to the prophetic statements of some of our latter-day prophets, seers, and revelators.

Joseph Smith on the Future of the United States

Only days before his martyrdom, Joseph Smith declared: "I call God and angels to witness that this people shall have their legal rights or my blood shall be spilt upon the ground—but if there is one drop of blood shed on this occasion, the sword shall never again be sheathed until Christ comes to reign over the earth. . . . Peace shall be taken from the land which permits these crimes against the Saints to go unavenged." (Christopher Layton, "Life of Christopher Layton," edited by Myron W. McIntyre and Noel R. Barton [Salt Lake City: Christopher Layton Family Organization, 1966], pp. 19–21.) Brigham Young quoted Joseph Smith as saying: "You will see the sorrows and misery of the world and the misery that will be upon this land, until you will turn away and pray that your eyes may not be obliged to look upon it. . . . There are men in this council that will live to see the affliction that

26

will come upon this nation, until your hearts sink within you."
(*Journal of Discourses*, 8:325.) Joseph also said: "My heart faints
within me when I see, by the visions of the Almighty, the
end of this nation, if she continues to disregard the cries and
petitions of her virtuous citizens, as she has done, and is now
doing. . . . Since Congress has decided against us, the Lord
has begun to vex the nation, and he will continue to do so,
except they repent; for they now stand guilty of murder,
robbery and plunder, as a nation, because they have refused
to protect their citizens and to execute justice according to
their own constitution. . . . I prophesy, in the name of the
Lord God of Israel, unless the United States redress the
wrongs committed upon the Saints in the State of Missouri
and punish the crimes committed by officers, that in a few
years the government will be utterly overthrown and wasted,
and there will not be so much as a potsherd left for their
wickedness in permitting the murder of men, women and
children, and the wholesale plunder and extermination of
thousands of her citizens to go unpunished, thereby perpe-
trating a foul and corroding blot upon the fair name of this
great republic, the very thought of which would have caused
the high-minded and patriotic framers of the constitution of
the United States to hide their faces with shame." ("Historical
Record," Church Archives, p. 514.)

Of course, as most Latter-day Saints should be aware from
studying Church history, such redress as Joseph desired from
the United States government was never made. Neither the
Church nor its individual members were ever reimbursed for
their loss of property, nor were the perpetrators of the gross
crimes committed against the Church and its members in
Missouri and Illinois ever brought to justice. Thus, these
prophecies of Joseph's stand binding upon this land today,
just as they did when he uttered them a hundred and fifty

years ago. In fact, with awful finality Joseph made additional remarks, which contain no conditional clauses whatsoever.

He said: "I prophesy, in the name of the Lord God of Israel, anguish and wrath and tribulation and the withdrawing of the Spirit of God from the earth await this generation, until they are visited with utter desolation. This generation is as corrupt as the generation of the Jews that crucified Christ; and if He were here today, and should preach the same doctrine He did then, they would put him to death." (*History of the Church of Jesus Christ of Latter-day Saints,* 2nd ed. rev., edited by B. H. Roberts, 7 vols. [Salt Lake City: The Church of Jesus Christ of Latter-day Saints, 1932–51], 6:58.) "And now I am prepared to say by the authority of Jesus Christ, that not many years shall pass away before the United States shall present such a scene of bloodshed as has not a parallel in the history of our nation; pestilence, hail, famine, and earthquake will sweep the wicked of this generation from off the face of the land, to open and prepare the way for the return of the lost tribes of Israel from the north country." (Ibid., 1:315–16.)

From Brigham Young

Following Joseph's death, Brigham Young reiterated the same theme of warning. He stated: "This nation shall feel the heavy hand of judgement. They have shed the blood of prophets and saints and have been the means of the death of many." (Edward W. Tullidge, *Life of Brigham Young* [New York, 1877], p. 37.)

He also said: "Do you think there is calamity abroad now among the people? Not much. All we have yet heard and all we have experienced is scarcely a preface to the sermon that is going to be preached. When the testimony of the Elders ceases to be given, and the Lord says to them, 'Come home; I will now preach my own sermons to the nations of the earth,' all you now know can scarcely be called a preface to the sermon that will be preached with fire and sword, tempests, earthquakes, hail, rain, thunders and lightnings, and fearful destruction. What matters the destruction of a few railway cars? You will hear of magnificent cities, now idolized by the people, sinking in the earth, entombing the inhabitants. The sea will heave itself beyond its bounds, engulfing mighty cities. Famine will spread over the nations, and nation will rise up against nation, kingdom against kingdom, and states against states, in our own country and in foreign lands; and they will destroy each other, not caring for the blood and lives of their neighbors, or their families, or for their own lives. They will be like the Jaredites who preceded the Nephites upon this continent, and will destroy each other to the last man, through the anger that the devil will place in their hearts, because they rejected the words of life and are given over to Satan to do whatever he listeth to do with them." (*Journal of Discourses*, 8:123.)

Not the Civil War

It might reasonably be argued that the dire prophecies we have related thus far were fulfilled with the destruction and misery brought on by America's Civil War. And certainly some of them were. The trouble with assuming that all this prophesied warfare is now in the past comes when we examine the statements of prophets who have presided since 1865, when the Civil War came to a close.

For instance, John Taylor, who followed Brigham Young as president of the Church, stated: "Were we surprised when the last terrible war took place here in the United States? No. Good Latter-day Saints were not, for they had been told about it. Joseph Smith had told them where it would start, that it should be a terrible time of bloodshed, and that it should start in South Carolina. But I tell you today the end is not yet. You will see worse things than that, for God will lay his hand upon this nation, and they will feel it more terribly than even they have done before. There will be more bloodshed, more ruin, more devastation than ever they have seen before. Write it down! You will see it come to pass; it is only just starting in. And would you feel to rejoice? No; I would feel sorry. I knew very well myself when this last war was commencing and could have wept and did weep; but there is yet to come a sound of war, trouble and distress, in which brother will be arrayed against brother, father against son, son against father, a scene of desolation and destruction that will permeate our land until it will be a vexation to hear the report thereof. . . . Would you help to bring [this destruction] about? No, I would not. I would stop it if I could. I would pour in the oil and the wine and the balm and try to lead people in the right path that will be governed by it, but they won't. Our Elders would do the same, and we are sending them forth doing all that we can, selecting the very best men we can put our hands upon—men of faith, men of honor, men of integrity—to go forth to preach the Gospel to this nation and to other nations." (Ibid., pp. 356–57.)

On another occasion, he wrote, "Knowing that there are other judgments in store for the earth, we will venture a prediction, that there shall be storm and hail enough to cause a famine, and show the whole of the earth that Jesus Christ, and not the Mormons, vexes the nation." (*Nauvoo Neighbor*, August 6, 1845.)

And again: "A terrible day of reckoning is approaching the nations of the earth; the Lord is coming out of his hiding place to vex the inhabitants thereof; and the destroyer of the gentiles, as prophesied of, is already on his way. . . . Already combinations are being entered into which are very ominous for the future prosperity, welfare, and happiness of this great republic. The volcanic fires of discordant and anarchial elements are beginning to manifest themselves and exhibit the internal forces that are at work among the turbulent and unthinking masses of the world." (*Journal of Discourses*, 23:62.)

Not the Last Two World Wars

We today might believe that the destruction these brethren described, the destruction the Lord has promised, was fulfilled by the devastation wrought by the First and Second World Wars. But besides the fact that nothing in those two wars comes even remotely close to fitting President Taylor's descriptions of conditions here in America, a statement by an even more modern prophet lays that idea to rest with great finality. President George Albert Smith stated: "I fear that the time is coming . . . unless we can call the people of this world to repent of their ways, the great war that has just passed [World War II] will be an insignificant thing, as far as calamity is concerned, compared to that which is before us." (*Improvement Era*, November 1946, p. 763.)

The Constitution to Hang by a Thread

If all this warfare is to sweep over America in the near future, destroying our government and bringing wrath and chastisement upon our people, then what about Joseph Smith's famous prophecy that the U.S. constitution would hang by a thread but that the elders would save it? Doesn't that mean there will be no war, or at least that our government won't be destroyed?

After a little research, we came as close as we think we will to pinning down this rather elusive prophecy. Sometime in either 1840, 1843, or 1844, Howard and Martha Jane Knowlton Coray recorded in their "Notebook" these remarks by Joseph Smith: "Even this nation will be on the very verge of crumbling to pieces and tumbling to the ground and when the constitution is upon the brink of ruin this people will be the Staff upon which the Nation shall lean and they shall bear the constitution away from the very verge of destruction." (Andrew F. Ehat and Lyndon W. Cook, eds., *The Words of Joseph Smith* [Provo UT: Brigham Young University Religious Studies Center, 1980], p. 416.)

Some two weeks later, James Burgess, who was present when the prophecy was made but who took a little longer to record it, wrote that Joseph stated: "The time would come when the Constitution and Government [of the United States] would hang by a brittle thread and would be ready to fall into other hands but this people the Latter day Saints will step forth and save it." (Ibid., p. 279.)

Because there is a question concerning the date of the Coray entry, as well as some evidence of slight changes in the Coray manuscript, and because it is the only known contemporary account of Joseph's remarks, the entire prophecy has become suspect. So we looked to other sources for reminiscence accounts and found several. The preponderance of these being essentially the same, it is our opinion that Joseph indeed made a prophecy of some sort about the constitution and the Church members' part in preserving it. The interpretation of that prophecy we will leave to the prophets, who have said much about it.

Orson Hyde, an apostle who was also there when Joseph made his remarks, stated: "It is said that Brother Joseph in his lifetime declared that the Elders of this Church should step forth at a particular time when the Constitution should be in danger, and rescue it, and save it. This may be so; but I do not recollect that he said exactly so. I believe he said something like this—that the time would come when the Constitution and the country would be in danger of an overthrow; and said he, If the Constitution be saved at all, it will be by the Elders of this Church. I believe this is about the language, as nearly as I can recollect it." (*Journal of Discourses*, 6:152.)

President Brigham Young declared: "Will the Constitution be destroyed? No: it will be held inviolate by this people; and as Joseph Smith said, 'The time will come when the destiny of the nation will hang upon a single thread. At that critical juncture, this people will step forth and save it from the threatened destruction.' It will be so." (Ibid., p. 15.)

Brigham Young also said: "I tell you further, Elders of Israel, that you do not know the day of your visitation, neither do you understand the signs of the times, for if you did you would be awake to these things. Every organization of our government, the best government in the world, is crumbling to pieces. Those who have it in their hands are the ones who are destroying it. How long will it be before the words of the prophet Joseph will be fulfilled? He said if the constitution of the United States were saved at all it must be done by this people. It will not be many years before these words come to pass." (Ibid., 12:204.)

According to President John Taylor: "We have got to have . . . political power. . . . We have got to establish a government upon the principle of righteousness, justice, truth and equality and not according to the many false notions that exist among men. And then the day is not far distant when this nation will be shaken from centre to circumference. And now, you may write it down, any of you, and I will prophesy it in the name of God. And then will be fulfilled that prediction to be found in one of the revelations given through the Prophet Joseph Smith. . . . When the people shall have torn to shreds the Constitution of the United States the Elders of Israel will be found holding it up . . . and proclaiming liberty and equal rights to all men." (Ibid., 21:8.)

He also said: "The Prophet Joseph Smith said that 'The Constitution of the United States was given by the inspiration of God.' But good, virtuous and holy principles may be perverted by corrupt and wicked men. . . . This nation abounds

33

with traitors who ignore that sacred palladium of liberty and seek to trample it under foot. Joseph Smith said that they would do so, and that when deserted by all, the elders of Israel would rally around its shattered fragments and save and preserve it inviolate." (Ibid., p. 31.)

Finally, President George Q. Cannon, counselor to John Taylor in the First Presidency, stated: "This is another prediction of Joseph Smith's—I want to remind you of it, my brethren and sisters, when good government, constitutional government—liberty—will be found among the Latter-day Saints, and it will be sought for in vain elsewhere. . . . The day will come when the Constitution, and free government under it, will be sustained and preserved by this people." (Ibid., 23:104.)

Again he said, "It seems like a very strange thing to say, but on all proper occasions I say it with a great deal of pleasure . . . that the day would come when republican institutions would be in danger in this nation and upon this continent, when, in fact, the republic would be so rent asunder by factions that there would be no stable government outside of the Latter-day Saints; and that it is their destiny as a people, to uphold constitutional government upon this land." (Ibid., pp. 122–23.)

As may be noted, while memories vary somewhat, the theme is the same. Obviously Joseph Smith prophesied that in a coming day this continent will be torn asunder by war—whether from within or without seems immaterial; in fact it may be both. He also said that whatever constitutional principles remain intact will have been preserved by righteous Latter-day Saints. In no way, then, does this contradict the statements and prophecies we have presented thus far. Apparently this land will yet be decimated by war, and the government as we know it will be overthrown and wasted away. At that juncture, righteous Latter-day Saints will be found clinging to and upholding within their hearts, homes, and communities the true principles of freedom and self-government embodied in our divinely inspired constitution.

From President Ezra Taft Benson

As President Ezra Taft Benson has declared, while citing the prophecy discussed above: "We are fast approaching that moment prophesied by Joseph Smith. . . . We must, with sadness, say that we have not been wise in keeping the trust of our Founding Fathers. For the past two centuries, those who do not prize freedom have chipped away at every major clause of our Constitution until today we face a crisis of great dimensions. . . . To all who have discerning eyes, it is apparent that the republican form of government established by our noble forefathers cannot long endure once fundamental principles are abandoned." (*The Constitution: A Heavenly Banner* [Salt Lake City: Deseret Book Company, 1986], pp. 24–27.)

While what President Benson has said thus far is timely and enlightening in terms of history and responsibility, it is by no means as bold a declaration as what immediately follows. He states prophetically: "Momentum is gathering for another conflict—a repetition of the crisis of two hundred years ago. This collision of ideas is worldwide. Another monumental moment is soon to be born. The issue is the same that precipitated the great premortal conflict—will men be free to determine their own course of action or must they be coerced? We are fast approaching that moment prophesied by Joseph Smith when he said: 'Even this nation will be on the very verge of crumbling to pieces and tumbling to the ground, and when the Constitution is upon the brink of ruin, this people will be the staff upon which the nation shall lean, and they shall bear the Constitution away from the very verge of destruction.' " (Ibid., pp. 27–28.)

Safety in the Promised Land

Another question we asked ourselves concerned the fact that America is a promised land and has the promise of the Lord's protection upon it. If that is so, we reasoned, then how can war come upon it? In examining the scriptural promises concerning this land, however, in every instance we found that the Lord's promise was made with a warning. Further, this warning is so stern that for the wicked it seems safer to live almost anywhere else than in one of the Lord's lands of promise.

Speaking specifically of America, for instance, to the Brother of Jared the Lord swore in his wrath (in other words, by laws of judgment and justice) that whosoever should possess this land should serve God or be swept off when the fulness of his wrath should come upon them. And the fulness of his wrath would come every time they allowed themselves to ripen in iniquity. And it is not until the fulness of iniquity exists among them that they are swept off. And then Moroni gave this warning: "And this cometh unto you, O ye Gentiles, that ye may know the decrees of God – that ye may repent, and not continue in your iniquities until the fulness come, that ye may not bring down the fulness of the wrath of God as the inhabitants of the land have hitherto done. Behold, this is a choice land, and whatsoever nation shall possess it shall be free from bondage, and from captivity, and from all other nations under heaven, if they will but serve the God of the land, who is Jesus Christ, who hath been manifested by the things which we have written." (Ether 2:7–12.)

In mighty vision the prophet Nephi saw the Americas, his land of promise, and he watched the future unfold upon the land from his day to ours. In chapters twelve through fourteen of First Nephi, he described the tumultuous history of the Americas, but from our day forward he was forbidden to leave a written record of what he saw – that being the mission of John the Revelator. Nephi did warn us, however, that in our day there would be "two churches only; the one is the church of the Lamb of God, and the other is the church of the devil; wherefore, whoso belongeth not to the church of the Lamb of God belongeth to that great church, which is the mother of abominations; and she is the whore of all the earth." (1 Nephi 14:10.) He also warned that in our day "the wrath of God [would be] poured out upon the mother of harlots, which is the great and abominable church of all the earth" (1 Nephi 14:17) "insomuch that there [would be] wars and rumors of wars among all the nations and kindreds of the earth." (1 Nephi 14:15.) So there would be wars poured out upon that church, wherever it existed. In spite of that, however, Nephi declared that "the power of the Lamb of God [would descend] upon the saints of the church of the Lamb, and upon the covenant people of the Lord . . . [arming them] with righteousness and with the power of God in great glory." (1 Nephi 14:14.)

More Than Membership by Baptism

How do we tell which church we are members of, and if we can expect such power and protection when war comes to this land? Again according to Nephi: "Behold the gold, and the silver, and the silks, and the scarlets, and the fine-twined linen, and the precious clothing, and the harlots, are the desires of [the members of] this great and abominable church. And also for the praise of the world do they destroy the saints of God, and bring them down into captivity." (1 Nephi 13:8-9.) In other words, membership, and therefore protection, seems to have less to do with baptism than it does with righteousness; less to do with church names than it does with attitudes and efforts. Are we worldly, or are we not? Are we members of Christ's church, or are we otherwise?

Lehi declared to his sons: "Wherefore, this land is consecrated unto him whom [God] shall bring. And if it so be that they shall serve him according to the commandments which he hath given, it shall be a land of liberty unto them; wherefore, they shall never be brought down into captivity; if so, it shall be because of iniquity; for if iniquity shall abound cursed shall be the land for their sakes, but unto the righteous shall it be blessed forever." (2 Nephi 1:7.)

Moroni adds: "The Lord did pour out his blessings upon this land, which was choice above all other lands; and he commanded that whoso should possess the land should possess it unto the Lord, or they should be destroyed when they were ripened in iniquity; for upon such, saith the Lord: I will pour out the fulness of my wrath." (Ether 9:7.)

The Promised Land Today

To members of the Church of Jesus Christ in the last days, the Lord says: "I hold forth and deign to give unto you greater riches, even a land of promise, a land flowing with milk and honey, upon which there shall be no curse when the Lord cometh; And I will give it unto you for the land of your inheritance, if you seek it with all your hearts. . . . But, verily I say unto you, teach one another according to the office wherewith I have appointed you; and let every man esteem his brother as himself, and practice virtue and holiness before me. . . . And if ye seek the riches which it is the will of the Father to give unto you, ye shall be the richest of all people, for ye shall have the riches of eternity; and it must needs be that the riches of the earth are mine to give; but beware of pride, lest ye become as the Nephites of old." (D&C 38:18–19, 23–24, 39.)

In other words, promised lands are blessings only to those who practice virtue and holiness before the Lord by esteeming their neighbors as themselves while they seek only the riches of eternity. To all others, no matter their religious affiliation, such lands are cursed, for because of their wickedness, because of the pride generated through their great abundance, like the Nephites of old the modern inhabitants thereof will experience ultimate destruction.

All this is according to the wrath and indignation, the judgments and justice, of Almighty God.

6

A Land of Desolation

If warfare comes to America as it will also come to the rest of the world, what can we expect? Will it be a small thing, or will it be more terrible than we can imagine? Will America become a land of desolation such as the Nephites encountered when they discovered the destruction of the Jaredites? Or will there be remnants left, as there were after the destruction of the Nephites? Will there be invasion from foreign powers, or will the strife be primarily internal? Let us once again turn to the words of our latter-day prophets and apostles to see how the Lord responds to these questions.

In terms of what sort of warfare we can expect to encounter, Joseph Smith stated: "I saw men hunting the lives of their own sons, and brother murdering brother, women killing their own daughters, and daughters seeking the lives of their mothers. I saw armies arrayed against armies. I saw blood, desolation, fires. The Son of Man has said that the mother shall be against the daughter, and the daughter against the mother. These things are at our doors. They will follow the Saints of God from city to city. Satan will rage, and the spirit of the devil is now enraged. I know not how soon these things will take place; but with a view of them, shall I cry peace? No, I will lift up my voice and testify of them. How long you will have good crops, and the famine kept off, I do not know; when the fig tree leaves, know then that summer is nigh at hand." (*History of the Church*, 3:391.)

Brigham Young spoke of the same things, mentioning that cities would sink and entomb their inhabitants, seas would heave themselves beyond their bounds and engulf other mighty cities, famine would spread over the nations, and here in America "states [will turn] against states, in our own country . . . and they will destroy each other, caring not for the blood and lives of their neighbors, of their families, or for their own lives. They [the wicked] will be like the Jaredites who preceded the Nephites upon this continent, and will destroy each other to the last man." (*Journal of Discourses*, 8:123.)

From Heber C. Kimball

Brigham Young's counselor, Heber C. Kimball, made the following remarks, which seem almost startling in light of conditions in present-day Utah. He says: "An army of Elders will be sent to the four quarters of the earth to search out the righteous and warn the wicked of what is coming. All kinds of religions will be started and miracles performed that will deceive the very elect if that were possible. Our sons and daughters must live pure lives so as to be prepared for what is coming. After a while the gentiles will gather by the thousands to this place, and Salt Lake City will be classed among the wicked cities of the world. A spirit of speculation and extravagance will take possession of the Saints, and the results will be financial bondage. Persecution comes next and all true Latter-day Saints will be tested to the limit. Many will apostatize and others will be still not knowing what to do. Darkness will cover the earth and gross darkness the minds of the people. The judgments of God will be poured out on the wicked to the extent that our Elders from far and near will be called home, or in other words the gospel will be taken from the Gentiles and later on carried to the Jews. The western boundary of the State of Missouri will be swept so clean of its inhabitants that as President Young tells us, when you return to that place, there will not be left so much as a yellow dog to wag his tail. Before that day comes, however, the Saints will be put to tests that will try the integrity of the best of them. The pressure will become so great that the more righteous among them will cry unto the Lord day and night until deliverance comes. Then the prophet and others will make their appearance and those who have remained faithful will be selected to return to Jackson County, Missouri, and take part in the upbuilding of that beautiful city, the New Jerusalem." (*Deseret News*, May 23, 1931.)

What we find interesting about Brother Kimball's prophecy is that it is specific enough that we can tell with near exactness where we are today. Utah newspaper headlines indicate that Salt Lake City has its wickedness just as do other cities of the world. These headlines scream of local crime often enough that they rival the headlines of newspapers in almost any other city in America. At the same time, a spirit of speculation and extravagance has indeed taken possession of many of the Saints, the result of which is, as Brother Kimball says, "financial bondage," an endless stream of bankruptcies, fraud and conspiracy trials, failed businesses, and loss of homes that ought to be providing security and comfort to the families who are losing them.

Interestingly, the next step in Brother Kimball's prophecy is persecution: "All true Latter-day Saints will be tested to the limit." Are we firm enough in our faith to stand against such testing, such persecution? Brother Kimball says that many won't be but will apostatize and join with the perse-cutors. We would do well to reflect upon where we will be when the choice comes to us.

From Wilford Woodruff

Concerning what we have yet to face in this land, consider also the following remarks made by President Wilford Wood-ruff: "The Lord is not going to disappoint either Babylon or Zion, with regard to famine, pestilence, earthquake or storms, he is not going to disappoint anybody with regard to any of these things, they are at the doors. . . . Lay up your wheat and other provisions against a day of need, for the day will come when they will be wanted, and no mistake about it. We shall want bread, and the Gentiles will want bread, and if we are wise we shall have something to feed them and ourselves when famine comes." (*Journal of Discourses*, 18:121.)

He also said: "The wickedness committed today in the Christian world in twenty-four hours is greater than would have been committed in a hundred years at the ratio of fifty years ago. And the spirit of wickedness is increasing, so that I no longer wonder that God Almighty will turn rivers into blood; I do not wonder that he will open the seals and pour out the plagues and sink great Babylon, as the angel saw, like a millstone cast into the sea, to rise no more forever. I can see that it requires just such plagues and judgments to cleanse the earth, that it may cease to groan under the wicked-ness and abomination in which the Christian world welters today." (*Journal of Discourses*, 14:3.)

And again: "[The judgments of God] will come down like the judgments of Sodom and Gomorrah. And none but the Priesthood will be safe from their fury. God has held the angels of destruction for many years, lest they should reap down the wheat with the tares (D&C 86:5). But I want to tell you now, that those angels have left the portals of heaven, and they stand over this people and this nation now, and are hovering over the earth waiting to pour out the judgments. And from this very day they shall be poured out. Calamities and troubles are increasing in the earth, and there is a meaning to these things. Remember this, and reflect upon these matters. If you do your duty, and I do my duty, we'll have protection, and shall pass through the afflictions in peace and safety." (*Young Woman's Journal*, 5:512–13.)

A Remarkable Vision

One of the most graphic accounts of what we can expect once these judgments begin in earnest was also provided by Wilford Woodruff. Though his account is lengthy, we would like to quote it in its entirety as he entered it in his journal, leaving his spelling and punctuation intact:

"A Vision

"Salt Lake City, Night of Dec 16, 1877

"I [ ] went to bed at my usual hour half past nine o'clock. I had been reading the Revelations in the French language. My mind was Calm, more so than usual if possible to be so. I Composed myself for sleep but Could not sleep. I felt a strange stupor Come over me and apparently became partially unconscious. Still I was not asleep, nor awake With strange far away dreamy feelings.

"The first I recognized was that I was in the Tabernacle at Ogden sitting on the back seat in the Corner for fear they would Call upon me to Preach, which after singing the second time, they did, by Calling me to the Stand.

"I arose to speak and said I did not Know that I had any thing special to say Except to bear my Testimony to the Truth of the Latter Day work when all at once it seemed as though I was lifted out of myself, and I said 'Yes, I have sumthing to say, it is this—some of my brethren present have been asking me what is Coming to pass, what is the wind blowing up. I will answer you right here what is Coming to pass shortly.

"I was immediately in Salt lake City wandering about the streets in all parts of the City and On the door of every house I found a badge of mourning, and I Could not find a house but what was in mourning. I passed by my own house and saw the same sign there, and asked, 'Is that me that is dead?' Sumthing gave me answer, 'No, you [shall] live through it all.'

"It seemed strange to me that I saw no person [on] the street in my wandering about through the City. They seemed to be in their houses with their Sick and Dead. I saw no funeral procession, or any thing of that kind, but the City looked very Still and quiet as though the people were praying and had Controll of the disease what ever it was.

"I then looked in all directions over the Territory, East west North and South, and I found the same mourning in every place throughout the Land. The next I knew I was Just this side of Omaha. It seemed as though I was above the Earth, looking down to it as I passed along on my way East and I saw the roads full of people, principally women, with just what they Could Carry in bundles on their backs traveling to the mountains on foot. And I wondered how they Could get there, with nothing but a small pack upon their backs. It was remarkable to me that there were so few men among them. It did not seem as though the Cars were running. The rails looked rusty, and the road abandoned, And I have no conception how I traveled myself.

"As I looked down upon the people I Continued Eastward through Omaha and Council Bluffs which were full of disease, and women every whare. The States of Missouri and Illinois were in turmoil and Strife, Men killing each other, and women joining in the fight, family against family Cutting each other to pieces in the most horrid manner.

45

"The next I saw was Washington, and I found the City a desolation, The White House Empty, the Halls of Congress the same Everything in ruins. The people seemed to have fled from the City and left it to take Care of itself.

"I was next in the City of Baltimore and in the square where the Monument of 1812 Stands, in front of St Charles and other Hotels I saw the Dead piled up so high as to fill the square. I saw Mothers Cut the throats of their own Children for the sake of their blood, which they drank from their veins, to quench their thirst and then lie down and die. The waters of the Chesapeake and of the City were so stagnant and such a stench arose from them on account of the putrefaction of Dead bodies that the very smell Caused Death and that was singular again I saw no men except they were dead, lying in the streets, and vary few women, and they were Crazy mad, and in a dying Condition. Every whare I went I beheld the same all over the City, And it was horrible, beyond description to look at.

"I thought this must be the End. But No I was seemingly in Philadelphia, and there every thing was Still. No living soul was to be seen to greet me, and it seemed as though the whole City was without an inhabitant. In arch and Chestnut Street and in fact Every whare I went the putrefaction of the Dead bodies Caused such a stench that it was Impossible for any Creature to Exhist alive, nor did I see any living thing in the city.

"I next found myself in Broad way New York and here it seemed the people had done their best to overcome the disease. But in wandering down Broadway I saw the bodies of Beautiful women lying stone dead, and others in a dying Condition on the side walk. I saw men Crawl out of the Cellars and rob the dead bodies of the valuables they had on and before they Could return to their coverts in the cellars they themselves would roll over a time or two and die in agony.

On some of the back streets I saw Mothers kill their own Children and Eat raw flesh and then in a few minutes die themselves. Wharever I went I saw the same scenes of Horror and Desolation rapine and Death. No Horses or Carriages, No busses or Street Cars, but Death and Destruction every whare.

"I then went to the Grand Central Park and looking back I saw a fire Start and just at that moment a mighty East wind sprang up and Carried the flames west over the City, and it burned untill there was not a single building left Standing whole Even down to the wharfs. And the shipping all seemed to be burned and swallowed up in the Common destruction and left Nothing but a Desolation whare the great City was a short time before. The Stench from the bodies that were burning was so great that it Carried a great distance across the Hudson River and bay, and thus spread disease and death wharever the flames penetrated. I Cannot paint in words the Horror that seemed to Encompass me around. It was beyond description or thought of man to Conceive.

"I supposed this was the End but I was here given to understand, that the same horror was being enacted all over the Country, North South East and West, that few were left alive. Still there were some.

"Immediately after I seemed to be standing on the west bank of the Missouri River opposite the City of Independence but I saw no City. I saw the whole States of Missouri & Illinois and part of Iowa were a Complete wilderness with no living human being in them. I then saw a short distance from the river Twelve men dressed in the robes of the Temple Standing in a square or nearly so. I understood it represented the Twelve gates of the New Jerusalem, and they were with hands uplifted Consecrating the ground and laying the Corner Stones. I saw myriads of Angels hovering over them and around about them and also an immens pillar of a Cloud over them and I heard the singing of the most beautif[ul] music the words 'Now is established the Kingdom of our God and His Christ, and He shall reign forever and Ever, and the Kingdom shall never be Thrown down for the Saints have overcome.' And I saw people Coming from the River and different places a long way off to help build the Temple, and it seemed that the Hosts of the angels also helped to get the material to build the Temple. And I saw some Come who wore their Temple . . . robs to help build the Temple and the City and all the time I saw the great pillar of Cloud hovering over the place.

"Instantly I found I was in the Tabernacle at Ogden yet I Could see the building going on and got quite animated in Calling to the people in the Tabernacle to listen to the beautiful music that the Angels were Making. I Called to them to look at the Angels as the House seemed to be full of them and they were saying the same words that I heard Before 'Now is the Kingdom of our God Esstablished forever & Ever.' And then a voice said 'Now shall Come to pass that which was spoken by Isaiah the Prophet 'that seven women shall take hold of one man, saying &c (Isaiah 4:1). [The full text of Isaiah 4:1 is: 'And in that day seven women shall take hold of one man, saying, We will eat our own bread, and wear our own apparel: only let us be called by thy name, to take away our reproach.']

"At this time I seemed to Stagger back from the pulpit & F D Richards and some one els Caught me and prevented me from falling when I requested Brother Richards to apologize to the audience for me because I stoped so adruptly and tell them I had not feinted but was exhausted. I rolled over in my bed and heard the City Hall Clock Strike Twelve." (*Wilford Woodruff's Journal, 1833–1898*, ed. Scott G. Kenney, 9 vols. [Midvale UT: Signature Books], 7:419–23.)

Elder Orson Pratt

Orson Pratt, a nineteenth-century apostle and gospel scholar, made the coming destruction by warfare even more clear when he described it on March 9, 1879: "What then will be the condition of [the American] people, when this great and terrible war shall come? It will be very different from the war between the North and the South. Do you wish me to describe it? I will do so. It will be a war of neighborhood against neighborhood, city against city, county against county, state against state, and they will go forth destroying and being destroyed, and manufacturing will, in a great measure, cease, for a time, among the American nation. Why? Because in these terrible wars, they will not be privileged to manufacture; there will be too much bloodshed — too much mobocracy — too much going forth in bands and destroying and pillaging the land to suffer people to pursue any local vocation with any degree of safety." (*Journal of Discourses*, 20:151.)

Elder Bruce R. McConkie

More recently, Elder Bruce R. McConkie, speaking in general conference, said: "I stand before the Church this day and raise the warning voice. It is a prophetic voice, for I shall say only what the apostles and prophets have spoken concerning our day. . . . It is a voice calling upon the Lord's people to prepare for the troubles and desolations which are about to be poured out upon the world without measure. For the moment we live in a day of peace and prosperity but it shall not ever be thus. Great trials lie ahead. All of the sorrows and perils of the past are but a foretaste of what is yet to be. And we must prepare ourselves temporally and spiritually. . . . Peace has been taken from the earth, the angels of destruction have begun their work, and their swords shall not be sheathed until the Prince of Peace comes to destroy the wicked and usher in the great Millennium. . . . There will be wars in one nation and kingdom after another until war is poured out upon all nations and two hundred million men of war mass their armaments at Armageddon. . . . Bands of Gadianton robbers will infest every nation, immorality and murder and crime will increase, and it will seem as though every man's hand is against his brother." (*Ensign*, May 1979, pp. 92–93.) He also said: "Nor are the days of our greatest sorrows and our deepest sufferings all behind us. They too lie ahead. We shall yet face greater perils, we shall yet be tested with more severe trials, and we shall yet weep more tears of sorrow than we have ever known before. . . . We tremble because of the sorrows and wars and plagues that shall cover the earth. We weep for those in the true Church who are weak and wayward and worldly and who fall by the wayside as the caravan of the kingdom rolls forward. . . . All that is yet to be shall go forward in the midst of greater evils and perils and desolations than have been known on earth at any time. . . . Amid tears of sorrow – our hearts heavy with forebodings – we see evil and crime and carnality covering the earth. Liars and thieves and adulterers and homosexuals and murderers scarcely seek to hide their abominations from our view. Iniquity abounds. There is no peace on earth. We see evil forces everywhere uniting to destroy the family, to ridicule morality and decency, to glorify all that is lewd and base. We see wars and plagues and pestilence. Nations rise and fall. Blood and carnage and death are everywhere. Gadianton robbers fill the judgment seats in many nations. An evil power seeks to overthrow the freedom of all nations and countries. Satan reigns in the hearts of men; it is the great day of his power." (*Ensign*, May 1980, pp. 71, 73.)

The Words of the Lord

Interestingly, the Lord, in the scriptures, warns us of the same events, in enough detail that we should not be confused when we see them surrounding us. When they come, there-fore, we shall recognize them.

He declares: "Not many days hence and the earth shall tremble and reel to and fro as a drunken man; and the sun shall hide his face, and shall refuse to give light; and the moon shall be bathed in blood; and the stars shall become exceed-ingly angry and shall cast themselves down as a fig that falleth from off a tree. And after your testimony [the labors of our missionaries, perhaps?] cometh wrath and indignation upon the people. For after your testimony cometh the testimony of earthquakes that shall cause groanings in the midst of her, and men shall fall upon the ground and shall not be able to stand. And also cometh the testimony of the voice of thun-derings, and the voice of lightnings, and the voice of tempests, and the voice of the waves of the sea heaving themselves beyond their bounds. And all things shall be in commotion; and surely men's hearts shall fail them; for fear shall come upon all people." (D&C 88:87–91.)

"There shall be earthquakes also in divers places, and many desolations; yet men will harden their hearts against me, and they will take up the sword, one against another, and they will kill one another." (D&C 45:33.)

"I the Lord God will send forth flies upon the face of the earth, which shall take hold of the inhabitants thereof, and shall eat their flesh, and shall cause maggots to come in upon them; and their tongues shall be stayed that they shall not utter against me; and their flesh shall fall from off their bones, and their eyes from their sockets; and it shall come to pass that the beasts of the forest and the fowls of the air shall devour them up." (D&C 29:18–20.)

Truly, then, will this become a land of desolation to the wicked or unrepentant inhabitants thereof; the desolation of abomination, which the Lord has emphatically warned us, is coming. (D&C 84:117; 88:85.)

A Thought-provoking Twist

In addition to the calamities we have already mentioned, there is to be an interesting twist in the upcoming "fulness of wrath and indignation" that is to be poured out upon the wicked in our day, and that twist seems to be worldwide in the scope of its destruction as well as its preservation. Concerning our day, Nephi says: "The time soon cometh that the fulness of the wrath of God shall be poured out upon all the children of men, for he will not suffer that the wicked shall destroy the righteous. Wherefore, he will preserve the righteous by his power, even if it so be that the fulness of his wrath must come, and the righteous be preserved, even unto the destruction of their enemies *by fire*. Wherefore the righteous need not fear, for thus saith the prophet, they shall be saved, *even if it so be as by fire*." (1 Nephi 22:16–17; italics added.)

"Behold, my brethren, I say unto you, that these things must shortly come; yea, even blood, and fire, and vapor of smoke must come; and it must needs be upon the face of this earth; and it cometh unto men according to the flesh if it so be that they will harden their hearts against the Holy One of Israel." (1 Nephi 22:18.)

"For the time speedily shall come that all churches which are built up to get gain, and all those who are built up to get power over the flesh, and those who are built up to become popular in the eyes of the world, and those who seek the lusts of the flesh and the things of the world, and to do all manner of iniquity; yea, in fine, all those who belong to the kingdom of the devil are they who need fear, and tremble, and quake; they are those who must be brought low in the dust; they are those who must be consumed as stubble; and this is according to the words of the prophet." (1 Nephi 22:23.)

"The time speedily cometh that the Lord God shall cause a great division among the people, and the wicked will he destroy; and he will spare his people, yea, even if it so be that *he must destroy the wicked by fire.*" (2 Nephi 30:10; italics added.)

Nuclear Fire?

Along with the warfare that apparently must shortly come to pass in this land and elsewhere, there will be an added element of God's wrath—fire! God has used fire before in limited areas, such as Sodom, Gomorrah, perhaps Capernaum, and certain exceedingly wicked Nephite cities such as Zarahemla, Jacobugath, Laman, Josh, Gad, and Kishkumen. But the scriptures declare that in these last days the whole world will be cleansed by fire, and the thought of that is staggering. We don't know what sort of fire this will be. We are not told. Many believe it will be nuclear, and in our day that seems to be a logical possibility. In fact, Elder McConkie said: "It may be, for instance, that nothing except the power of faith and the authority of the priesthood can save individuals and congregations from the atomic holocausts that surely shall be." (*Ensign*, May 1979, p. 93.)

Destroyed or Preserved—by Fire

The truly interesting thing about this fire, whether it is nuclear or not, is that the righteous, those who are willing to constantly repent of their sins and believe in Jesus Christ with all their hearts, should not fear it. Instead they should rejoice in it, for their lives will be spared through the safety that this consuming fire will provide for them as it destroys their enemies.

No wonder God continually pleads with us to repent! Obviously he would rather that we not be destroyed by war and by fire; that we have power in our priesthood, power in our faith. Is it any wonder that Joseph Smith, as he dedicated the Kirtland Temple, prayed, "We know that thou hast spoken by the mouth of thy prophets terrible things concerning the wicked, in the last days—that thou wilt pour out thy judgments, without measure. Therefore, O Lord, deliver thy people from the calamity of the wicked; enable thy servants to seal up the law, and bind up the testimony, that they may be prepared against the day of burning." (D&C 109:45–46.)

7

This Is Not the Lord's
Peace

We can almost hear the questioning: "But wait! All of Eastern Europe is striking for and obtaining the freedoms that we enjoy. They are finding safety as they escape from their long captivity, which movement will surely bring peace. Even the premier of Russia is advocating peace and safety, at last allowing our missionaries to actively spread the gospel among the Russian people! How can these present trends possibly lead to such terrible war as the prophets have described?"

That is a fair question, and one that we will approach as nonpolitical, it being spiritual in nature. Therefore, it seems more than appropriate to examine the word of God and attempt to determine if he has already given us an answer, or at least some clues, from which we can obtain understanding about what to expect from the political upheavals and peace movements of our day.

When Peace Is Deceptive

The Apostle Paul, speaking of the days prior to the Second Coming, said: "For yourselves know perfectly that the day of the Lord cometh as a thief in the night. For when they shall say, Peace and safety; then sudden destruction cometh upon them . . . and they shall not escape." (1 Thessalonians 5:2–3.) Jeremiah, also speaking of the last days, stated: "Then said I, Ah, Lord God! surely thou hast greatly deceived this people . . . saying, Ye shall have peace; whereas the sword reacheth unto the soul." In other words, when the world expects to see peace, instead they shall be devastated by war. Finally, Daniel, speaking of a latter-day anti-Christ world leader, said: "Through his policy also he shall cause craft to prosper in his hand; and he shall magnify himself in his heart, and by peace shall destroy many." (Daniel 8:23–25.)

These prophecies are clear enough: the peace that the world is clamoring for now, will not be permanent! Nor will Satan's well-laid schemes for the destruction of all mankind be so easily thwarted. As Elder Bruce R. McConkie put it: "It is one of the sad heresies of our time that peace will be gained by weary diplomats as they prepare treaties of compromise, or that the Millennium will be ushered in because men will learn to live in peace and to keep the commandments, or that the predicted plagues and promised desolations of latter days can in some way be avoided." (*Ensign,* May 1979, p. 93.)

A Temporary Peace to Be Used with All Diligence

Meanwhile, how we thrill as we consider the temporary possibility of world peace and global safety that seems to be moving to front and center stage in the world today. With the tumbling of so many Communist borders, and with so many more likely to fall in the near future, surely the Lord has opened the way, and the gospel is being spread into many new lands.

Speaking prophetically through Enoch, the Lord said of our time: "the day shall come that the earth shall rest, but before that day the heavens shall be darkened, and a veil of darkness shall cover the earth; and the heavens shall shake, and also the earth; and great tribulations shall be among the children of men, but my people will I preserve; and righteousness will I send down out of heaven; and truth will I send forth out of the earth, to bear testimony of mine Only Begotten; his resurrection from the dead; yea, and also the resurrection of all men; and righteousness and truth will I cause to sweep the earth as with a flood, to gather out mine elect from the four quarters of the earth." (Moses 7:61–62.)

That is an interesting statement: righteousness will come down out of heaven. Might this mean that we all came from heaven to our births, having been foreordained to be righteous missionaries, and to prepare others to be righteous missionaries? And that truth will come forth from the earth — an obvious reference to the Book of Mormon. Then those two things, righteousness and truth, are to sweep the earth as with a flood. And all of this must happen while the Lord's people are being preserved from the great tribulations of the last days. Obviously we have our assignment: missionary work. The question is, are we willing and able to do it?

The Ways of the World Are Interfering

Brother Hugh Nibley writes: "In the TV documentary on missionaries . . . a General Authority declared that 'more is expected of us than any other generation,' yet nothing could be further from the minds of these young people [who are being called to go forth as missionaries] than the teaching of the Prophet Joseph: 'The things of God are of deep import; and time, and experience, and careful and ponderous and solemn thoughts can only find them out. Thy mind, O man, . . . must stretch as high as the utmost heavens' (*Teachings of the Prophet Joseph Smith*, p. 137). They don't seem to realize that we need such knowledge even for survival: 'The Saints ought to lay hold of every door . . . to obtain foothold on the earth, and be making all the preparation that is within their power for the terrible storms that are now gathering in the heavens. . . . Any among you who aspire after their own aggrandizement, and seek their own opulence . . . cannot be benefited by the intercession of the Holy Spirit' (Ibid., p. 141). [Prospective missionaries] today greet such statements as alien and hostile." (*Approaching Zion* [Salt Lake City and Provo UT: Deseret Book Company and Foundation for Ancient Research and Mormon Studies, 1989], p. 259.)

Why do so many of our young people feel this way? Why have these deep things of the Spirit become so distant to us and our children? At least partially it is because a large number of us are caught up in the vain things of the world. Brigham Young said: "Elders of Israel are greedy after the things of this world. If you ask them if they are ready to build up the kingdom of God, their answer is prompt—'Why, to be sure we are, with our whole souls; but we want first to get so much gold, speculate and get rich, and then we can help the church considerably. We will go to California and get gold, go and buy goods and get rich, trade with the emigrants, build a mill, make a farm, get a large herd of cattle, and then we can do a great deal for Israel." (*Journal of Discourses*, 1:164.)

Of course, such an attitude is unrighteous. As the Lord declares, "I command thee that thou shalt not covet thine own property." (D&C 19:26.) And: "Let them repent of all their sins, and of all their covetous desires, before me, saith the Lord; for what is property unto me? saith the Lord." (D&C 117:4.) Once again Brigham Young, in an address titled "Holy Ghost Requisite To Teach The Truth," states: "I am sorry that this people are worldly-minded. . . . Their affections are upon . . . their farms, upon their property, their houses and possessions, and in the same ratio that this is the case, the Holy Spirit of God – the spirit of their calling – forsakes them, and they are overcome with the spirit of the evil one." (*Journal of Discourses*, 11:216.)

Brother Hugh Nibley wrote: "We've certainly [attributed to God] the puritanical doctrine that God has promised prosperity to the righteous; therefore, if you prosper, you must be righteous. Wilford Woodruff came down on that very hard when he said that that is a special doctrine favored by the Latter-day Saints to justify wealth. There are many who really feel very strongly that those who prosper are good and those who don't deserve what they have. So we talk about the deserving rich; well, there are no deserving rich. To be rich is to have more than you need. No one deserves more than he needs, as King Benjamin said. We define the word [prosperous] as money in the bank, rather than progressing in whatever path you're following, which is what the word means." ("Hugh Nibley In Black and White," *BYU Today*, May 1990, p. 41.)

"Every step in the direction of increasing one's personal holdings," Brother Nibley states in another place, "is a step away from Zion, which is another way of saying, as the Lord has proclaimed in various ways, that one cannot serve two masters: to the degree in which he loves the one he will hate the other, and so it is with God and business, for mammon is simply the standard Hebrew word for any kind of financial dealing." (*Approaching Zion*, p. 37.) As Joseph Smith declared, "The greatest temporal and spiritual blessings which always come from faithfulness and concerted effort, never attended individual exertion or enterprise." (*Teachings of the Prophet Joseph Smith*, ed. Joseph Fielding Smith [Salt Lake City: Deseret Book Company, 1976], p. 183.) Even worse, Joseph declared that coveting the things of the world sealed the heavens and closed the mind to personal revelation from God. (Ibid., p. 9.) Perhaps this is why so many of us, young and old alike, lack spirituality and spiritual power to accomplish God's latter-day work.

Indeed the Lord has opened the way, but will we go forth to do the work with power? Will we forsake the world in order to accomplish what we have covenanted to do? The answer, of course, is up to each of us, for salvation is a totally individual effort.

The Time Is Now

Speaking of sweeping the earth as with a flood, President Ezra Taft Benson has said: "The Book of Mormon is the instrument [of truth] that God designed to 'sweep the earth as with a flood, to gather out [his] elect.' (Moses 7:62.) The time is long overdue for a massive flooding of the earth with the Book of Mormon. . . . In this age of electronic media and mass distribution of the printed word, God will hold us accountable if we do not now move the Book of Mormon in a monumental way. We have the Book of Mormon, we have the members, we have the missionaries, we have the resources, and the world has the need. The time is now! . . . my good Saints, we have a great work to perform in a very short time." (*Ensign*, November 1988, pp. 4–5.)

President Benson did not say why he feels such an urgency. He stated only that he knows it is to be done now, "in a very short time." In his words: "I do not know why God has preserved my life to this age, but I do know this: That for the present hour He has revealed to me the absolute need for us to move the Book of Mormon forward now in a marvelous manner. You must help with this burden and with this blessing which He has placed on the whole Church, even all the children of Zion." (Ibid., p. 6.)

As President Gordon B. Hinckley pointed out in the 1989 First Presidency Christmas Devotional on Temple Square, the Lord surely seems to be opening the way for dramatic advancements in missionary work in the world of today. He stated: "Not in a long while has there been a Christmas quite comparable to this. Notwithstanding serious conflicts in many areas, I am convinced that the spirit of the Christ is brooding over much of the earth. We have witnessed in the past few months miracles undreamed of only a short time ago. The shackles of enslavement are falling. The ruthless atheism that in some areas has hung as a cloud of darkness for decades is now being dissipated. Wrote Paul to the Corinthian saints: 'Where the spirit of the Lord is, there is liberty.' (2 Cor. 3:17) Paul said also to the Galatians: 'Stand fast therefore in the liberty wherewith Christ hath made us free, and be not entangled with the yoke of bondage.' (Gal. 5:1) Paul was speaking of the bondage of sin, yes, but he also had known something of another kind of bondage. Tiberius Caesar then governed the known world. It was *Pax Romana,* the peace of Rome. But it was an enforced peace, held together by the ruthless power of the Roman legions. It was the light of Christ that heralded the dawning of a brighter day in that oppressive age. So in our time millions of voices in the nations of eastern Europe are boldly speaking out with faith in God against the oppression of the past, calling for liberty and freedom. It is so tremendous a thing that is happening that it is difficult to comprehend. It is a Christmas present of gigantic proportions to millions who have been under a yoke of bondage. We are celebrating here in the United States the 200th anniversary of the adoption of the Bill of Rights. Today another bill of rights is being crafted as the spirit of Christ broods over great areas of Europe and millions of her people. Like a glorious sunburst through dark clouds, there is emerging freedom of worship, freedom of assembly, freedom of expression, freedom to choose those who will govern.

"In these nations, where new chapters of law and new constitutions of liberty are being written, there is a strong residual of faith in the Lord Jesus Christ. Decades of oppression have not stamped it out. Through all the dark fabric of the past there has remained a silver thread of faith. Quietly, in hushed tones, it has been passed from generation to generation. From this seed will spring new truth as the revealed word of the Lord Jesus Christ is taught as opportunity comes. And come it surely will. It is a non-violent revolution that is taking place. It will open the way for a new day and a new revelation of eternal truth." ("First Presidency's Christmas Devotional," December 1989, pp. 4–6.)

But Now Will Be Brief

The Lord does indeed seem to be granting the world a wondrous blessing in terms of peace; he does indeed seem to be granting the members of the Church a wonderful opportunity to be of missionary service to their fellow beings. But all that notwithstanding, from what has been written by the prophets and apostles, scripturally and prophetically, it seems that this period of peace and prosperity will be brief and will be followed by a difficult period of trouble and turmoil. Then, probably little missionary work will be allowed or even possible. As has been prophesied by Heber C. Kimball and others (*Deseret News*, May 23, 1931), at that time the missionaries will be called home and the world will be left in readiness for the judgments of God. The Lord's missionary work will be "cut short in righteousness." (D&C 84:97; 109:59; 52:11; Romans 9:28.) Might this be why President Benson has felt such a sense of urgency to stress missionary work now and to flood the earth with copies of the Book of Mormon? Perhaps this great book, which the Lord declares to be true

(D&C 17:6) and which Joseph Smith declared to be the most correct book on the face of the earth will continue its ordained work of gathering Israel even when we as a people are rendered temporarily incapable of helping to further the work ourselves. The Book of Mormon could certainly do the job, but it can do so only if enough copies have been spread abroad to do the work—if enough youthful and no-so-youthful elders and sisters have been sent forth to place these copies where they need to go.

A Classic Example

Concerning how to become involved in this great and urgent latter-day work, consider the following account from an elderly couple who, because of poor health, were not able to go on a regular mission. Therefore, they called themselves on what they called a three-year "Book of Mormon mission." They wrote of their experience: "We decided to stop our many travels. We also cut out most non-vital expenses and turned a large part of our cash savings over to our Book of Mormon mission. Also we began living more economically. We started our mission by having the Family-to-Family Book of Mormon program send out 200 books per month to the missions in Mexico, Central and South America. Before long, we learned that one convert baptism was resulting from each ten to twenty of our books. . . . We have received reports of convert baptisms from Mexico, Central and South America, Portugal and Spain. These reports have been sent by mission presidents, missionaries, and converts themselves. All are sincere expressions of appreciation, and we treasure them. When our mission was nearly half over, we were so thrilled with the joys and blessings of the Lord to us, that we decided to triple the number of books provided each month. The interesting thing is that this resulted in tripling the number of convert baptisms reported to us! Our three-year mission will be concluded in a few days. The total number of convert baptisms reported to us is 757, and we feel sure that there are many more that have not been reported. This is quite a contrast to my three-year mission to Germany in the early Twenties, where my companions and I had only three baptisms. My wife and I are convinced that this three-year mission has afforded us some of the happiest years of our lives." (Names withheld at writers' request.)

If we are willing to involve ourselves in this work, we will be exceedingly blessed. As the Lord declared to Joseph Smith in a revelation about the parable of the wheat and the tares, His instructions to the destroying angels are: "Let the wheat and the tares grow together until the harvest is fully ripe; then ye shall first gather out the wheat from among the tares, and after the gathering of the wheat, behold and lo, the tares are bound in bundles, and the field remaineth to be burned. Therefore, thus saith the Lord unto you, with whom the priesthood hath continued through the lineage of your fathers—blessed are ye if ye continue in my goodness, a light unto the Gentiles, and through this priesthood, a savior unto my people Israel." (D&C 86:7–8, 11.)

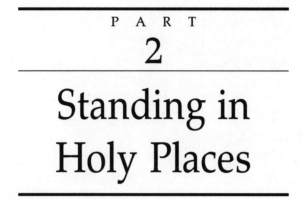

P A R T

2

Standing in
Holy Places

8

Safety Only in Zion

If all the prophecies presented thus far are true, and if what appears to be peace ultimately deteriorates into an all-consuming global war bringing "a full end of all nations" (D&C 87:6), will there be safety anywhere for any of us? Of course there will, at least in a sense, for the Church must survive; and that means that the more righteous portion of its members must also survive.

In the words of Wilford Woodruff: "The Prophet [Joseph Smith] said, 'Brethren, I have been very much edified and instructed in your testimonies here tonight, but I want to say to you before the Lord, that you know no more concerning the destinies of this church and kingdom than a babe upon its mother's lap. You don't comprehend it.' I was rather surprised. He said, 'It is only a handful of Priesthood you see here tonight, but this Church will fill North and South America — it will fill the world. Among other things he said, 'It will fill the Rocky Mountains. There will be tens of thousands of Latter-day Saints who will be gathered in the Rocky Mountains, and there they will open the door for the establishing of the gospel among the Lamanites, who will receive the gospel and their endowments and the blessings of God. This people will go unto the Rocky Mountains; they will there build temples to the Most High. They will raise up a posterity there, and the Latter-day Saints who dwell in those mountains will stand in the flesh until the coming of the Son of Man. The Son of Man will come to them while in the Rocky Mountains.' " (*Conference Report,* April 1898, p. 57.)

In other words, the Church, as well as many of its more goodly members, will make it through the turmoil that lies ahead. Brigham Young added, "[The Rocky Mountains have] been designated, for many generations, to hide up the Saints in the Last Days, until the indignation of the Almighty be over." (*Deseret Evening News,* May 1, 1861, p. 1.)

But does this mean that if we can just live in the mountains, all will be well for us? Hardly! President Joseph Fielding Smith quoted a prophecy by Wilford Woodruff wherein he said that the time was coming when Utah would be a pretty good place in which to live. Then President Smith said: "Now I can't take time to read more of it, but he raised this warning voice, and I believe Utah will be a pretty good place to live in, and other stakes of Zion, for I don't believe President Woodruff intended to confine this to the borders of Utah, but to the stakes of Zion. But the judgments of the Almighty are being poured out, and they shall continue, for the Prophet of God has said it." (*Conference Report,* April 1937, p. 62.)

Not Where, but How

Elder Harold B. Lee said: "I was down in Kelsey, Texas, last November, and I heard a group of anxious people asking, 'Is now the day for us to come up to Zion, where we can come to the mountain of the Lord, where we can be protected from our enemies?' I pondered that question. I prayed about it. What should we say to those people who are in their anxiety? I have studied it a bit, I have learned something of what the Spirit has taught, and I know now that the place of safety in this world is not in any given place; it doesn't make so much difference where we live; but the all-important thing is how we live, and I have found that . . . security can come to Israel only when they keep the commandments, when they live so that they can enjoy the companionship, the direction, the comfort, and the guidance of the Holy Spirit of the Lord, when they are willing to listen to these men whom God has set here to preside as His mouthpieces, and when we obey the counsels of the Church." (*Conference Report,* April 1943, p. 129.)

Elder Bruce R. McConkie said: "We do not know when the calamities and troubles of the last days will fall upon any of us as individuals or upon bodies of the Saints. The Lord deliberately withholds from us the day and hour of his coming and of the tribulations which shall proceed it—all as part of the testing and probationary experiences of mortality. He simply tells us to watch and be ready. We can rest assured that if we have done all in our power to prepare for whatever lies ahead, he will then help us with whatever else we need. He rained manna from heaven upon all Israel, six days each week for forty years, lest they perish for want of bread. . . . (Exodus 16:3–4). During forty years in the wilderness the clothes worn by all Israel waxed not old and their shoes wore not out. . . . (Deut. 29:5). When there was a famine in the land, at Elijah's word, a certain barrel of meal did not waste, and a certain cruse of oil did not fail, until the Lord sent again rain on the earth. And it is worthy of note, as Jesus said, that though there were many widows in Israel, unto only one was Elijah sent (1 Kings 17:10–16). We do not say that all of the Saints will be spared and saved from the coming day of desolation. But we do say there is no promise of safety and no promise of security except for those who love the Lord and who are seeking to do all that he commands." (*Ensign,* May 1979, p. 93.)

In other words, safety will exist only for those who are a Zion people, for those who have become pure in heart (D&C 97:21; 101:18) by striving to live a celestial law (D&C 105:5, 32). But this is an individual issue, not a collective or group issue. As Hugh Nibley writes: "Prophecy tells us that things are going to change and that there is nothing we can do to stop it. Certain things are certainly going to happen. Must we therefore resign ourselves to our fate? Not at all. There is a vital rule that leaves the door wide open to effective individual repentance and escape. We have Professor Heisenberg to thank for that. He found that though you can predict with absolute certainty how masses of particles are going to act, you can never predict how any one particle is going to behave. That is the Heisenberg Uncertainty Principle, which used to be called 'the free will of the atom.' The single particle is unpredictable; only the mass is absolutely bound to behave according to the unimpeachable laws of physics. In the same way one can prophesy with absolute certainty what a nation or people or society is going to do: you can talk about aggregates and predict the behavior of masses, but you can never deny any individual the freedom to repent and go the other way. 'Thou shalt not follow a multitude to do evil.' The prophets and Professor Heisenberg show us the way out. You do not have to wait for the group to change, for the society to repent, nor do you have to change your ways to comply with theirs; the individual is free to ignore the multitude, and only he is free. Only an individual can repent. Repent is a reflexive verb—you can't repent somebody else or force somebody else [to repent]; you just repent. The clear rule for assuring desirable change is set forth in 2 Nephi: 'As many of the Gentiles as will repent are the covenant people of the Lord; and as many of the Jews who will not repent shall be cast off; for the Lord covenanteth with none save it be with them that repent and believe in his Son' (2 Nephi 30:2)." (*Approaching Zion,* pp. 416–417.)

Stand Ye in Holy Places

Specifically, then, what is each of us to do? As the Lord puts it, "Verily I say unto you all [of the Church]: Arise and shine forth, that thy light may be a standard for the nations; and that the gathering together upon the land of Zion, and upon her stakes, may be for a defense, and for a refuge from the storm, and from wrath when it shall be poured out without mixture upon the whole earth." (D&C 115:5–6.) "Wherefore, *stand ye in holy places,* and be not moved, until the day of the Lord come; for behold, it cometh quickly, saith the Lord." (D&C 87:8; italics added.)

So, to be delivered from the judgments and calamities that will be poured out upon the wicked without measure in the coming days, we must each stand in holy places. And what does this mean? Where are these holy places in which we are commanded to stand?

President Ezra Taft Benson has said: "We . . . live in the midst of economic, political and spiritual instability. When these signs are observed—unmistakable evidences that His coming is nigh—we need not be troubled, but 'stand in holy places, and be not moved, until the day of the Lord come' (D&C 87:8). Holy men and women stand in holy places, and these holy places consist of our temples, our chapels, our homes, and stakes of Zion, which are, as the Lord declares, 'for a defense, and for a refuge from the storm, and from wrath when it shall be poured out without mixture upon the whole earth' (D&C 115:6). We must heed the Lord's counsel to the Saints of this dispensation: 'Prepare yourselves for the great day of the Lord' (D&C 133:10). This preparation must consist of more than just casual membership in the Church.

We must be guided by personal revelation and the counsel of the living prophet so we will not be deceived. Our Lord has indicated who, among Church members, will stand when He appears: 'At that day, when I shall come in my glory, shall the parable be fulfilled which I spake concerning the ten virgins' (D&C 45:56). There is a real sifting going on in the Church, and it is going to become more pronounced with the passing of time. It will sift the wheat from the tares, because we face some difficult days, the like of which we have never experienced in our lives. And those days are going to require faith and testimony and family unity, the like of which we have never had." (*The Teachings of Ezra Taft Benson* [Salt Lake City: Bookcraft, 1988], pp. 106–7.)

How to Do It

Specifically, in the above statement President Benson lists the following items that we need to be aware of; needs and spiritual skills that we must perfect within our own lives if we are to be listed among the "wise virgins," the 50 percent that Jesus declared would be prepared to receive their Lord. They are, in the order we would like to discuss them:

1. The obtaining and strengthening of a personal testimony.

2. Developing personal faith through sincere and humble repentance.

3. Diligent Church activity and a willingness to follow the Lord's living prophet.

4. Regular temple attendance.

5. Continual reception of personal revelation.

6. A consistent effort to develop unified, spiritual families.

All of these are eternally important if we are to be found standing in holy places. If we ignore these important matters, it doesn't matter where we are standing—in temple, chapel, or any other place. If we are not holy, it will not be a holy place *for us*. President Joseph Fielding Smith said it this way: "We shall not escape [the calamities of the last days] unless we repent, turn to the Lord, honor our Priesthood and our membership in this Church, and be true and faithful to our covenants." (*Conference Report*, April 1937, p. 62.) Only if we follow the Lord in righteousness will we be delivered!

9

The Need for a Personal Testimony

We find it interesting that the more we learn about the gospel of Jesus Christ, the more overwhelmed we are by it. We are awed by the power that living the gospel places in our hands—power to teach and to bless as well as to receive blessings. We are troubled by the scope and complexity of God's laws and of the eternal rewards and punishments affixed to them. We say we are troubled, but that is only because we have so frequently chosen to allow ourselves to become victims of those eternal consequences. Beyond our own troublesome natures, we are in awe of God's incredibly complete organization, his laws and his church. And finally, we are in reverence of the power of the atonement and the infinite mercy associated with Christ's mission for us, two of his struggling servants.

In short, the gospel of Jesus Christ overwhelms us, for it

Some of the material in this chapter has been excerpted from: Blaine and Brenton Yorgason, *Binding the Lord* (Orem UT: Keepsake BookCards, 1989).

is much more vast and deep than we had ever supposed—or, frankly, are even yet capable of grasping.

Yet as we look at it, we see a complete whole of truth made up of many small parts called doctrines or teachings. If a member of the Church will examine each small part or portion of the gospel or the Church until he or she gains a thorough understanding of it, using the techniques of study given us by God through the prophet Moroni (Moroni 10:4–5), then the eternal truthfulness of that small portion will be known. And once a person *knows,* he or she need never again be dissuaded from his or her knowledge of that truth. Combined, such small portions of known truth become the basis for a person's testimony.

A Knowledge of Truth

Elder Bruce R. McConkie said that a personal testimony should consist of three things:

1. A witness that Jesus is real and that he is the Christ, the Son of the Living God. (D&C 46:13.)

2. A witness that Joseph Smith was a prophet of God and that there is a living prophet of God on the earth today. (Amos 3:7.)

3. A witness that The Church of Jesus Christ of Latter-day Saints is the only true and living church on the face of the earth (D&C 1:30) and that it teaches the complete gospel of Jesus Christ. (*Mormon Doctrine* [Salt Lake City: Bookcraft, 1966], pp. 785–86.)

A Personal Revelation

It is important to understand three things about this personal witness or testimony. First, it is not something that we only *think* is true, or that we have "conjured up" in our minds. If the source is from within ourselves, it is not a witness or testimony but only an idea. Therefore, it does not have the power to change our behavior or to bring about our salvation. A true testimony, on the other hand, is pure, heavenly knowledge, granted by the power of the Holy Ghost. It is direct revelation from God and can be called by no other term. Because of the divine source of this revelation, it can and does motivate a person to change, for it is a direct gift from God and thus has the power of salvation within it. (See Moroni 10:5.)

Joseph Smith declared: "Now if any man has the testimony of Jesus, has he not the spirit of prophecy? And if he has the spirit of prophecy, I ask, is he not a prophet? And if a prophet, he can receive revelation! And any man that does not receive revelation for himself must be damned, for the testimony of Jesus is the spirit of prophecy." (*The Words of Joseph Smith*, ed. Andrew F. Ehat and Lyndon W. Cook [Provo UT: Brigham Young University Religious Studies Center, 1980], p. 230.)

That's a pretty bold statement. But to support Joseph Smith, President John Taylor added: "When the light that is in heaven communicates with the light within us, when the Spirit that dwells in the bosom of the Almighty dwells in ours, and an intercourse is opened between heaven and us, we are then placed in a position to understand that which it would be impossible to comprehend upon any natural principle known to us, and hence it is written, 'For what man knoweth the things of a man, save the spirit of man which is in him? even so the things of God knoweth no man, but the Spirit of God.' (1 Corinthians 2:11)." (*The Gospel Kingdom* [Salt Lake City: Bookcraft, 1987], p. 45.)

Alma the younger said: "I testify unto you that I do know that these things whereof I have spoken are true. And how do ye suppose that I know of their surety? Behold, I say unto you they are made known unto me by the Holy Spirit of God. Behold, I have fasted and prayed many days that I might know these things of myself. And now I do know of myself that they are true; for the Lord God hath made them manifest unto me by his Holy Spirit; and this is the spirit of revelation that is in me." (Alma 5:45–46.)

Nephi's younger brother, Jacob, who became a remarkable orator in his day, said: "Great and marvelous are the works of the Lord. How unsearchable are the depths of the mysteries of him; and it is impossible that man should find out all his ways. And no man knoweth of his ways save it be revealed unto him; wherefore, brethren, despise not the revelations of God." (Jacob 4:8.)

Concluding this thought about a person's testimony being nothing more nor less than personal revelation, the Lord says: "If thou shalt ask, thou shalt receive revelation upon revelation, knowledge upon knowledge, that thou mayest know the mysteries and peaceable things – that which bringeth joy, that which bringeth life eternal." (D&C 42:61.)

Testimony Must Be Diligently Sought

Personal revelation from God does not 'just come.' A conviction of the truth of the gospel, a testimony, must be diligently sought if it is to be found. As Elder John A. Widtsoe once declared: "It does not come as the dew from heaven. It is the result of man's eagerness to know truth. Often it requires battle with traditions, former opinions and appetites, and a long testing of the gospel by every available fact and standard." (*Evidences and Reconciliations* [Salt Lake City: Bookcraft, 1960], p. 15.)

Moroni said: "When ye shall receive these things, I would exhort you that ye would ask God, the Eternal Father, in the name of Christ, if these things are not true; and if ye shall ask with a sincere heart, with real intent, having faith in Christ, he will manifest the truth of it unto you by the power of the Holy Ghost. And by the power of the Holy Ghost ye may know the truth of all things." (Moroni 10:4–5.)

Thus it should be seen that diligent effort is required if a true testimony is to be obtained. This principle is clearly illustrated by the example of the four sons of Mosiah. When they departed on their fourteen-year missions, they too had to seek their own testimonies, and they did so by fasting much and praying much (Alma 17:9–10), obtaining their testimonies by exercising diligent effort. In response, the Holy Ghost gave them a feeling of comfort and then led them, blessed them with incredible missionary success, and gave them protection throughout their entire missions. But first they had to pay the price!

During his Sermon on the Mount, Jesus said, "Ask, and it shall be given you; seek, and ye shall find; knock, and it shall be opened unto you." (Matthew 7:7.) The Savior promises direct responses or testimony, but only to those who initiate the action. Ask; seek; knock. Each of us puts forth his or her best effort, and then and only then will the heavens respond.

Once the Lord has responded, is that the end of the matter? We do not think so. President Harold B. Lee quoted one of the other apostles as saying that a person was not truly converted but needed to seek after and increase his or her testimony until "it goes down in his heart like fire." (*Stand Ye in Holy Places* [Salt Lake City: Deseret Book Company, 1975], p. 63.) That means we are obligated to continually pray for and seek after our testimonies, even after we have come to believe and know certain things, until the divine witnessing of the Holy Ghost becomes such a very powerful experience within us that it can only be described as being "like fire," burning within us time and time again.

Our personal experiences with revelation can become daily more powerful, but only as we make ourselves more pure and committed to keeping the commandments. And our goal, in terms of personal worthiness, of course, is to "let thy bowels also be full of charity towards all men, and to the household of faith, and let virtue garnish thy thoughts unceasingly." (D&C 121:45–46.) Then the promise is made that "the Holy Ghost [shall] be thy constant companion." (Ibid.) And that, for any of us, would be a wonderful blessing indeed.

By Personal Study

Besides keeping the commandments, another area that requires a sincere and diligent effort if we are going to obtain and then strengthen our own personal testimony is that of personal study. Before we can know the gospel is true, we must learn it, understand it, and comprehend the relationship of its principles. The scriptures must become our daily guide, and we must long each day to learn more of God's will from them.

Again Elder Widtsoe wrote: "It is a paradox that men will gladly devote time every day for many years to learn a science or an art; yet will expect to win a knowledge of the gospel, which comprehends all sciences and arts, through perfunctory glances at books or occasional listening to sermons. The gospel should be studied more intensively than any school or college subject. They who pass opinion on the gospel without having given it intimate and careful study are not lovers of truth, and their opinions are worthless." (*Evidences and Reconciliations*, pp. 16–17.)

Adding to this, President Joseph Fielding Smith said: "It is our duty to seek the Lord, to obey his laws, to keep his commandments, to put away from us light-mindedness, foolishness, and the false theories, notions and philosophies of the world, and to accept with fullness of heart and in humility these solemn, God-given principles which will bring us into eternal life in the Celestial Kingdom. There is no knowledge, no learning that can compensate the individual for the loss of his belief in heaven and in the saving principles of the

79

Gospel of Jesus Christ. An education that leads a man from these central truths cannot compensate him for the great loss of spiritual things." (*Doctrines of Salvation* [Salt Lake City: Bookcraft, 1954], pp. 321–22.)

By Pondering

Once we have begun our sincere personal study of God's holy writ, we must not neglect that quiet aspect of study, the process of pondering, or deep prayerful thinking. To truly obtain our testimony of fire, we need to make pondering what we have read and prayed about our constant pastime. This should be the lullaby we fall asleep to; the anthem that stirs our wakening hearts and souls each morning. Pondering should not be accompanied by the radio or other distractions but should be done in silence, when we are alone with ourselves, our thoughts, and the Spirit of the Lord.

The great prophet Nephi writes: "My soul delighteth in the scriptures, and my heart pondereth them. . . . Behold, my soul delighteth in the things of the Lord; and my heart pondereth continually upon the things which I have seen and heard." (2 Nephi 4:15–16.) When the resurrected Christ visited the Nephites, he said to them: "Go ye unto your homes, and ponder upon the things which I have said, and ask of the Father, in my name, that ye may understand." (3 Nephi 17:3.) And the Lord said to the elders at Kirtland, "I leave these sayings with you to ponder in your hearts, with this commandment which I give unto you, that ye shall call upon me while I am near." (D&C 88:62.)

Pondering, therefore, is the quiet time in this noisy world of ours when the Holy Ghost is finally able to penetrate the ears of our understanding. A "testimony of fire" can never be obtained without this essential, scripturally advocated focus of activity.

By Prayer

Though we will deal with prayer in greater detail later on, it should go without saying that a person will not normally obtain personal revelation without asking for it in prayer. Elder John A. Widtsoe once said: "The seeker for a testimony must recognize his own limitations. He is on a royal road, traveling towards the palace of truth, in which all human good may be found. There are truths beyond the material universe. Indeed, a testimony may be said to begin with the acceptance of God, who transcends as well as encompasses material things. The seeker for a testimony feels the need of help beyond his own powers, as the astronomer uses the telescope to enlarge his natural vision. The seeker for a testimony prays to the Lord for help. Such a prayer must be as insistent and constant as the desire. They must move together as the palm and back of the hand. Then help will come." (*Evidences and Reconciliations*, p. 16.)

Further, besides the fact that the four sons of Mosiah "fasted much, and prayed much," we learn from Moroni that if we are to learn truth, we must "ask God, the Eternal Father, in the name of Christ." Of course, this can only mean simple, sincere prayer.

By Practice

Additionally, we must practice keeping the commandments and living the principles of the gospel of Jesus Christ if we are to obtain a testimony of its truthfulness. The Savior declared: "My doctrine is not mine, but his that sent me. If any man will do his will, he shall know of the doctrine, whether it be of God, or whether I speak of myself." (John 7:16–17.)

The Verb "Chosen"

In the scriptures, the Lord frequently uses the phrase "called and chosen" (Revelation 17:14; Alma 13:3; D&C 24:1; 52:1; 55:1; 95:5; 121:34) in reference to His Saints. One of the more enlightening of these references states: "There are many who have been ordained among you, whom I have called; but few of them are chosen. They who are not chosen have sinned a very grievous sin, in that they are walking in darkness at noon-day." And, "If you keep not my commandments, the love of the Father shall not continue with you, therefore you shall walk in darkness." (D&C 95:5-6, 12.)

Because the Lord is telling us that not being chosen is a grievous sin, then he is also saying that being chosen is a factor of *our* agency, not his. In other words, we are the ones who decide if we are to be chosen, not God. And how do we make that decision? By whether or not we choose to walk in darkness at noon-day, or, in other words, how we choose to respond to God's commandments. Thus the word *chosen* becomes an action verb to us and an adjective to God, rather than vice-versa as so many people seem to think. Plainly stated, God doesn't do the choosing—we do.

We might paraphrase the Lord's words, likening them to ourselves: "There are many called, but few are chosen. And why are [we] not chosen? Because [our] hearts are set so much upon the things of this world, and aspire to the honors of men . . . [in doing which we undertake to] cover our sins, [to] gratify our pride, our vain ambition, [and] to exercise control or dominion or compulsion upon the souls of the children of men, in . . . unrighteousness." (See D&C 121:34–37.) Once again, we become chosen only if we choose to live righteously.

Now, permit us to bring this conversation full circle. Diligently seeking after a testimony, and then diligently seeking to increase its strength would encompass the process of "becoming chosen." This would include willingly repenting of all sins, keeping the commandments with a whole and joyful heart, studying the scriptures with an intent desire to know their meaning, serving others selflessly, and offering up constant, sincere prayers in behalf of self and others. Or, as the Lord says, becoming "chosen." And only the chosen will be found standing in holy places during the coming days of trial and judgment.

By Our Fruits

How do we know if we have become chosen? The answer, again according to the scriptures, is by how we live; by the choices we make every day; by the little things we choose to do — not only for a living but in our spare time as well. Patterns of daily living reflect our inner beliefs; this has always been the case and undoubtedly will always be so.

Jesus said it this way: "Ye shall know them by their fruits. Do men gather grapes of thorns, or figs of thistles? Even so every good tree bringeth forth good fruit, but a corrupt tree bringeth forth evil fruit. A good tree cannot bring forth evil fruit, neither can a corrupt tree bring forth good fruit. Every tree that bringeth not forth good fruit is hewn down, and cast into the fire. Wherefore by their fruits ye shall know them." (Matthew 7:16–20.)

And Moroni adds: "I remember the word of God which saith by their works ye shall know them; for if their works be good, then they are good also. For behold, God hath said a man being evil cannot do that which is good; for if he offereth a gift, or prayeth unto God, except he shall do it with real intent it profiteth him nothing. For behold, it is not counted unto him for righteousness." (Moroni 7:5–7.) But on the other hand, "every thing which inviteth and enticeth to do good, and to love God, and to serve him, is inspired of God." (Moroni 7:13.) Therefore, "if ye will lay hold upon every good thing, and condemn it not, ye certainly will be a child of Christ" (Moroni 7:19), for "in Christ there should come every good thing" (Moroni 7:22).

With such clarity of instructions, each of us should know exactly where we stand in terms of a sound personal testimony. Do we keep the commandments, or do we selectively break them? Do we keep all Church rules and policies, or do we pick and choose and set ourselves up as our own master when in fact we have covenanted to be faithful servants of Christ and his mortal administrators? Do we spend our spare time contemplating and pondering the deep things of God, or do we waste it upon worldly trivia or even worse activities? Watching our own actions, listening to our own words, and being aware of our own thoughts, all will give us clear indication of the depth and reality of our own witness or testimony.

A Testimony Can Be Lost

Just as we can gain a testimony, just so surely can we also lose it. Since a testimony is a living entity that requires feeding, if such nourishment stops, the testimony will wither up and finally starve to death. Starvation of a testimony usually begins with failure to keep in touch with the Lord, with not praying. Once regular and continual prayer stops, a person's desire to learn and grow in the gospel soon weakens. Ere long, sacred covenants diminish in importance until they are forgotten entirely, and almost any activity available will preempt study of the gospel. Church participation takes on less and less importance, and finally such a person is unable to see that he or she has wandered from the truth.

As Alma declared to Zeezrom: "It is given unto many to know the mysteries of God," but "he that will harden his heart, the same receiveth the lesser portion of the word . . . until they know nothing concerning his mysteries; and then they are taken captive by the devil, and led by his will down to destruction. Now this is what is meant by the chains of hell." (Alma 12:9–11.) And, as the Lord further declared to Joseph Smith, "that wicked one cometh and taketh away light and truth, through disobedience, from the children of men, and because of the tradition of their fathers." (D&C 93:39.)

In other words, losing one's testimony is a process, not an event, and coincides with losing the Spirit. And that, the scriptures plainly teach, occurs only when we are disobedient to the principles of the gospel that we have already learned, through personal revelation, are true.

"The dying testimony," Elder Widtsoe wrote, "is easily recognized. The organizations and practices of the Church are ignored; the television takes the place of the Sacrament meeting; golf or motion pictures, the Sunday worship; the cup of coffee instead of the Word of Wisdom; the cold, selfish hand instead of helpfulness, charity for the poor and the payment of tithing. Soon, the testimony is gone, and the former possessor walks about . . . sour and discontented, and always in his heart, unhappy. He has lost his most precious possession, and [there is] nothing to replace it. He has lost inward freedom, the gift of obedience to law." (*Evidences and Reconciliations*, p. 40.) So we must watch ourselves and be forever on our guard that such will never be our lot.

Testimony Not Sufficient for Salvation

According to the Lord, we are not saved simply by virtue of a testimony. (D&C 3:4.) But a testimony is the only beginning (and only the beginning) of real spiritual progress. With it comes a greater desire to serve God, to keep his commandments, and to walk according to the light that we have received through personal revelation. (See D&C 82:2–4.)

But a Testimony Is Required
If We Are to Stand in Holy Places

From what the Lord revealed to Joseph Smith, we learn that it is only those who obtain and then are valiant in their testimonies who are then able to work out their salvation. These are the "chosen," the people who by becoming independent of the world find themselves standing in holy places before the Lord. On the other hand, those "who are not valiant in the testimony of Jesus" will experience the judgments of God unto destruction. They will then be assigned an eternal inheritance, not in the celestial kingdom but in the terrestrial kingdom or below. (See D&C 76:79.)

CHAPTER

10

Sincere and Humble Repentance

A close friend of ours, while serving as a bishop, recorded the following in his journal: "I had a rather unusual interview today. A young man, whose name I will not record, made an appointment over a week ago to meet with me. This afternoon, after a few moments of chit-chat, he proceeded to unburden himself of boxcars full of sins, most of them having to do with drugs and sexual promiscuity. Most recently he has been fornicating with a live-in girlfriend. They have now decided to get married, and since both are from L.D.S. families, they want to marry in the temple.

"I listened silently until he was through—over an hour's worth of unburdening of some very gross sins, and then I stared in amazement as he made the following remark.

" 'Whew!' he sighed with real relief. 'I'm glad that's over.

Some of the material in this chapter has been excerpted from: Blaine and Brenton Yorgason, *How To Repent* (Orem UT: Keepsake BookCards, 1989) and from: Blaine and Brenton Yorgason, *Satan and His Host* (Orem UT: Keepsake BookCards, 1989).

You know, bishop, it feels real good to have repented. Now I can't wait to go to the temple.'

" 'Who has repented?' I asked, setting him back on his heels just a little.

" 'Uh . . . I have,' he replied, sounding confused. 'I just told you everything I've been doing that's bad. I don't think I left anything out, so I've repented. You know—confessed? That's repenting, isn't it?'

"Needless to say, the young man and I then had another long talk, with me doing most of the speaking, while I taught him that repentance consists of doing a great deal more than simply confessing a bunch of sins before some priesthood authority and then waltzing off into the temple. I believe he now knows that it takes real effort to repent, and he was a mighty sober young man when he finally walked out of my office. Of course it will remain to be seen whether or not he has the courage to really repent."

A Knowledge of Unworthiness

Once we have begun to gain or develop a personal testimony, then an understanding of our own personal unrighteousness or unworthiness before God will begin to fill our hearts and minds. As this painful knowledge grows in scope, we will long with ever greater fervor to become totally cleansed. The seeking of such a cleansing, granted only through the atoning blood of Jesus Christ, is called repentance.

As the young man mentioned above learned, repentance is the process whereby a mortal soul—unclean and stained with sin—is enabled, through the love of Christ and the Father, to cast off his burden of guilt, wash away the filth of his iniquity, and become clean every whit, entirely free of the bondage of sin. (See *Mormon Doctrine*, p. 630.) But remember—repentance is a process, not an event! In other words, it takes time, and it requires certain kinds of efforts. Therefore, it is the process whereby we can once again become worthy to return to the presence of Heavenly Father. The Lord says, "He who has repented of his sins, the same is forgiven, and I, the Lord, remember them no more." (D&C 58:42.)

Repentance, however, isn't just an optional portion of the gospel that we can take or leave at our whim. Instead it is a commandment, and the Lord is very forceful in his declarations regarding it. He says: "Remember that he that persists in his own carnal nature, and goes on in the ways of sin and rebellion against God, remaineth in his fallen state and the devil hath all power over him. Therefore he is as though there was no redemption made, being an enemy to God; and also is the devil an enemy to God." (Mosiah 16:5.)

Can you imagine being an enemy to God, and in the same class as Satan? And all because we won't choose to repent. Nephi calls it being a member of the church of the devil (1 Nephi 14:10) and records that the angel told him that members of the devil's church were characterized by the fact that gold, silver, silks, scarlets, fine-twined linen, precious clothing, immorality, and praise of the world, were important to them (1 Nephi 13:7–9), no matter which church they had been baptized into. "O ye workers of iniquity," the Lord says, "ye that are puffed up in the vain things of the world, ye that have professed to know the way of righteousness nevertheless have gone astray, as sheep having no shepherd, notwithstanding a shepherd hath called after you and is still calling after you, but ye will not hearken unto his voice." (Alma 5:37.)

Vain Things of the World

So God has been calling after us to keep us from being his enemies, members of the church of the devil, and he will surely continue to do so. But why won't we listen to his calls;

why won't we repent? Again, because we are puffed up in the vain things of the world. In another place he says, "Can ye be puffed up in the pride of your hearts . . . and setting your hearts upon the vain things of the world, upon your riches?" (Alma 5:53.) Apparently, then, such worldly things as power or position, fame, expensive homes, cars, boats, clothing, or anything else that might stroke our vanity or deflect our attention from God's service are great stumbling blocks to repentance. If people, Latter-day Saints or otherwise, are caught up in serving these idols then repentance is going to be very difficult for them, if not impossible.

The "Little Sins"

That brings us to the next point in this issue. Alma said, "Come and fear not, and lay aside every sin, which easily doth beset you, which doth bind you down to destruction, yea, come and go forth, and show unto your God that ye are willing to repent of your sins and enter into a covenant with him to keep his commandments." (Alma 7:15.) Now notice: to repent, each of us must lay aside every sin. That means all of them, all of the time. Sadly, many of us don't do that. Instead, we spend our days being pretty good about most things but still desperately clinging to our favorite sins, the "little" things that we enjoy in secret and are certain are not serious enough to have any eternal impact upon us.

Those who have such habits are ignoring the Lord's word and are blissfully marching down the road to misery, sorrow, and perhaps destruction. More immediate, and more pertinent to our discussion, they are not repenting and so are taking the position of becoming an enemy to God, members of what the prophet Nephi described as the church of the devil.

What are these "little" sins we speak of? Virtually anything that, in one way or another, is contrary to God's instructions and commandments. "Little white lies" would certainly be one of them, as would attending movies or watching videos that we know are not conducive to the Lord's Spirit. Losing our temper with our children or companion is surely not the Lord's way, nor are gossiping, backbiting, profaning or being vulgar, and carrying in our hearts our favorite grudges because we have been so innocently wronged. The Lord declares, "Let the wicked forsake his way, and the unrighteous man his thoughts: and let him return unto the Lord, and he will have mercy upon him, and to our God, for he will abundantly pardon." (Isaiah 55:7.)

Is the message clear? Here the Lord defines the terms *wicked* and *unrighteous*. A wicked person does things wrong, while an unrighteous person thinks wrong things. And both wicked and unrighteous people have great need of cleansing themselves through repentance, for they are not clean before the Lord.

How many of us have problems with our thoughts, with being filled with pride and arrogance, with not always telling the complete truth, with mentally ridiculing or simply ignoring God's ordinances or commandments?

Where Much Is Given

In putting this discussion in perspective, perhaps such sins as just described are not serious to a prostitute, or to a hardened criminal. But are they not serious to an active, endowed member of the Church? To those who have been sealed to eternal mates in the holy temple of God? What about to those who have made solemn covenants to live the highest laws of the kingdom of God?

The Lord has said, "Of him unto whom much is given much is required; and he who sins against the greater light shall receive the greater condemnation." (D&C 82:3.) As seminary teachers we heard this phrase quoted many times, but rarely did we hear it quoted correctly. Many of our students said the word "expected" instead of "required," which dramatically lessens the impact. The trouble with that, of course, is that they are mistaken. Clearly the Lord says that where "much is given much is required," and He means it. And what is required? Obedience — obedience to all of God's laws and commandments. And that most surely includes no longer doing wicked things or thinking unrighteous thoughts.

Alma declared, to those of us who would prefer clinging a while longer to our favorite sins because they can't possibly be that serious: "Our words will condemn us, yea, all our works will condemn us; we shall not be found spotless; and our thoughts will also condemn us." (Alma 12:14.) And, in a powerful conclusion to this thought, King Benjamin stated, as he was about to conclude his great, final admonition to his people: "If you do not watch yourselves, and your thoughts, and your words, and your deeds, and observe the commandments of God, and continue in the faith . . . even unto the end of your lives, ye must perish. And now . . . remember, and perish not." (Mosiah 4:30.)

Perhaps our "little" sins committed knowingly are in some ways worse than the major sins committed by such unhappy people as prostitutes and criminals who may not know any better. Therefore, if we desire to repent and thus stop being an enemy to God, we must repent of even the tiniest of our sins, thoughts and actions both, and become "clean every whit" (John 13:10) before the Lord.

Flaxen Cords

There is, though, another reason why the "little" sins we cling to are so dangerous. Nephi said, referring to those of us who live in the latter days: "The Gentiles are lifted up in the pride of their eyes, and have stumbled, because of the greatness of their stumbling block, that they have built up many churches; nevertheless, they put down the power and miracles of God, and preach up unto themselves their own wisdom and their own learning, that they may get gain and grind upon the face of the poor. And there are many churches built up which cause envyings, and strifes, and malice. And there are also secret combinations, even as in times of old, according to the combinations of the devil, for he is the founder of all these things; yea, the founder of murder, and works of darkness; yea, and he leadeth them by the neck with a flaxen cord, until he bindeth them with his strong cords forever." (2 Nephi 26:20–22.)

Nephi talks about the pride that the people in the latter days, including, of course, members of the Church, are going to struggle with. According to President Ezra Taft Benson, this pride is actually an enmity between the proud and God, which is why people sometimes have a hard time accepting spiritual things. Instead, President Benson says, they are rebellious, hard-hearted, stiff-necked, puffed up, easily offended, and unrepentant. (See *Ensign*, April 1989, p. 4.)

Next Nephi talks about secret works of darkness that were founded by the devil. From our limited experience, we have found that those who are attracted to "works of darkness" often get involved with activities after dark, when people can't see what they are up to. According to Nephi, the devil will lead such people by a flaxen cord until he can finally bind them with his strong cords forever. Put into modern language, people who do not sincerely try to keep God's commandments drift from good to bad and from bad to worse, without ever really thinking that they are doing anything wrong. Or, put another way, the more we sin, the easier it gets. In Nephi's words, Satan is leading such people along, carefully, gently, with "flaxen cords." And he does that until a person's unrighteous habits are so deeply ingrained that he no longer needs to worry about that person, at which time those cords of his have become "strong."

Sadly, many people don't even know what is happening to them. In fact, many teenagers and adults alike hardly believe in the devil, or just laugh at him. Sadly, Satan and his host laugh right back and wrap their flaxen cords more tightly.

All who knowingly commit a sin help wrap one of the devil's flaxen cords around their own necks. If they commit a sin without knowing better, then they are not as accountable and will eventually be taught better. But every person is born with the light of Christ, which teaches right from wrong. (D&C 88:7; Moroni 7:19; and D&C 88 heading.) That light becomes brighter as we live the gospel, and dimmer as we stray from keeping the commandments. Of course, we can douse the light altogether by ignoring the promptings of the Holy Ghost, and that is when Satan's cords become strong enough to lead us to destruction.

It takes time for Satan's flaxen cords to become strong, and during that time, repentance is a fairly simple option. If those so bound will recognize what is happening to them and decide immediately to repent, the Lord will help them remove Satan's cords. On the other hand, if they have not decided to repent, or choose not to when the wisdom of it is pointed out, then before long they may stop attending church, or, if they do attend, they may become argumentative during classes. Meanwhile, fear will play a bigger and bigger role in their lives, they drive the Spirit further and further away, and all of this will go on until finally, as the Lord puts it, they are left unto themselves, to kick against the pricks, to persecute the saints, and to fight against God. (See D&C 121:38.)

The Guilty Taketh the Truth to Be Hard

Such unrepentant people are recognizable even before such drastic things occur. Consider, for example, the case of Laman and Lemuel. The record states: "After I, Nephi, had made an end of speaking to my brethren, behold they said unto me: Thou hast declared unto us hard things, more than we are able to bear. And it came to pass that I said unto them that I knew that I had spoken hard things against the wicked, according to the truth; and the righteous have I justified, and testified that they should be lifted up at the last day; wherefore, the guilty taketh the truth to be hard, for it cutteth them to the very center. And now, my brethren, if ye were righteous and were willing to hearken to the truth, and give heed unto it, that ye might walk uprightly before God, then ye would not murmur because of the truth, and say: Thou speakest hard things against us." (1 Nephi 16:1–3.)

When Nephi said that truth cutteth the wicked to the very center, he meant that it hurt their feelings or pricked their consciences right to the core of their emotions. Someone who is defensive or easily offended by some gospel truth or other may also be in need of repentance. According to the scriptures, it is that simple.

Satan Is As Real As Christ

An understanding of repentance cannot be complete without an understanding of the reality and role of Lucifer or Satan, who with his followers is known as the devil. Just as Jesus Christ is the author of salvation, Satan is the author of evil. As Christ is the Father of truth, Satan is the father of lies. As Christ is the source of all light, so Satan is the author of darkness. As Christ sends forth angels and mortal servants to accomplish his righteousness through the power of the Holy Ghost (Moroni 7:29–31), so Satan sends forth his emissaries, both spiritual and mortal, to accomplish the destruction of the souls of men through the power of evil.

To believe otherwise is ludicrous. If the Savior's work is going forward, then Satan's opposing work must also be prospering. And, if truth is revealed, great righteousness brought to pass, and people's hearts lifted to Christ by the power of God, then by the power of the evil one are wrought sorceries, witchcrafts, magics, and every form of evil abomination. (See Mormon 1:19.)

Satan's Ambition

Even though we know that the devil will ultimately be overcome, Lucifer must be an eternal egotist. Apparently his ego did not diminish after he failed to dethrone God during the grand council in heaven, for Moses learned that one of his greatest aims, then as well as now, is still to persuade people to worship him. (Moses 1:12; Moses 6:49.) In this, tragically, he has met with great success. Claiming to be "the god of this world," he has the support and, though they might not realize it, the adoration and worship of all those who live after the manner of the world, including some Latter-day Saints. Let us explain.

As we worship God through obedience to his commandments, so also do we worship Satan if we obey his directives. If, for instance, our mouths are filled with profanity or deceit, if our hearts and minds are filled with lust and thoughts of immorality, if our money is spent on filth or time-wasting products or materials, if our goals are wealth and power before or in place of building the kingdom, then no matter how often we pray or go to church or serve missions, Satan remains our god because we are obeying his commandments rather than Heavenly Father's. We then are members of Satan's church, Nephi's aptly described "church of the devil" (1 Nephi 13), and until we repent it does us little good to have been baptized a member of Christ's earthly kingdom.

Satan's Laughter

If all this darkness reigns, then according to what Moses learned, Satan is very pleased. Moses saw that the devil "had a great chain in his hand, and it veiled the whole face of the earth with darkness; and he looked up and laughed, and his angels rejoiced." (Moses 7:26.) It is difficult for us to imagine such intense evil, but we know it is real, and has been, since before the foundation of the earth.

How Evil Spirits Act upon Mortals

Apparently the pattern of abuse of an evil spirit upon a mortal is to come at the person over and over from the outside, afflicting, tormenting with fears and temptations, wearing at the person in the area of the spirit's assignment or the individual's weakness. This continues until the victim gets rid of the spirit through righteousness and rebuking, or succumbs to it and partakes of the sin. Once a person has succumbed, the spirit is apparently allowed to gain entry to his body, where it is able to exert even more power and influence than before. In this manner many diseases occur, marriages are broken up, testimonies are lost, missions are abandoned, families are destroyed, callings are not fulfilled, and even people's lives are taken before their time.

Nephi says: "At that day shall he rage in the hearts of the children of men, and stir them up to anger against that which is good. And others will he pacify, and lull them away into carnal security, that they will say: All is well in Zion; yea, Zion prospereth, all is well — and thus the devil cheateth their souls, and leadeth them away carefully down to hell. And behold, others he flattereth away, and telleth them there is no hell; and he saith unto them: I am no devil, for there is none — and thus he whispereth in their ears, until he grasps them with his awful chains, from whence there is no deliverance." (2 Nephi 28:20–22.)

Concerning this scripture, LDS scholar Dennis L. Largey writes: "A closer look at some of the key words used in this passage is helpful to broaden our understanding of how Satan

operates: First, he pacifies, which means he appeases or pla-
cates. Second, he cheats, swindles, misleads, fools, or practices fraud upon, which means he deceives by trickery. Third,
he flatters, which means he compliments excessively and in-
sincerely, especially to win favor, to feed vanity, or to persuade that what one wants to believe is the case. Fourth, he
leads the way by going in advance, by conducting, escorting,
or directing, by causing one to follow a certain course of action
or line of thought. All of this—the pacifying, the cheating,
the flattering, and the leading—is done carefully, which is
synonymous with thoroughly, painstakingly, and conscien-
tiously. Satan thus customizes his dishonesty according to
the susceptibility of his target. His favorite approach is whatever works. In the pride of his heart, he does not drive from
the rear but leads from the front. Knowing only a few would
follow him if his true identity and design were manifested,
he carefully draws people into the false conclusion of sup-
posing they are winning when, in fact, they are slowly, but
nevertheless effectively being destroyed." ("The Enemies of
Christ," in *The Book of Mormon: Second Nephi, The Doctrinal
Approach* [Provo UT: Brigham Young University Religious
Studies Center, 1989], pp. 297–98.)

Remember, the evil spirit's only purpose in doing this nefarious work is to make the mortal person as miserable as
that spirit already is. Remember how Moses saw the spirits
laughing and rejoicing? That is why Alma taught his youngest
son that wickedness could never be happiness. (Alma 41:10.)
Wickedness and happiness are opposite poles on the same
compass, and the one can never be experienced while participation in the other is going forward.

Avoiding Satanic Afflictions

The next question, of course, is: "What can I do about
Satan?" Joseph Smith can help with this question. He had

some very interesting things to say about Lucifer, his powers, and how to avoid problems with him. He said: "Before the foundation of the earth in the Grand Council . . . the spirits of all men were subject to oppression & the express purpose of God in giving [man] a tabernacle was to arm [him] against the power of Darkness — for instance Jesus said Get behind me Satan Also the apostle [James] said Resist the Devil & he will flee from you." (*The Words of Joseph Smith*, p. 62. See also Luke 4:8, James 4:7.)

On another occasion Joseph said: "All beings who have bodies have power over those who have not. The devil has no power over us only as we permit him; the moment we revolt at anything which comes from God the devil takes power." (*The Words of Joseph Smith*, p. 60.)

Also he stated: "Satan cannot seduce us by his enticements unless we in our hearts consent and yield — our organization [the structure of our physical bodies] is such that we can resist the devil. If we were not so organized we would not be free agents." (Ibid., p. 65. See also *Return from Tomorrow*, by George G. Ritchie [Lincoln VA: Chosen Books, 1978], for some interesting examples of how this mortal protection works and how it is broken down when we give up personal control through substance abuse and other bodily evils.)

Finally, the *Times and Seasons* of June 1, 1841, reported that Joseph "observed that satan was generally blamed for the evils which we did, but if he was the cause of all our wickedness, men could not be condemned. The devil cannot compel mankind to evil — all was voluntary. Those who resist the spirit of God, are liable to be led into temptation, and then the association of heaven is withdrawn from those who refuse to be made partakers of such great glory — God would not exert any compulsory means [over mankind] and the Devil could not; and such ideas as were entertained by many were absurd." (P. 72.)

Joseph, then, is simply telling us that our physical bodies were designed by God as a shield or a protection for our spirits against Satan; and the only one who has the power to weaken or pull aside that shield is ourselves.

The Law Governing Satan and His Host

The Lord says, "That wicked one cometh and taketh away light and truth, through disobedience, from the children of men." (D&C 93:39.) Because we have been given our agency, everything we do, or everything that we allow Satan to do, is voluntary. It hinges upon our obedience or our disobedience. From what the ancient as well as modern Church leaders have instructed, the eternal law under which Satan and his hosts function is that they are governed by each of us individually, just as we choose to govern them.

As we exercise agency, we either give them power through our disobedience to God's laws, or we take power away from them by our righteous obedience. The more we choose to sin, the more we give them permission to afflict us. The less we choose to sin, the more free of them we will be. That is why Christ's gift of repentance is so dramatically important. If we want to get Satan and his host of servants off our backs, all we need to do is repent and become clean—and then stay that way, which absolutely robs the old serpent of his power over us.

By the Priesthood

Joseph Smith remarked, "It would seem . . . that wicked spirits have their bounds, limits, and laws by which they are governed or controlled . . . and it is very evident that they possess a power that none but those who have the Priesthood can control." (Ibid., p. 208.)

Therefore, if evil spirits are to be discerned and controlled, it must be by the priesthood, which is also used by personal righteousness. (D&C 121:36.) And for those who are worthily endowed in the temple and have received the keys of the priesthood, there are given even greater powers of detection. Joseph again said: "There [are] keys of the kingdom, certain signs and words by which false spirits and personages may be detected from true, which cannot be revealed to the Elders till the Temple is completed." (*Words of Joseph Smith*, pp. 20–21.) In other words, the understanding of, as well as the righteous discerning and rebuking of, these wicked spirits, is part of the gift that we receive in the temple, which is called the endowment. But once again, this gift can be exercised only upon the principles of righteousness.

Heber C. Kimball, Brigham Young's counselor, once said: "I do not fear anything. I fear nothing that is in heaven, or that is upon the earth. I do not fear hell nor its combinations; neither hell nor the devil, nor any of his angels has power over me, or over you, only as we permit them to have. If we permit the devil to have power over us . . . then he will have dominion over us. Upon the same principle, we let sin have power over us, but it has no power over us unless we subject ourselves to it." (*Journal of Discourses*, 1:204.)

Diligently Fulfilling Callings

The Lord gives us one other key of understanding in our quest to conquer Satan. It's very simple, really, and very basic. In fact, it goes along with all we have discussed from Joseph Smith and the Doctrine and Covenants. But this pearl of wisdom came to us from the prophet Mormon, who wrote to his son Moroni: "My beloved son, notwithstanding their hardness, let us labor diligently; for if we should cease to labor, we should be brought under condemnation; for we have a labor to perform whilst in this tabernacle of clay, that we may conquer the enemy of all righteousness, and rest our souls in the kingdom of God." (Moroni 9:6.)

Thus it should clearly be seen that by diligently fulfilling our Church callings, great or small, including our family responsibilities, we can conquer the devil and obtain rest with God. And conversely, if we don't labor diligently in our callings, then Satan may obtain power over us.

Children in Zion Greedy

The Lord declares: "Inasmuch as parents have children in Zion, or in any of her stakes which are organized, that teach them not to understand the doctrine of repentance, faith in Christ the Son of the Living God, and of baptism and the gift of the Holy Ghost by the laying on of the hands, when eight years old, the sin be upon the heads of the parents. For this shall be a law unto the inhabitants of Zion, or in any of her stakes which are organized. And they shall also teach their children to pray, and to walk uprightly before the Lord. Now I, the Lord, am not well pleased with the inhabitants of Zion, for there are idlers among them; and their children are also growing up in wickedness; they also seek not earnestly the riches of eternity, but their eyes are full of greediness." (D&C 68:25–26, 28, 31.)

As some members of the Church struggle just to have a desire to be obedient to God's word, it appears obvious that they haven't been taught properly about Satan's role, repentance, and having faith in Jesus Christ sufficient unto forgiveness. Nor do many have an understanding about praying or walking uprightly before the Lord. But the problem that is so evident around us is that, as the Lord says, many of the youth of the Church are growing up in wickedness, ignoring the riches of eternity and letting their eyes remain full of greediness.

We are confident that many of our young people do not think that they have seen a lot of greed among their peers, but we believe that is only because these people don't understand the full definition of the word. After all, isn't greed just another word for selfishness? For a moment, why don't we consider just one tiny aspect of this wickedness or greed that seems so rampant among our youth. We don't mean fancy cars, expensive clothes, cliquish friends, and so on, all of which certainly qualify as symbols of greed and selfishness. We are speaking of something that the Lord declares is even more serious.

Consider, for a moment, the person who seeks to take away another's chastity or virtue. When such evil-designing persons become aggressive in taking their partner's chastity to satisfy their own lustful habits and desires, we could say that this person was exhibiting the height of selfishness. And after all, isn't that wickedness and greed?

Moroni recorded: "Notwithstanding this great abomination of the Lamanites [enforced cannibalism upon the bodies of family members], it doth not exceed that of our people in Moriantum. For behold, many of the daughters of the Lamanites have they taken prisoners; and after depriving them of that which was most dear and precious above all things, which is chastity and virtue . . . " (Moroni 9:8–9.)

Moroni's account helps us see how serious this form of greed actually is. In our day, this greediness is truly rampant. And why did the Lord say that such wickedness and greed existed among the youth of the Church? Because at least some of the parents of such youth, apparently being idle (less than diligent) in their parental roles, have not taught them enough about faith, or repentance, or how to pray with power, or why they should walk uprightly before the Lord, or about what Satan desires to do to them. And perhaps they haven't taught them enough because they haven't understood or participated in such things themselves. This is tragic, especially when we consider the many young people in the Church today who are struggling with immorality.

The Precious Blood of Christ

This brings up another problem. Every living person is filled, to one degree or another, with wickedness and unrighteousness. King Benjamin said, "The natural man is an enemy to God, and has been from the fall of Adam, and will be, forever and ever." (Mosiah 3:19.) Seems very bleak, doesn't it.

But wait! There is hope, even for the natural man; the selfish, the greedy, the wicked, the unrighteous; those bound with Satan's cords. And that hope? The precious blood of Jesus Christ. But how does that great and eternal sacrifice become operative for the natural man, who is an enemy to God? Again the Book of Mormon provides the answer. The great missionary Ammon declared: "What natural man is there that knoweth these things? I say unto you, there is none that knoweth these things, save it be the penitent. Yea, he that repenteth and exerciseth faith, and bringeth forth good works, and prayeth continually without ceasing." (Alma 26:21–22.) And King Benjamin concluded his statement concerning the natural man being an enemy to God forever with these words: " . . . unless he yields to the enticings of the Holy Spirit, and putteth off the natural man and becometh a saint through the atonement of Christ the Lord, and becometh as a child, submissive, meek, humble, patient, full of love, willing to submit to all things which the Lord seeth fit to inflict upon him, even as a child doth submit to his father." (Mosiah 3:19.) Only then will we no longer be natural men, enemies to God.

According to Our Desires

We ask, "But how does one start to repent?" And the Lord answers, "Simply by wanting to start, because you will be granted exactly what you truly want." In other words, desiring it. Alma says: "I know that [God] granteth unto men according to their desire, whether it be unto death or unto life; yea, I know that he allotteth unto men, yea, decreeth unto them decrees which are unalterable, according to their wills, whether they be unto salvation or unto destruction. Yea . . . he that knoweth good and evil, to him it is given according to his desires, whether he desireth good or evil, life or death, joy or remorse of conscience." (Alma 29:4-5.) And later he concluded his thought by saying, "If [a person] hath repented of his sins, and desired righteousness until the end of his days, even so he shall be rewarded unto righteousness." (Alma 41:6.)

One of the greatest accounts of desire toward repentance in all scripture is the story of a young man named Enos. He recorded: "I will tell you of the wrestle which I had before God, before I received a remission of my sins. . . . The words I had . . . heard my father speak concerning eternal life . . . sunk deep into my heart. And my soul hungered." (Enos 1:2-4.) Yes, Enos's soul hungered—he yearned, he longed, he ached—with all his heart he wanted a remission of his sins. In fact, he struggled so much with it, and with his natural self, that he called it a "wrestle . . . before God."

But finally he said, "I kneeled down before my Maker, and I cried unto him in mighty prayer and supplication for mine own soul." (Enos 1:4.) And here is another key to repentance—our desire. Once our desire, our hunger for a remission of our sins, is great enough, then we will drop to our knees in mighty prayer and supplication in behalf of our eternal soul.

How long will it take to get an answer? Who knows? For each person it will be different. But Enos reported, "All the day long did I cry unto him; yea, and when the night came I did still raise my voice high that it reached the heavens." (Enos 1:4.) That, finally, was determined sufficient by God, for at last the Lord's voice told Enos that his sins had been

105

forgiven and he would be blessed "according to thy desires, and because of thy faith." (Enos 1:5, 12.)

The message? True repentance, and with it a remission of sins, is granted only to those who desire it with all their hearts and souls and who willingly pay the price to obtain it!

11

Following the Lord's Living Prophets

On one occasion, while Brent was serving in a stake presidency, he had the opportunity to interview a man who had been excommunicated for practicing plural marriage. Brent says of that interview: "Much of what the man stated bothered me, and it was not difficult to tell that he did not have the gift or companionship of the Holy Ghost. He was very logical in his arguments, but all his logic was 'on tilt,' just not quite square with what I have come to appreciate as truth.

"For instance, he pointed out in great detail, and I might add with great accuracy, that Joseph Smith, Brigham Young, and John Taylor had all practiced and advocated plural marriage. Therefore, he reasoned, it was proper to practice it today.

"I asked him where Wilford Woodruff's 'Manifesto' fit into the picture, and he quickly informed me that Wilford Woodruff had become a fallen prophet when he issued it. Therefore, he said, the Manifesto was not binding on this man or on the

Church. So also was every prophet since Wilford Woodruff a fallen prophet, including Ezra Taft Benson, for none had sanctioned the current practice of plural marriage, which the first three prophets had sanctioned.

"I pointed out to him that the keys of the kingdom, the right to the oracles of God or the revelations of God in behalf of the Church, belong always to the Presidency of the High Priesthood (D&C 81:2); that Joseph never lost them, but that they had also been passed along to subsequent prophets (D&C 90:3–4); and that there was only one man on the earth at a time who had the right to the full use of such keys and revelation (D&C 132:7); that one man being the living prophet of God.

"My reasoning didn't affect my friend any more than his had me, and I left our meeting sorrowing for him. But I do know, by the power of the Holy Ghost, that we are to follow the living prophet. That is the very reason we have a living prophet on the earth. Situations change, governments change, the Second Coming draws closer, and God reveals to our living prophet exactly how we are to respond to situations from day to day, making it far more easy to spiritually survive these difficult times than if we had no such continual guidance. And for right now, despite how eternally correct the doctrine of plural marriage may be, the living prophet has told us not to practice it. Since that is the most current revelation from God, we have only to obey, and we will be blessed."

A Wonderfully Important Choice

For those of us who live during this period of history which the Lord has designated as the last days, perhaps the most eternally significant decision we will ever make is how consistently we will follow the Lord's living prophet. As Elder Bruce R. McConkie says: "It seems easy to believe in the prophets who have passed on and to suppose that we believe and follow the counsel they gave under different circumstances and to other people. But the great test that confronts us, as in every age when the Lord has a people on earth, is whether we will give heed to the words of his living oracles and follow the counsel and direction they give for our day and time." (*Ensign,* May 1974, pp. 71–72.)

Is the Prophet Really God's Mouthpiece?

As Brent's friend argued, what if these men who come to the head of the Church become "fallen prophets?" What if an unrighteous man reaches this position? Or what if a man turns unrighteous after he has become prophet? How can we know that such is not the case, and that we can place our confidence in our leaders?

Actually, the answers to these questions become one answer: we will know that the prophet is God's mouthpiece in the same way that we know the truthfulness of all things — through the personal revelations we receive from the Holy Ghost. If the gospel is true, if the Church is Christ's, then the president of the Church is divinely selected and sustained, and we can have confidence in him. In other words, it all boils down to faith. As Harold B. Lee put it: "[The Lord] knows whom he wants to preside over this church, and he will make no mistake. The Lord doesn't do things by accident. . . . Let's keep our eye on the President of the Church." (Harold B. Lee, *Conference Report,* October 1970, p. 152.) President Spencer W. Kimball said: "It is reassuring to know that [a new prophet is] . . . not elected through committees and conventions with all their conflicts, criticisms, and by the vote of men, but [is] called of God and then sustained by the people. . . . The pattern divine allows for no errors, no conflicts, no ambitions, no ulterior motives. The Lord has re-

served for himself the calling of his leaders over his church."
(*Ensign*, January 1973, p. 33.)

In other words, through the process that we call death,
the Lord releases from mortality certain of the brethren. By
doing so, he preserves in life and brings to the forefront and
presidency of the apostleship others—each particular leader
who has been foreordained to lead the Church at any precise
time in world history. This prophet then succeeds the pre-
ceding one, who has been released from his labors through
the death of his physical body. And because God controls
the lives and deaths of all of us, there can be no accidents
here. That is why we can say that God does the calling. As
President Benson has said: "I have witnessed the refining
processes through which the Lord chips, buffs, and polishes
those whom He has selected to hold the keys of His kingdom. . . . This is particularly true in the case of those who
have become presidents of the Church. Each president has
been uniquely selected for the time and situation which the
world and Church needed. . . . Contemplate the miracle of
that foreordination and preparation. . . . Though called and
given keys many years prior to the time that the mantle fell
upon him, the President was always the right man in the
right place for the right time. This miracle alone is one of the
marks of the divinity of the Church." (Ezra Taft Benson, Salt
Lake City, Utah, January 19, 1977.)

What About Their Teachings?

Because this choice of whether or not to follow the prophet
is so important, it is never made without difficulty. In fact,
it is sometimes as though the prophets themselves, through
the things they teach, intentionally make following them more
difficult. As Elder Neal A. Maxwell put it: "Prophets have a
way of saying what the people need to hear, not what they
want to hear. . . . There are, or will be, moments when pro-

phetic declarations collide with our pride, or our seeming personal interests. . . . For the participants, such painful episodes tend to force home the question: Do I believe in the living prophet even when he speaks on matters affecting me and my specialty directly? Or do I stop sustaining the prophet when his words fall in my territory? If the latter, the prophet is without honor in our own country." (Neal A. Maxwell (*Things As They Really Are* [Salt Lake City: Deseret Book, 1978], pp. 72–73.) President Lee said: "We must learn to give heed to the words and commandments that the Lord shall give through his prophet. . . . You may not like what comes from the authority of the Church. It may contradict your political views. It may interfere with some of your social life. . . . [But] your safety and ours depends upon whether or not we follow the ones whom the Lord has placed to preside over his church." (Harold B. Lee, *Conference Report*, October 1970, p. 152.)

Safety in Obedience to the Living Prophet

Safety — the very thing we are seeking as we make our way through the perilous times of the last days. And here we learn that such safety depends upon whether or not we choose to follow the prophets. But how can obedience to the words of our living prophets bring safety? Because their inspired utterances are the words of the Lord and are the very things that will preserve us during the perilous times through which we must live. "Whatever counsel the Presidency of this church have been led to give unto this people," Wilford Woodruff said, "it has been dictated by the Spirit and power of God, and our safety and salvation lies in obeying that counsel and putting it into practice." (As quoted in Neal A. Maxwell, *All These Things Shall Give Thee Experience* [Salt Lake City: Deseret Book Company, 1979], pp. 120–21.)

Once we know these things through the power of the Spirit to our own souls, then we will begin to eagerly seek out and put into practice the words of our living prophets. Doing so, we find numerous topics that might be addressed in a chapter concerning following the living prophets—almost an unlimited number. Though we do not intend to address them all, there are four issues that we feel merit discussion, four topics concerning spiritual and temporal survival in the last days that the living prophets of today have repeatedly raised and continue to raise. These are surely pertinent to an individual's desire to be found standing in holy places when the Lord comes.

CHAPTER

12

Following the Lord's
Living Prophets — Food
Storage

Elder Bruce R. McConkie once said: "For the moment we live in a day of peace and prosperity, but it shall not ever be thus. Great trials lie ahead . . . and we must prepare ourselves temporally and spiritually. . . . Our temporal preparation consists in using the good earth in the way the Lord designed and intended so as to supply all our just wants and needs. It is his purpose to provide for his Saints for all things are his, but, he says, it must needs be done in his own way (D&C 104:14–18). . . . He commands both the Church and its members 'to prepare and organize' their temporal affairs according to the law of his gospel, 'that through my providence,' saith the Lord, 'notwithstanding the tribulation which shall descend upon you, that the church may stand independent above all other creatures under the celestial world. . . . The Church, which administers the gospel, and the Saints who have received the gospel, must be independent of all the powers of earth, as they work out their salvation — temporally and spiritually — with fear and trembling before the Lord." (*Ensign,* May 1979, pp. 92–93.)

"Knowing what we know," Elder McConkie continues, "and having the light and understanding that has come to us, we must — as individuals and as a Church — use our talents, strengths, energies, abilities, and means to prepare for whatever may befall us and our children. . . . Relying always on the Lord, we must become independent of the world. We must be self-reliant." (Ibid., p. 93.)

Why, it might be asked, must we be independent of such temporal or worldly activities? And what have these to do with food storage? And the answer: If all that we have discussed is to come to pass — and it surely must if the gospel of Jesus Christ is true — then the world may at some time be in such chaos that it will no longer be able to supply all our wants and needs, or to sustain any of us in the manner to which we have become accustomed. It seems to us that, from what has been prophesied, wicked men will be in control when there is any control at all; world economy will be in Satan's control with no buying or selling except to those who have the mark or number of the beast in their hands or foreheads; famines and drought will waste the earth; pestilence and diseases such as AIDS and drug addiction will sweep away entire populations; bloody invasions and mobocracy will create worldwide anarchy; and all these plus a host of natural disasters will, in our opinion, help bring a complete halt to what so many of us call our consumer society. Knowing that these things are coming, perhaps soon, it is easy to see why the Lord has counseled us to stand independent of the world by securing our own supply of food and other day-to-day essentials.

Since at least the days of Brigham Young, the Saints have

been directed to lay up necessary stores in preparation for a day of want. He declared, "The time will come that gold will hold no comparison in value to a bushel of wheat." (*Journal of Discourses*, 1:250.) President Wilford Woodruff declared: "Lay up your wheat and other provisions against a day of need, for the day will come when they will be wanted, and make no mistake about it. We shall want bread, and the Gentiles will want bread, and if we are wise we shall have something to feed them and ourselves when famine comes." (*Journal of Discourses*, 18:121.)

From then until now, the counsel has not been altered; we are to lay up at least a year's worth of essential items such as food, clothing, fuel, and so forth. President Ezra Taft Benson feels strongly enough about this that he stated, "The revelation to produce and store food may be as essential to our temporal welfare today as boarding the ark was to the people in the days of Noah." (*Conference Report*, October 1980, p. 27.) "Then store at least a year's supply of basic food, clothing, and fuel. Then you will find these blessings will accrue: You will not be confronted with the danger of losing all you have because of inflation or depression. You will have security that no government can provide—savings and supplies for emergencies." (*The Teachings of Ezra Taft Benson* [Salt Lake City: Bookcraft, 1988], p. 263.) And finally: "We must do more to get our people prepared for the difficult days we face in the future. Our major concern should be their spiritual preparation so they will respond with faith and not fear. 'If ye are prepared, ye shall not fear' (D&C 38:21). Our next concern should be for their temporal preparation. When the economies of nations fail, when famine and other disasters prevent people from buying food in stores, the Saints must be prepared to handle these emergencies. This is a matter of concern." (Ibid., p. 264.)

Can anyone doubt the message in these statements? Hardly, not if we intend to be found standing in holy places.

13

Following the Lord's Living Prophets—The Bondage of Debt

The Lord has commanded us to stand independent above all other creatures under the celestial world, and for that reason his laws forbid us to get into debt to our enemies. (See D&C 64:27.) Obviously, once we are in debt, we are no longer independent of the world.

So far as we are able to understand, the word *enemies* in this context refers to all who seek, no matter the cost to us, to make a profit from our indebtedness. The way to tell who might be enemies and who might not would be to see how they react to a debtor's misfortunes or mistakes. Patience, kindness, tolerance, gentleness, and even outright forgiveness of debt would characterize one who is not an enemy.

We should recognize immediately that this list reads very

Some of the material in this chapter has been excerpted from: Blaine and Brenton Yorgason, *Seeking Wealth* (Orem UT: Keepsake BookCards, 1989).

much like the qualities of a righteous priesthood holder as described by the Lord in section 121 of the Doctrine and Covenants. (See D&C 121:41–44.)

Enemies and Friends

We read a few other scriptural references to the word *enemy*, and of course Satan is the major enemy the Lord mentions. (See Mosiah 4:14; Mosiah 16:5; Alma 34:23; Moroni 7:12; Moroni 9:6.) But the Lord also points out, through King Benjamin, that all transgressors of God's commandments become enemies of righteousness. (Mosiah 2:37.) In the scriptures these people are referred to as "the natural man" (1 Corinthians 2:14; Mosiah 3:19; Alma 26:21; D&C 67:12), and every "natural man" is an "enemy to God" (Mosiah 3:19). So, if our enemies are natural men and women rather than simply Satan himself, then they are those who will not yield to the enticings of the Holy Spirit. (Ibid.) Instead, they purposely ignore God's commandments while they exhibit unrighteous tendencies in their interactions with others. In terms of this discussion, such tendencies would be greed, lust, avarice, anger, hatred, and so forth. And that is as opposed to those who exhibit the qualities of godliness mentioned earlier — the people whom the Lord calls his friends. (See D&C 93:45.)

To illustrate, God's enemies loan money selfishly, their overriding concern being only to get it back and to make a great deal of money from the borrower. God's friends, on the other hand, either loan or give money to help those less fortunate, with interest earnings or even paybacks being of little or no concern. Their primary concern is for the borrowers, their fellow beings. (Mosiah 2:17.) As Brother Hugh Nibley puts it: "The most common way of taking advantage of another's need is loaning money at interest, and [in Hebrew law] this is strictly forbidden, though it is the cornerstone of our present-day economy (Deuteronomy 23:19)." (*Approach-*

ing Zion, p. 194.) We have known people who truly have this unselfish orientation in the way they provide financial assistance for those around them; but we have also found that lenders of this caliber are few and far between.

Now, we know that banks and other institutions are organized to make money with money, and it is not our intention to indict the banking industry. They have collection and repossession policies so they can preserve themselves in our society, and people who work for them, many of whom are great and righteous people, have no choice but to follow their employers' policies. Neither are we saying that we shouldn't borrow money from banks or other lending institutions. What we are saying is that, for so long as society continues to ignore God's economic policies in favor of Satan's, we had better be aware of what we are doing when we borrow anything from *anybody!* At least in our present society, people have the right to do as they wish with their credit and their financial desires. We will all make our choices, and we will all reap the rewards of those choices. The scripture declares it a forbidden practice to go into debt to an enemy, but it is up to each of us to determine who our enemies are.

Avoid All Debt

To make this directive even easier for us to live in the world of today, however, most of the prophets since Joseph Smith have reconfirmed the Lord's statement and have counseled Latter-day Saints to avoid all debt, except under certain extreme conditions. Why all debt? We suppose at least partially it is because so many lenders either cannot or will not follow the Lord's guidelines for the righteous exercise of power, in lending or anything else. Therefore, these have become the enemy the Lord speaks of, and in today's society it is almost impossible to avoid them. President Benson says simply: "Get out of debt if it is at all humanly possible." (*The Teachings of*

Ezra Taft Benson, p. 288.) We believe that he has given us scripturally sound advice.

Being Bond-Servants

But, it might be asked, what if I have no choice but to go into debt? What if conditions force debt upon me? Very well— go into debt, but do it with total awareness of what you are doing. President Benson says: "I do not mean to say that all debt is bad. Of course not. [In this present society] sound business debt is one of the elements of growth. Sound mortgage credit is a real help to a family that must borrow for a home." (Ibid., p. 290.) But remember, President Benson said "sound debt." He adds: "But is it not apparent that in the areas of both public and personal debt the limitations of soundness have been seriously strained?" (Ibid.)

"Seriously strained soundness" may be the understatement of this chapter, considering the things many of us enter debt to acquire. Considering that any debt takes away that independence we have been commanded to maintain, we should be as careful as possible that what we are considering going into debt for is really necessary. But as we said, if it is necessary, Latter-day Saints should still be aware that such debt is literally a bondage. By our signatures we agree to be in servitude to someone else, which means that we are no longer independent of the world. As the sage declared: "The borrower is servant to the lender." (Proverbs 22:7.) Thus we should choose very carefully when and to whom we would like to become a bond-servant.

That is why the prophets say that the best way possible for us to live is to avoid debt altogether! "The Lord desires His Saints to be free and independent in the critical days ahead," states President Benson. "But no man is truly free who is in financial bondage. 'Think what you do when you run in debt,' said Benjamin Franklin; 'you give another power

119

over your liberty.' 'Pay thy debt, and live,' said Elisha (2 Kings 4:7). And in the Doctrine and Covenants the Lord says, 'It is my will that you shall pay all your debts' (D&C 104:78)." (*The Teachings of Ezra Taft Benson*, p. 288.) Thus speaks the prophet of today. And to Joseph Smith the Lord declared that, "It is not right that any man should be in bondage one to another." (D&C 101:79.) Thus, if we are to stand independent in the coming days of turmoil and judgment, we should not go into debt!

Sadly, many of us don't see the terrifying aspects of giving up our independence and becoming bond-servants. Instead, we swallow the ways of the world—hook, line, and sinker! We are converted to debt through all sorts of fine-sounding words: *tax shelters, home-equity loans, risk-free investment opportunities, extended credit-card limits, buy now—pay later plans, deficit spending, the big deal (while families suffer in want while they wait), financial players,* and *tax laws and loopholes* that we can take advantage of if we would just acquire nicer, more expensive cars, a boat, or a few other "toys." Again according to President Benson: "One reason for the increase in debt causes great concern. This is the rise of materialism as contrasted with spiritual values. Many a family, in order to make a 'proper showing,' will commit itself for a larger and more expensive house than is needed, in an expensive neighborhood." (*The Teachings of Ezra Taft Benson*, p. 290.) So we run out and place the entire security of our families squarely in the hands of our enemies, just so that we can look good in the eyes of the people we are trying to impress. In other words, we selfishly accumulate massive amounts of debt, which the Lord specifically commands us not to do, and we do it because of pride, which is the worst possible reason for going into debt. Nevertheless we do it, and thus we place ourselves in bondage.

In a message directed specifically toward younger families,

President Benson states: "The need for education or material things does not justify the postponing of children in order to keep the wife working as the breadwinner in the family. I remember the counsel of our beloved prophet Spencer W. Kimball to married students. He said: 'I have told tens of thousands of young folks that when they marry they should not wait for children until they have finished their schooling and financial desires. . . . They should live together normally and let children come. . . . I know of no scripture where an authorization is given to young wives to withhold their families and go to work to put their husbands through school. There are thousands of husbands who have worked their own way through school and have reared families at the same time.' Sometimes the mother works outside of the home at the encouragement, or even insistence, of her husband. It is he who wants the items or conveniences that the extra income can buy. Not only will the family suffer in such instances, brethren, but your own spiritual growth and progression will be hampered." (Ibid., p. 506.)

The Troubles We Incur

Why is such debt a bondage? Because when we enter into debt, we give to another the control of our financial resources. Tragically, the minute we lose the ability to release or at least maintain the bondage or debt we have contracted (remember how positive we were, due to our increased or even two-worker income, that we could pay it back?), our cars, our homes, and every other thing we own will be stripped away from us, essentially leaving us helpless and dependent upon others for our very existence. "Credit is a willing but a cruel master," says President Benson. "A large proportion of families with personal debt have no liquid assets whatsoever to fall back on. What troubles they invite if their income should be suddenly cut off or seriously reduced." (Ibid.) Anyone who has ever gone through such an experience will testify that the word *trouble* is terribly inadequate.

Of course, the "enemy" money-lenders in today's society don't care about such troubles, or the reasons why our debts might not be paid. They feel little or no concern for us or for our families. That isn't what "business" is all about. Their primary concern is their money and how to get it back without losing it, and at the highest interest they can get away with. If this recovery process leads to rudeness or pain or threats or any other form of oppression or intimidation, then we must respond willingly to it.

We Are to Blame

The irony is that in spite of the unrighteous ways of these people, if we choose to get into debt to them, we really cannot blame them, nor should we rant and rave every time they come at us with their dunners, their summonses to court, and their officers of the law. Every decision to accumulate debt was our own and was made freely, and we are accountable for our problems, not those enemies who hold our notes. They will ultimately answer to God for how they treat their debtors, not to us, and he will judge them justly. Meanwhile, we have no right to judge them at all. Just remember, every ounce of power those people hold over us, we gave to them. They didn't force us into servitude. We sold our independence for a mess of pottage, and if the pottage has turned out to be less than we thought, we have no right to complain.

An Empire Instead of the Kingdom

Why are so many of us caught up in worldly things and are therefore in bondage, unable to exercise our independence from the world? The answer is to be found within the covenants we have made, wherein we have covenanted to give our all to build God's earthly kingdom until it can be joined in righteousness with his heavenly one. (See D&C 65:5–6.) Instead, however, a tragic number of us dedicate our lives to building up our own personal empires, building God's kingdom only peripherally in our spare time; and we wonder as we do so why it is so difficult to grow spiritually. Obviously, we have somehow missed the point. While the accumulation of money and property is often our highest priority, it seems to be the lowest item possible on God's list. Instead, sufficiency seems to be all he is concerned with; that and how well his children keep his commandments and love each other — or strive for independence and equality among themselves. (D&C 49:20; Jacob 2:17.)

And why is having more substance than another person such a problem? At least one reason is that poor people must always strive upward for equality. But, if the more wealthy are not also righteously striving downward for the same equality (which is what the Lord desires of the rich, as explained in D&C 104:16), then the only avenue left open for the poor to obtain their desires is through debt. It is the old dilemma of the "haves" versus the "have-nots." In other words, debt ranks people according to class, and all over the world people use such positions of class or status to oppress, enslave, and make money from those beneath them. This is nearly always so, and inevitably such philosophies or doctrines, if accepted by the people, lead to the same end — war, bloodshed, and the dissolution of society. (Alma 60:16–32.) This, we believe, leads to Samuel's Law.

Samuel's Law

Anciently, obsession with things of the world led to destruction, and it is certain that it will do the same thing today. Brother Nibley calls this the operation of Samuel's Law. He says: "The Prophet Samuel the Lamanite sets forth the interesting rule that when 'the economy' becomes the main and engrossing concern of a society—or in the routine Book of Mormon phrase, when 'they begin to set their hearts upon their riches'—the economy will self-destruct. This is how [Samuel] puts it: 'Ye do always remember your riches. . . . Your hearts are not drawn out unto the Lord, but they do swell with great pride . . . envyings, strifes, malice, persecutions and murders, and all manner of iniquities' (Helaman 13:22). Note well the sequence of folly: first we are well pleased with ourselves because of our wealth, then comes the game of status and prestige (careerism becomes the order of the day in a business-society of 'many merchants . . . and also many lawyers, and many officers . . . the people . . . distinguished by ranks, according to their riches and their chances for learning') (3 Nephi 6:11–12), leading to competitive maneuvers, hatred, and dirty tricks, and finally the ultimate solution (of murder). Where wealth guarantees respectability, principles melt away as the criminal element rises to the top: (The Gadianton Protective Association soon became the biggest business in America! . . . as the more part of the Nephites did unite with those bands of robbers [Ibid., p. 383. Also, Helaman 6:21.]). 'For this cause hath the Lord God caused that a curse should come upon the land, and also upon your riches' (Helaman 13:23). 'And behold, the time cometh that he curseth your riches, that they become slippery, that ye cannot hold them; and in the days of your poverty ye cannot retain them' (Helaman 13:31). [This] ends in utter frustration and total insecurity as morals and the market collapse together and the baffled [economic] experts surrender." (*The Prophetic Book of Mormon*, pp. 349–50.)

The Real Issues

Why are all of our economic experts baffled by what is happening to us today? Frankly, it is because they have not learned the nature of the real issues that face this world. As

President Benson says: "The fate of humanity and all civilization hinges on whether man will use his free agency to govern himself or ignore eternal laws at his own peril and reap the consequences. The real issues of today are, therefore, not economic. . . . They are spiritual—meaning that man must learn to conform to the laws which God has given to mankind." (*The Teachings of Ezra Taft Benson*, pp. 83–84.) If we don't conform, then we may be in for some very troublesome times.

Of course, few of us ever intentionally break such covenants as our promise to live the law of consecration. Instead, we are led to do so a little at a time, being led carefully along by the devil's flaxen cords until they become strong cords forever. (2 Nephi 26:22.) Remember, flaxen means soft, smooth, and silky. And those words describe exactly how the situations feel that lead us to break the promises of consecration we make in the temple. We are attracted to the things of the world that have been so enticingly packaged. We obtain a few of them and enjoy them but find they are not enough to fully satisfy. We then become greedy for more, we obtain more, we want even more, and without realizing it we become raised up in our pride because of what we have managed to accumulate. We continue to want more than ever because such wealth somehow seems our right, and besides, it is so very comfortable. Lo and behold, we have broken our covenants; we have become intent on building our own empires rather than the kingdom we covenanted to build. As the Book of Mormon says, we become lifted up unto pride and boastings because of our exceedingly great riches (3 Nephi 6:10), and we set our hearts upon those riches rather than upon the things of God (Psalm 62:10; Proverbs 23:5; Mosiah 12:29; Alma 1:30; 4:8; 7:6; 17:14; Helaman 6:7; 7:21; 13:20–21). And because that behavior is contrary to what we have covenanted to do in the temple, the Lord can't bless us and protect us from the power of Satan. Neither can we enjoy the protection promised the righteous in these latter days of turmoil and destruction.

A Hope in Christ

So, are we ever to seek for riches – the wealth of this earth? Actually, the message rings out clearly that such a quest is foolish and dangerous. Further, according to Jacob, it most likely won't occur even after we have obtained the "hope in Christ" that connotes having been born again and having experienced the mighty change. Why? Because then we will seek riches only to give them to others – we won't want them for ourselves. If there is an eternal law that governs this (and we must assume that there is), we would call it the law of wealth. Simply stated, it would be that the more we freely give away so that others will be blessed, the more the Lord will return back to us so that we can give it away again. When we do this, we will always have more than we need. (See JST, Genesis 14:39–40.)

But until we have made such spiritual progress by obtaining a hope in Christ and then striving to bring about absolute economic equality among our family, friends, and associates, seeking wealth or riches for any reason is a definite no-no.

The Riches of Eternity

We feel that instead we should focus on obtaining what the Lord calls the riches of eternity, for only in that kind of wealth will we find protection and safety. The Lord says: "Seek not for riches but for wisdom; and behold, the mysteries of God shall be unfolded unto you, and then shall you be made rich. Behold, he that hath eternal life is rich." (D&C 11:7; D&C 6:15.) "Behold and lo," he says again, "my eyes are upon you, and the heavens and the earth are in my hands, and the riches of eternity are mine to give." (D&C 67:2.)

If we are seeking the riches of eternity, then we seek these things: strong families whose children are not growing up in wickedness with eyes full of greediness (see D&C 68:31); whatever education or skills we feel from prayer need to be gained; the paying off and staying free of debt; the serving and building up of our associates and neighbors; the righteous fulfillment of our employment obligations; and the time and spiritual power to serve diligently in whatever Church callings the Lord might give us. In other words, we seek to do the things the prophets have told us to do — which have nothing to do with worldly wealth. But above all else, we should earnestly seek the face of Christ — through study, prayer, and sincere, constant repentance unto greater righteousness. (See D&C 101:38.)

If we do these things, thinking always of others before ourselves as we conduct our daily walk before God, then we will not only be blessed with the riches of eternity but we will also have sufficient for our needs of this world's goods. Such sufficiency will come without unrighteous "seeking," and it will come miraculously when the storms of the last days descend upon the world, making our normal pattern of living impossible.

Trust in the Lord

Once we truly obtain a hope in Christ, we will have learned to trust the Lord sufficiently that we will desire with all our hearts to turn our financial affairs over to him. Our whole desire will be to give service to him and our fellow beings, and we won't have time to seek after the things of the world. Then, while we are serving him with all our heart, might, mind, and strength, the Lord can prosper us as he deems best for our eternal well-being — much or little, whichever he chooses, for whichever day he chooses. And not for one minute will it matter to us! We will have learned to trust the Lord's infinite knowledge of our eternal needs.

Blessed with that sort of righteous prosperity, no matter what is going on around us by way of judgments and destruction, we too will be among "the [happiest] people among all the people who had been created by the hand of God." (4 Nephi 1:16.) Further, we will be standing in holy places when the end comes.

14

Following the Lord's Living Prophets — The Word of Wisdom

If we were to give a concise definition of the Word of Wisdom, we would say that it is divine counsel that advocates self-control while decrying self-indulgence. As President Benson has taught, the Lord says "that we should use moderation in all . . . things . . . [which use of moderation, that is, the Word of Wisdom] leads to clean habits, thoughts and actions." (*The Teachings of Ezra Taft Benson*, pp. 475–76.) To Joseph Smith the Lord said, "No one can assist in this work except he shall be humble and full of love, having faith, hope and charity, being temperate in all things." (D&C 12:8.) This direction to be temperate was also given by Alma to the people of Gideon (Alma 7:23), was repeated by the Lord to Oliver Cowdery as he began his work as scribe for Joseph Smith in the translating of the Book of Mormon (D&C 6:19), and corresponds with the theme of exercising prudence in what we put into our bodies as stated specifically in the Word of Wisdom (D&C 89:11).

But modern society, being unwittingly guided and directed by Lucifer and his minions, advocates just the opposite approach. Today individuals and families are being torn apart and destroyed by pervasive self-indulgence. Instead of developing self-control, many spend their lives not earnestly seeking the riches of eternity but rather allowing their eyes to be full of greediness for the pleasures of the world. (D&C 68:31.) Pleasure and happiness are considered the main goals of life. Pleasure-seeking behavior and avoidance of pain are the very human instincts of the natural man, but, as we know, the natural man is an enemy to God. (Mosiah 3:19.) Phrases like "Whatever turns you on" and "If it feels good, do it" are absolutely contrary to the temperate doctrines of Christ. Yet they are widely subscribed to even by many within the Church—even though we know full well that acceptance of such immediate gratification is detrimental to our long-range, eternal goals.

On the national and global front, we live in what we call a dynamic society, a progressive, competitive, acquisitive, self-indulging mingling of cultures that must always be expanding to survive. However, as Brigham Young has shown, in the long run this will turn out to be a physical impossibility. (See *Journal of Discourses,* 12:160; 16:65; 17:41.) But still we keep indulging ourselves. Hugh Nibley points out: "We have contrived a way to keep things going by destroying our natural resources at an accelerating pace as long as there are any left, while assuring an expanding market by ever more extravagant excesses of Madison Avenue unreality, inventing outrageous needs for pernicious products. To keep producing what we do not need, not only high-powered advertising but deliberate obsolescence is necessary." (*Approaching Zion,* p. 273.)

When we were children, our mother did her entire month's grocery shopping in a small store that would hardly fit into the cold-cereal department of a modern supermarket. And we had more than sufficient. But whom is a modern supermarket "super" for? The self-indulging consumers who can never fully satisfy their wants, or the gain-seeking suppliers of pernicious products who have advertised their way into our pocketbooks? Doesn't it seem possible that this is part of the conspiracy of which the Lord warned us when he gave the Church the Word of Wisdom?

The Plop-Plop, Fizz-Fizz Society

In today's permissive world, we and our children are taught to listen to and think about whatever we want, to do "whatever turns us on," and to open our mouths and find instant gratification and relief. Widely promoted, for instance, is the self-indulging philosophy that sexual intimacy is a way of saying to an instantly vanishing partner, "I briefly noticed you; thank you for noticing me, but you owed me one anyway because I probably noticed you first." It means a great deal more than this even to most animals.

Also promoted are prescription drugs for "minor aches and pains," "tension headache," "night cough," "tired blood," and a variety of other ailments and symptoms. For those needing even more help, "extra strength" preparations are available. The message is clear: the answer to whatever ails you can usually be found in capsule or syrup form. Is it any wonder that illicit drugs and the illicit use of prescription drugs have become so popular among all age groups in our society?

A Secret Combination in the Last Days

Moroni, in abridging the writings of Ether, issued a rather stern warning to us of the latter days. He said: "Whatsoever nation shall uphold such secret combinations, to get power and gain, until they shall spread over the nation, behold, they shall be destroyed; for the Lord will not suffer that the blood of his saints, which shall be shed by them, shall always cry unto him from the ground for vengeance upon them and yet he avenge them not. Wherefore, O ye Gentiles, it is wisdom in God that these things should be shown unto you, that thereby ye may repent of your sins, and suffer not that these murderous combinations shall get above you, which are built up to get power and gain — and the work, yea, even the work of destruction come upon you, yea, even the sword of the justice of the Eternal God shall fall upon you, to your over-throw and destruction if ye shall suffer these things to be. Wherefore, the Lord commandeth you, when ye shall see these things come among you that ye shall awake to a sense of your awful situation, because of this secret combination which shall be among you. . . . For it cometh to pass that whoso buildeth it up seeketh to overthrow the freedom of all lands, nations and countries; and it bringeth to pass the de-struction of all people, for it is built up by the devil, who is the father of all lies." (Ether 8:22–25.)

When speaking of secret combinations, Moroni uses the phrase "which shall be among you." In other words, this isn't an "if" sort of prophecy — there *is* a secret combination among us today, despite the movement toward political peace, which will murder the Saints and seek "to overthrow the freedom of all lands, nations and countries." Nephi the son of Lehi also prophesied that such a secret combination would be among us. He said: "The Gentiles are lifted up in the pride of their eyes, and have stumbled, because of the greatness of their stumbling block, that they have built up many churches; nevertheless, they put down the power and mir-acles of God, and preach up unto themselves their own wis-dom and their own learning, that they may get gain and grind upon the face of the poor. And there are many churches built up which cause envyings, and strifes, and malice. *And there are also secret combinations,* even as in times of old, according to the combinations of the devil, for he is the founder of all these things; yea, the founder of murder, and works of darkness; yea, he leadeth them by the neck with a flaxen cord, until he bindeth them with his strong cords forever." (2 Nephi 26:20–22; italics added.)

Alma prophesied that if such secret combinations do exist, then the land has a curse upon it that will ensure destruction to all who participate in such combinations and who by their apathy or greed uphold them. (Alma 37:28–31.) And finally Moroni again, in a thundering denunciation of prideful, uncommitted Latter-day Saints and others, asked in conclusion: "O ye pollutions, ye hypocrites, ye teachers, who sell yourselves for that which will canker, why have ye polluted the holy church of God? Why are ye ashamed to take upon you the name of Christ? Why do ye not think that greater is the value of an endless happiness than that misery which never dies, because of the praise of the world? Why do ye adorn yourselves with that which hath no life, and yet suffer the hungry, and the needy, and the naked, and the sick and the afflicted to pass you by, and notice them not? *Yea, why do ye build up your secret abominations to get gain,* and cause that widows should mourn before the Lord, and also orphans to mourn before the Lord. . . . Behold, the sword of vengeance hangeth over you; and the time soon cometh that he avengeth the blood of the saints upon you, for he will not suffer their cries any longer." (Mormon 8:38–41; italics added.)

These scriptures make it evident that this secret combination will exist in the last days, even among members of the Church who are filled with pride unto greediness, causing them to be deceived and to uphold it. The question is, just what is this secret combination, and what has it to do with our discussion of the Word of Wisdom?

A Different View

Much has been written about this latter-day secret combination. It has been identified as everything from political ideologies to religious organizations and dogmas. Any and all of these may indeed play a part in Satan's scheme. On the other hand, in recent years a global crisis has developed that the Lord himself refers to as an evil combination, and it is our opinion that this particular problem comes as close as anything we have ever studied to fitting the profile of the secret combination the ancient prophets warned us of.

Illicit Drugs—the Product of a Secret Combination

On February 27, 1833, the Lord gave to Joseph Smith a revelation that has become known in the Church as the Word of Wisdom. This is a heavenly directive "showing forth the order and will of God in the temporal salvation of all saints in the last days." (D&C 89:2.) In verse 4 we read: "In consequence of evils and designs which do and will exist in the hearts of conspiring men in the last days, I have warned you, and forewarn you, by giving unto you this word of wisdom by revelation." (D&C 89:4.) According to the Lord, evils and designs do (in 1833) and will (beyond 1833) exist in the hearts of conspiring men—their evils and designs having to do with substances that are designed to be taken within the human body. These substances will be both physically and spiritually harmful, even deadly, and are to be avoided at all costs by his people, even the weakest of those who consider themselves to be Saints.

Does this sound like a description of a secret combination? From the scriptures we learn concerning ancient secret combinations that it "was the object of all those who belonged to [these bands] to murder, and to rob, and to gain power [and this was their secret plan, and their combination]" (Helaman 2:8); that they are "built up to get power and gain" (Ether 11:15); that "their works were in the dark" (Moses 5:51); that the devil "stirreth up the children of men unto secret combinations of murder and all manner of secret works of darkness" (2 Nephi 9:9); that such a combination "is most abominable and wicked above all, in the sight of God" (Ether 8:18); that "whatsoever nation shall uphold such secret combinations, to get power and gain, until they shall spread over the nation, behold, they [the nation] shall be destroyed" (Ether 8:22); and that when we see these things come among us in our day, we must "awake to a sense of [our] awful situation, because of this secret combination which shall be among [us]" (Ether 8:24).

To Get Gain

Can anyone possibly argue that the designs of the alcohol, tobacco, and illicit drug "industries" is financial gain with a capital G, no matter the harm that their products bring to consumers? "Drugs, legal and otherwise, are big business. . . . The American tobacco and alcohol industries . . . gross . . . $27 billion a year. As impressive as these figures are, they are dwarfed by the profits from illegal drugs. It was estimated that in 1980 the retail, street-level transaction value of the illegal drug trade in the United States was about $79 billion, which was up 22% from 1979, with escalation continuing. When compared with sales of the largest U.S. business corporations in 1980, only Exxon at $103 billion was greater. Number five was Standard Oil of California, with sales of $40 billion. The profit motive for traffickers has been powerful and compelling." (Donald Ian MacDonald, *Drugs, Drinking, and Adolescents* [Chicago: Year Book Medical Publishers, 1984],

p. 92.) Concerning just the tobacco industry alone, a recent news article declared, "Smoking costs U.S. $52 billion a year." (*Deseret News,* February 20–21, 1990, p. A3.) Truly this is a conspiracy, a secret combination, and a plague of the worst order.

Further, can it possibly be denied by any thinking person that the products these "industries" dispense do nothing but cause pain and death? In the news article cited above, the Department of Health and Human Services stated that most of the $52 billion would be spent largely for health-care expenses. (Ibid.) And since bad health and death are the only results of using these products, and since this fact has been very well documented, shouldn't this be called what the Lord calls it — murder? Therefore, the desires of these "industries" that the Lord calls secret combinations, are to murder and get gain. This is what Brother Hugh Nibley calls the "Mahan principle," based upon the great secret that Satan taught Cain, making him Master Mahan. He writes: "The 'Mahan principle' is a frank recognition that the world's economy is based on the exchange of life for property." (*Approaching Zion,* p. 436.)

Finally, it is painfully obvious that some Latter-day Saints are, in one manner or another, involved with one or more of these "industries." Therefore, as both Nephi and Moroni prophesied, this secret combination is certainly "among us." The conclusion we are forced to draw, then, is that this particular secret combination, the world-wide as well as American alcohol-tobacco-illicit drug cartel, must be at least a major portion of the secret combination we have been so forcefully warned against by a loving Heavenly Father, both anciently and in modern scripture.

Drugs and Other Worldly Pollutants

We have become aware that Church members who use illicit drugs, both prescription and non-prescription, offer the excuse that "drugs aren't mentioned in the Word of Wisdom, so they must be all right." In light of such an attitude, consider the words of President Gordon B. Hinckley: "Some have even used as an alibi the fact that drugs are not mentioned in the Word of Wisdom. What a miserable excuse. There is likewise no mention of the hazards of diving into an empty swimming pool or of jumping from an overpass onto the freeway. But who doubts the deadly consequences of such? Common sense would dictate against such behavior.

"Regardless of the Word of Wisdom, there is a divinely given reason for avoiding these illegal substances. I am convinced that their use is an affront to God. He is our Creator. We are made in His image. These remarkable and wonderful bodies are His handiwork. Does anyone think that he can deliberately injure and impair his body without affronting its Creator? We are told again and again that the body is the tabernacle of the spirit. We are told that it is a temple, holy to the Lord. In a time of terrible conflict between the Nephites and the Lamanites, we are told that the Nephites, who had been strong, became 'weak, like unto their brethren, the Lamanites, and that the Spirit of the Lord did no more preserve them; yea, it had withdrawn from them because the Spirit of the Lord doth not dwell in unholy temples.' (Helaman 4:24.)

"Alma taught the people of Zarahemla: 'The Lord doth not dwell in unholy temples; neither can filthiness or anything which is unclean be received into the kingdom of God.' (Alma 7:21.) Can anyone doubt that the taking of these mind- and body-destroying drugs is an act of unholiness? Does anyone think that the Spirit of God can dwell in the temple of the body when that body is defiled by these destructive elements? If there be a young man [or woman] anywhere who is listening . . . who is tampering with these things, let him resolve forthwith, and with the strongest determination of

which he is capable, that he will never touch them again."
(*Ensign,* November 1989, p. 50.)

But despite what the Lord and his prophets have told us,
Satan continues to beat his deceptive drum: "Self-indulgence
is the way to happiness!" Using tobacco is made out to be
manly, macho, or (for women) beautifying and alluring. In a
recent news article, the R. J. Reynolds Tobacco Company
admitted targeting their advertisements of a new cigarette
brand "at poorly educated 18- to 20-year-old women whose
favorite pastimes include 'cruising,' 'partying,' and going to
'hot-rod shows' and 'tractor pulls' with their boyfriends."
(*Deseret News,* February 18, 1990, p. A19.) Alcohol is widely
promoted as a key part of all sorts of social and athletic activities. Fun is equated with smoking and drinking, and while
the handsomest models make big bucks posing for tobacco
billboards and advertisements, all great athletes look forward
to retirement so they can spend their time in bars arguing
over which beer is lightest. It was once a common belief in
this country that weekends were for family, church, and re-
laxation. Now the message is clearly that "weekends were
made for Michelob."

In a sobering warning to the entire Church, President Benson stated: "The Lord foresaw the situation of today when
motives for money would cause men to conspire to entice
others to take noxious substances into their bodies. Advertisements which promote beer, wine, liquors, coffee, tobacco
and other harmful substances are examples of what the Lord
foresaw. But the most pernicious example of an evil conspiracy in our time is those who induce [our] people into the
use of drugs. In all love, we give you warning that Satan and
his emissaries will strive to entice you to use harmful substances, because they well know if you partake, your spiritual
powers will be inhibited and you will be in their evil power."
(*The Teachings of Ezra Taft Benson,* pp. 478–79.)

Donald Ian MacDonald, M.D., associate clinical professor of pediatrics at the University of South Florida, writes: "During the decade of the 1960s and 1970s, an unprecedented and tragic increase in the use and abuse of psychoactive drugs occurred in this country. Its most dangerous impact was on young people, particularly teenagers. In earlier decades, though many adolescents smoked cigarettes and often began to experiment with alcohol, they were essentially drug-free so far as illicit drugs were concerned. By 1982, however, the percent of high school seniors who had some experience with illicit drugs climbed from essentially zero to over 65%." (*Drugs, Drinking, and Adolescents,* p. v.)

In a chapter titled "The Drug Epidemic," Dr. MacDonald traces the history of illicit drug abuse by American adolescents and their parents, showing not only the effects of various drug substances but also the apparent causes behind the growth in their use. He says, referring to adults in the 1960s and 1970s: "These people, also, were dealing with life chemically, but their chemicals were the legal tranquilizers and sedatives prescribed by their physicians for stress and anxiety. It was a frequent occurrence in the early 1970s for pediatricians to see in their offices glassy-eyed and tranquilized mothers of young children. These were respectable middle-class housewives, women whose physicians had prescribed diazepam (Valium) or chlordiazepoxide (Librium) to help them cope with the stress of their daily lives. Along with these and other exciting and less legal new drugs, the acceptability and use of alcohol continued to escalate. The hope of better living through chemistry seemed to have arrived." (Ibid., p. 3.)

Frightening Statistics

This acceptance of drug use was demonstrated by the Johnston-Bachman-O'Malley study, first commissioned by the National Institute on Drug Abuse in 1975. In that year, "the senior class had had only 17% of its members initiated [to marijuana] by the time they [had been] freshman. In startling contrast 34.1% of freshmen in 1975 had already tried pot. Of these, 16.2% had begun by the eighth grade." (Ibid., p. 4.)

Doctor MacDonald continues by pointing out that in 1979, 52 percent of male high-school seniors admitted to consuming five or more alcoholic drinks at one sitting within the previous two weeks. The percentage of use among females was only slightly less. (Ibid., p. 5.) Cigarette smoking was a different matter. In 1977 girls took the lead in cigarette consumption in America, which lead they continue to hold, according to the most recent studies. And this addiction, introduced into society for money, is deadly. "Over 200,000 Americans died in 1981 as a result of cigarette smoking, and the American Cancer Society estimates that by 1985 lung cancer will be the leading cause of death in American women." (Ibid., p. 6.) One has to wonder at the cigarette ad that says, "You've come a long way, baby."

Another survey conclusion states: "In 1979, more than 50 million Americans had tried marijuana at least once. Young adults (18–25 years) were the most frequent users (68%), followed by youths aged 12–17 years (31%) and adults aged 26 years and older (20%). . . . Within the youth group . . . females were more likely than males to be current cigarette smokers. . . . In 1980, the lifetime prevalances of marijuana, tobacco and alcohol outstripped those of all other drugs, at 60%, 71% and 93%, respectively. . . . Those students who show less successful adaptation to the educational environment (by low grades and truancy) show above-average drug use. Also, those who spend many evenings out for recreation and those with heavy time commitments to a job and with relatively high income report higher-than-average drug use. Lower-than-average drug use is reported by those with strong religious commitments and conservative political views." (Iris

F. Litt, ed., *Adolescent Substance Abuse*, Report of the Fourteenth Ross Roundtable on Critical Approaches to Common Pediatric Problems [Columbus: Ross Laboratories, 1983], pp. 3–5.)

Interesting findings, we feel. A more recent study (1988) prepared by the American Academy of Pediatrics states: "More than 90% of adolescents in the United States will have used alcohol before graduating from high school, and two thirds of seniors report drinking within the past month. Fifty percent of seniors report having ever used marijuana, and one fourth of seniors report having used it in the last thirty days. Approximately 5% of seniors use either marijuana or alcohol daily. Alcohol and marijuana use began before entrance to high school for approximately 30% and 10%, respectively, of seniors. Seventeen percent of seniors used cocaine, with 5% reporting using it within the past month. . . . Initial drug use is . . . now occurring at an earlier age. Ten times as many high school seniors report that they began drinking before leaving the sixth grade as did a decade ago. The percentage of students using drugs by the sixth grade has tripled since 1975. In the early 1960s, marijuana use was virtually nonexistent among 13-year-olds; at the present time, one in six 13-year-olds has used marijuana. 'Crack,' a highly addictive, inexpensive, smokable form of cocaine, is now widely available. Cocaine use among teenagers has increased: 17% of the senior class of 1985 reported that they had used cocaine in the past year. The 1986 National Household Survey of Drug Use reveals some potentially serious developments in patterns of drug abuse by 12–17-year-old youth, the youngest age group surveyed. Twenty-four percent of boys and 23% of girls in this age group had used an illicit drug within the last year. . . . Patterns of alcohol, tobacco and marijuana use among youth are of special concern because these three substances are often considered 'gateway' drugs. Most people

141

who become seriously involved with illicit drugs have started with these substances. . . . The pattern of use changes; risk remains a constant. For most young people, such risk arises through their own drug use; nonetheless, even that minority of youth who abstain from psychoactive drugs are not immune to the dangers created by their peers. These young people should not be deprived of our counsel and support as they attempt to maintain their lifestyle in an environment where drug use is the mode." (*Substance Abuse: A Guide For Health Professionals* [Elk Grove Village IL: American Academy of Pediatrics, 1988], introduction and p. 2.)

Untimely Death—a National Disaster

All of this abuse has resulted in a tragic national disaster. Doctor MacDonald states: "In the 15- to 24-year range, the leading causes of death are accidents, homicides, and suicides. All have a strong correlation with drug and alcohol use. Marvelous technical and medical advances in our society have produced declining death rates for all ages with each passing decade in this century, with one exception. Mortality rates in the 15- to 24-year age range have risen significantly in the last 20 years." (*Drugs, Drinking, and Adolescents*, p. 8.) "Of the 25,000 accidental deaths among youth annually, approximately 40%, or 10,000, are alcohol related. Homicide is the second leading cause of death among adolescents. Of the 5,500 adolescent homicide victims each year, 30% are intoxicated at the time they are killed. Drug use is a leading, if not the leading, cause of death among adolescents." (*Substance Abuse*, introduction.)

Doctor MacDonald continues: "The effect of drugs on the non-using population cuts much deeper than the mortality figures. Perhaps more important is the weakening of our national fibre in a number of measurable and fairly obvious ways. Areas affected include scholastic performance, work performance, family relationships, military readiness, the cost of goods and services, the crime rate, and the filling of our mental health institutions. Scholastic aptitude test (SAT) scores in this country fell for eighteen straight years following 1964, when less than 2% of the population had ever tried pot. . . . Drug use is related to truancy, sleeping in school, change in short-term memory, and attention ability. . . .

"In 1980, a worldwide survey of United States military personnel on active duty revealed that 5% used marijuana daily and 26% had used it within the past 30 days. In 1980 the Pentagon spent $95 million on drug and alcohol programs aimed at prevention, treatment and rehabilitation. In that year 25,000 servicemen were referred for treatment. . . . The National Institute on Alcohol Abuse and Alcoholism estimated that in 1980, alcohol-related industry losses were $30 billion. . . .

"Pediatricians have become increasingly concerned about child abuse and its disastrous effects on young people and families. They should be aware that more and more of the abused young people have parents who are chemically dependent. . . . A survey by an Oklahoma legislator revealed that 62% of all prisoners in that state were incarcerated for crimes directly related to alcohol and/or drug use. . . .

"Women who used marijuana during pregnancy were five times more likely to deliver infants with features compatible with the Fetal Alcohol Syndrome (mental retardation, microcephaly which means reduced or non-existent brain, and irritability), [which] suggests that the effects of alcohol and marijuana on the fetus may be additive." (*Drugs, Drinking, and Adolescents,* pp. 10, 11, 72.)

All Is Not Well in Zion

Having seen these things coming upon us, perhaps this is another reason why Nephi cried so many centuries ago: "Wo be unto him that is at ease in Zion! Wo be unto him that crieth: All is well!" (2 Nephi 28:24–25.) Certainly in our day and age, the last days, all is not well.

Self-Indulgence of the Mind

In another vein, but still dealing with damaging and often damning self-indulgence, can anyone possibly doubt that polluting our minds is just as contrary to the temperate doctrines of the Word of Wisdom as is polluting our bodies? Can it be supposed that the Holy Ghost will dwell in and inspire a mind filled and consumed with carnal filthiness? As President Benson stated: "Stay morally clean. This means that you keep a clean mind. Your thoughts will determine your actions, and so they must be controlled. It is difficult to control those thoughts if you submit yourself to temptation. So you will have to carefully select your reading material, the movies you see, and the other forms of entertainment in order to have good thoughts rather than unwholesome desires." (*The Teachings of Ezra Taft Benson*, p. 197.) On another occasion President Benson stated: "Consider carefully the words of the prophet Alma to his son, Corianton, 'Forsake your sins, and go no more after the lusts of your eyes' (Alma 39:9). 'The lusts of your eyes'—in our day what does that expression mean? Movies, television programs [which would probably include every episode of every soap opera in existence today], and video recordings that are both suggestive and lewd. Magazines and books that are obscene and pornographic. We counsel you . . . not to pollute your minds with such degrading matter, for the mind through which this filth passes is never the same afterward." (Ibid., p. 222.)

As Jesus taught the Nephites: "The light of the body is the eye; if, therefore, thine eye be single, thy whole body shall be full of light. But if thine eye be evil, thy whole body shall be full of darkness." (3 Nephi 13:22–23.) In our opinion, the resurrected Christ is saying that we become what we decide to look at, to watch, to allow our eyes to feast upon. Every waking minute of every day we have a choice, and we will quite literally become what we choose.

Many are familiar with the notorious serial killer Ted Bundy's last-minute admission to the deadly impact of pornography on his thinking and subsequent activities. In his last mortal interview, he stated: "This is the message that I want to get across, that as a young boy, and I mean a boy of 12 or 13 certainly, that I encountered . . . in the local grocery store, in a local drug store . . . soft-core pornography. . . . [In people's garbage] we would come across pornographic books of a harder nature . . . of a more graphic explicit nature. . . . This kind of literature contributed and helped mold and shape the kinds of violent behavior [I am here for]. . . . My experience with pornography . . . is once you become addicted to it . . . I would keep looking for more potent, more explicit, more graphic kinds of material. Like an addiction, you keep craving something that is harder, harder, something which . . . gives you a greater sense of excitement. Until you reach a point where the pornography only goes so far, you reach that jumping off point where you begin to wonder if maybe actually doing it would give you [a thrill] which is beyond just reading it or looking at it." (*Deseret News,* January 26–27, 1989, p. 4A.)

Need we say more about the satanically inspired dangers of polluting the mind with such filth? By the same token, Dr. Donald Ian MacDonald states concerning the dangers of polluting our minds with rock and heavy-metal music: "Rock music grew up in a time of youthful rebellion [in the 1960s and 1970s]. Interwoven with the music were messages of sex, drugs, and protest. More recently homosexuality and satanism have been added to these themes. Rock music has become the music of the young. . . . Many teenagers understandably enjoy the beat and the use of fascinating electronic effects. Much of the music, though, is definitely counterculture. Strong messages to 'let it all hang out,' 'do drugs,' and 'have sex' abound. Pleasure is king. Popular rock star Eric Clapton sings, 'Cocaine, cocaine, she's all right, she's OK.' Adults who largely ignore these media messages are seen by children as passively accepting them. Outrage might be more appropriate." (*Drugs, Drinking, and Adolescents,* p. 92.)

A Latter-day Saint, says President Benson, "should never permit himself to see a movie or cheap literature, or hear music that tends to interfere with or dampen the spirit. . . . There is ample evidence that rock music is offensive to the Spirit and affects adversely [our] spirituality." (*The Teachings of Ezra Taft Benson,* p. 202.) "Rock music, with its instant physical appeal, is an ideal door-crasher, for the devil knows that music has the power to ennoble or corrupt, to purify or pollute. He will not forget to use its subtle power against you. His sounds come from the dark world of drugs, immorality, obscenity, and anarchy. His sounds are flooding the earth. It is his day—a day that is to become as the days of Noah before the Second Coming, for the prophets have so predicted. The signs are clear. The signs are here in this blessed land. You cannot escape this mass media environment which is controlled by financial censorship. Records, radio, television, movies, magazines—all are monopolized by the money-managers who are guided by one ethic, the words wealth and power. . . . Don't listen to music that is degrading. Music can, by its tempo, by its beat, by its intensity [and I would add by its lyrics], dull the spiritual sensitivity of men and women. [Latter-day Saints] cannot afford to fill [their] minds with this unworthy, hard music of our day." (Ibid., p. 326.)

The Lord adapted the Word of Wisdom and its message of temporal care and moderation for our entire bodily system "to the capacity of the weak and the weakest of all saints, who are or can be called saints." (D&C 89:3.) If we indulge in self-gratification as we pollute our bodies with poisonous substances; if we pollute our minds with satanically inspired music, photographs, and movies; if we pollute God's earth through self-indulgent waste; can we think to consider ourselves Saints? Can we think to obtain deliverance from God's wrath and indignation as it is being poured out in these last days?

Joy Versus Happiness

This hedonism we have been discussing, so pervasive in modern society, has reached down to involve parenting and the desire of parents to see their children's desires gratified. When asking parents what they want their children to be when they grow up, be prepared for an answer that coincides with this desire. One single response to this question has become predominant. The all-too-common answer is, "I don't care what Charley becomes as long as he's happy." Happiness is great, but only when it is not sought in wickedness and self-indulgence. When "happiness" becomes the number-one goal in life, deferment of gratification, self-sacrifice, sharing, and caring about others will surely be pushed aside. Better goals, we believe, are to have children grow up feeling good about themselves, living up to their potential, having a spiritual awareness, and caring about other people—in short, exercising self-control. These interrelated goals are righteous, and therefore they will lead to true happiness (see Alma 41:10), which the Lord calls joy (see 2 Nephi 2:25). The joy of accomplishment and helping others is great. In fact, according to King Benjamin this is the way to serve God. (Mosiah 2:17.) Putting "happiness" first will absolutely prevent the attainment of such joy.

Families Are Being Destroyed

Unfortunately, the message of "happiness at all costs" seems to have become firmly entrenched in child-rearing practices from the nursery onward. Pediatricians and parents have subscribed increasingly to the belief that it is a parental responsibility to shield children from all trauma. Children are not to face death, discomfort, boredom, loneliness, frustration, or anxiety. Parents, in trying to shield children from these situations, have only postponed reality. These "traumas" are real, and the role of parenting should be helping a child learn to deal with them. Careful, loving, and age-appropriate teaching of the joyful message of the gospel of Jesus Christ allows children to learn from their own experiences.

President Ezra Taft Benson states: "Because parents have departed from the principles the Lord gave for happiness and success, families throughout the world are undergoing great stress and trauma. Many parents have been enticed to abandon their responsibilities in the home to seek after an elusive 'self-fulfillment.' Some have abdicated parental responsibilities for pursuit of material things, unwilling to postpone personal gratification in the interest of their children's welfare." (*The Teachings of Ezra Taft Benson,* p. 500.)

Such social and economic choices in a family certainly seem to increase the risk that children will break the commandments through self-indulgence. With the increasing number of single-parent or both-parents-working families, this pattern of inadequate supervision is becoming commonplace, and the damage is becoming apparent. Especially does this seem to create problems with keeping the Word of Wisdom. One recent study indicated that a large percentage of children first tried alcohol, tobacco, or drugs while they were home either alone or with friends, but without parental supervision or control. (*Adolescent Substance Abuse,* p. 7.) For this reason

148

alone, it would make sense to follow the counsel of the prophets.

President Benson has quoted President Kimball as saying: "The husband is expected to support his family, and only in an emergency should a wife secure outside employment. Her place is in the home, to build the home into a haven of delight. Numerous divorces can be traced directly to the day when the wife left the home and went out into the world into employment. Two incomes raise the standard of living beyond its norm. Two spouses working prevents the complete and proper home life, breaks into the family prayers, creates an independence which is not cooperative, causes distortion, limits the family, and frustrates the children already born. . . . I beg of you, you who could and should be bearing and rearing a family: Wives, come home from the typewriter, the laundry, the nursing; come home from the factory, the cafe. No career approaches in importance that of wife, homemaker, mother — cooking meals, washing dishes, making beds for one's precious husband and children. Come home, wives, to your husbands. Make home a heaven for them. Come home, wives, to your children, born and unborn. Wrap the motherly cloak about and, unembarrassed, help in a major role to create the bodies for the immortal souls who anxiously await. When you have fully complemented your husband in home life and borne the children, growing up full of faith, integrity, responsibility, and goodness, then you have achieved your accomplishment supreme, without peer, and you will be the envy [of all] through time and eternity." (Spencer W. Kimball, San Antonio Fireside, December 3, 1977, pp. 9–12. Quoted in *The Teachings of Ezra Taft Benson*, pp. 514–15.)

For many, knowing that over 50 percent of all American mothers are now employed in the work force, and feeling the tremendous economic pressures of our day, this counsel is considered "hard" doctrine. However, when we have the faith to be obedient to the counsel of our prophets, the Lord has promised that we can go to him and ask what we, as individuals, are to do about the above counsel, and receive direction. If the Spirit directs that we are to work, then so be it. If, on the other hand, we are constrained from leaving the home, then we, along with our children, will be economically sustained and spiritually united. Thus either way we will be found standing in holy places.

Not Just "Thou Shalt Nots"

We must understand that the Word of Wisdom is not simply a set of prohibitory rules, a list of "Thou shalt nots." Some things we are told to avoid, but others we are just as strongly instructed to use. As Elder Bruce R. McConkie put it, the Word of Wisdom's "affirmative provision gives direction for the use of meat and grain by both man and animals; its prohibitions direct man to refrain from the use of certain specified harmful things." (*Mormon Doctrine,* p. 845.) In other words, the Word of Wisdom is a set of wise instructions given by a loving Heavenly Father, which, if followed, will give us both bodily and spiritual strength to deal with the judgments that are coming upon the world. President Benson, our living prophet, says, "We can be grateful for the Word of Wisdom. Healthful foods, proper rest, adequate exercise, and a clear conscience can prepare us to tackle the trials that lie ahead." (*The Teachings of Ezra Taft Benson,* p. 476.)

A Key to Personal Revelation

Elder Boyd K. Packer states: "Our physical body is the instrument of our spirit. In that marvelous revelation, the Word of Wisdom, we are told how to keep our bodies free from impurities which might dull, even destroy, those delicate physical senses which have to do with spiritual communication. The Word of Wisdom is a key to individual revelation. It was given as 'a principle with a promise, adapted to the capacity of the weak and the weakest of all saints.' (D&C 89:3.) The promise is that those who obey will receive 'great treasures of knowledge, even hidden treasures.' (V. 19.) If we abuse our body with habit-forming substances, or misuse prescription drugs, we draw curtains which close off the light of spiritual communication. Narcotic addiction serves the design of the prince of darkness, for it disrupts the channel to the holy spirit of truth." (*Ensign*, November 1989, p. 14.)

Again quoting President Benson: "The Word of Wisdom leads to clean habits, thoughts, and actions. It will make you more receptive to the Spirit of God which cannot dwell in an unclean tabernacle (see Helaman 4:24)." (*The Teachings of Ezra Taft Benson*, p. 476.) And President Stephen L Richards, counselor in the First Presidency to David O. McKay, declared: "The Word of Wisdom is spiritual. It is true that it prohibits the use of deleterious substances and makes provision for the health of the body. But the largest measure of good derived from its observance is in increased faith and the development of more spiritual power and wisdom. Likewise, the most regrettable and damaging effects of its infractions are spiritual, also. Injury to the body may be comparatively trivial to the damage to the soul in the destruction of faith and the retardation of spiritual growth." (*Conference Report*, April 1949, p. 141.)

Divine Protection

Finally, in terms of temporal preparation for the conflict and turmoil that we must pass through during the next few years, few of the Lord's requirements have as specific a promise of temporal protection as does the Word of Wisdom.

Though this theme has been addressed by many of the latter day prophets and apostles, few provide a more poignant account of personal protection than does Elder William H. Bennett, formerly of the First Quorum of Seventy, who served in the South Pacific during World War II. From his own reminiscences, Elder Bennett discovered that his war years seemed to have a theme: obedience to the gospel, and specifically the Word of Wisdom. His understanding apparently began with his miraculous escape from a Japanese ambush on Morotai Island and the wide-ranging discussions of that escape, and the theme escalated rapidly after that. Hardly ever did more than a week pass that he did not note in his journal a conversation with one man or another, and sometimes whole groups of men, regarding the Lord's law of health.

Years later, after his call as a General Authority, he spoke in the Sydney Australia Area Conference, declaring: "I have a very personal testimony pertaining to the Word of Wisdom. Let me just say that my life was miraculously saved on four occasions that I'm aware of during World War II. I attribute that to three things. First of all, the teaching I received in my home as a boy from wise parents and my older brothers and my younger sisters, and also from my wonderful teachers that I had in the Church organizations. I learned the value of prayer very early in my life, and I want to tell you that I did a lot of praying under combat conditions. Second, I received my temple endowments in the Alberta Temple in Canada before I went into military service. I made up my mind that I was going to keep those covenants, including the wearing of the temple garments, and I testify to you that I received the protection that is promised to those who do keep that covenant.

"The third is the Word of Wisdom. Being interested in athletics, I've never had a problem with the Word of Wisdom. I demonstrated in the classroom and in athletics its value. But in World War II, I learned the meaning of that last verse:

'And I, the Lord, give unto them a promise, that the destroying angel shall pass by them, . . . and not slay them.' We were ambushed on one occasion under conditions that would have annihilated our small patrol group. Not a single man was killed.

"On another occasion, I came down with what the medical officer diagnosed as Japanese Scrub Typhus Disease, I had all of the symptoms and was sent quite a distance back to the rear to the medical aid station. I was there for four days, and for twenty-four hours of those four days I was under constant medical surveillance by the medical officers or nurses. I had all of the symptoms, but on the fourth day everything became normal; I was completely well. Medical people couldn't understand it, but I could. There was only one other LDS soldier in my outfit; Sergeant Leslie E. Milam. . . . I wasn't able to make contact with him to be administered to, but I still received a blessing. It means a great deal to me." (Blaine and Brenton Yorgason, *Here Stands a Man* [Salt Lake City: Deseret Book Company, 1990], pp. 294–95.)

In conclusion, living the Word of Wisdom protects us in two ways, one direct and the other indirect. Directly we are given the promise that the destroying angel will pass us by and not slay us, meaning that our lives will not be taken before our time. Indirectly we learn to avoid self-indulgence and through that the poisons introduced in our society by "conspiring men" whose hearts are filled with "evils and designs." Thus we become worthy of being filled with the power and influence of the Holy Ghost, who will give us needed direction and protection during the judgments that are even now descending upon our world.

15

Following the Lord's Living Prophets — Sexual Purity

Probably Satan advertises no product with greater alacrity and determination than he does illicit sex. Movies, videos, sitcoms, soap operas, magazines, newspapers, billboards, commercials, designer fashions, lingerie advertisements, novels, radio and television talk-show hosts, nonfiction books, rock and country music, music videos, even "good ol' boy" radio disk jockeys — all promote illicit sex, vulgarity, and promiscuity. In our present world, there is literally no way to escape it. How we respond to this nefarious campaign of Lucifer's will, in great measure, determine whether or not we are independent of the world.

Sadly, a great many Latter-day Saints don't escape. A friend of ours told us recently that at one point within the past couple

Some of the material in this chapter is excerpted from: Blaine and Brenton Yorgason, *The Problem With Immorality* (Orem UT: Keepsake BookCards, 1989).

of years, he did not have a single elder in his branch at the MTC who had not had some sort of moral problem. "Last year in my stake," a stake president told us a couple of years ago, "thirty-two girls became pregnant out of wedlock. I can only guess at the horrifying numbers of immoral young men and women who did not get caught." In many stakes in the Church, similar sins are being committed by similar numbers of people, both young and old alike, and Satan is laughing gleefully at the success of his glitzy campaign.

Regarding sexual purity, Joseph Smith said, "[Brethren and sisters], if they are pure and innocent, can come in the presence of God; for what is more pleasing to God than innocence; you must be innocent, or you cannot come up before God; if we would come before God, we must keep ourselves pure, as He is pure." (*Teachings of the Prophet Joseph Smith*, p. 227.)

This law is one of the two highest laws that people covenant to live and obey when they go through the temple, where God's most holy and sacred ordinances are revealed. President Benson says, "We covenant to live the law of chastity . . . [which] is virtue and sexual purity. This law places us under covenant to live this commandment strictly." (*The Teachings of Ezra Taft Benson*, p. 278.) Such covenanting is eternally serious, and if the covenant is later broken, or if it is made unworthily, then the individual has committed solemn mockery before God. And as the Lord says, "I, the Lord, am not to be mocked in the last days." (D&C 63:58.)

It seems to us that most members of the Church pay at least lip service to the law of chastity. Sadly, however, a great many must not understand the spiritual and physical consequences of breaking themselves against this commandment, either physically or mentally, for we suspect that, to one degree or another, it is abused by more members of the Lord's Church and kingdom than any other law.

A Difficult Question

Blaine states: "A few years ago when I was serving in a bishopric I was interviewing a young man, and out of the blue he became angry and posed what I found at the time to be a rather difficult question to answer. To the best of my memory, he stated: 'I don't see what the big deal is about morals. So somebody makes a mistake, or has a problem with sex. So what? I know of tons of kids who have had sex, and it's no big deal. They still go on their missions, even when they tell their bishops about it. And the girls get married in the temple, too. Sometimes they have to wait a year, but so what? A year's no big deal, either. I just don't see why people get so hyper about it.' "

As we have considered this young man's question in the years since he posed it, we believe that we have found the answer that should have been given him then but most likely wasn't because it wasn't clearly understood. We have concluded that if members of the Church, young and old alike, could only understand with greater clarity the negative impact that being immoral has upon them, now and in eternity, far fewer would allow themselves to fall. As the writer of Proverbs says, "Whoso committeth adultery . . . lacketh understanding: he that doeth it destroyeth his own soul." (Proverbs 6:32.) Samuel the Lamanite taught the same thing when he said, "Ye have sought for happiness in doing iniquity, which thing is contrary to the nature of . . . righteousness." (Helaman 13:38.)

Three Punishments

For those who choose to break this law, even if only to mentally lust after another by entertaining unrighteous thoughts or fantasies, the Lord specifically spells out, or promises, three separate and distinct consequences. He says, "He that looketh upon a woman to lust after her, or if any shall commit adultery in their hearts, they shall not have the spirit, but shall deny the faith and shall fear." (D&C 63:16; 42:23.)

Punishment #1 — Losing the Spirit

The first punishment, then, is that "they shall not have the Spirit." President Benson says of this prophetic promise: "No sin is causing the loss of the Spirit of the Lord among our people more today than sexual promiscuity. It is causing our people to stumble, damning their growth, darkening their spiritual powers, and making them subject to other sins." (*The Teachings of Ezra Taft Benson,* p. 279.)

This Spirit that departs when immorality occurs is the Holy Ghost, a member of the Godhead. The privilege of having his companionship is given to all who come through the waters of baptism, receive confirmation and the gift of the Holy Ghost, and then live according to what they have covenanted through baptism to live. He is the Comforter, Testator, Revelator, Sanctifier, Holy Spirit, Holy Spirit of Promise, Spirit of Truth, Spirit of the Lord, and Messenger of the Father and the Son. His companionship is the greatest gift, save eternal salvation, that mortals can enjoy, for he accomplishes for us each and all of the above titles or assignments.

If his presence is withdrawn because people choose to lust or commit other immoral acts, each and all of the above spiritual events or gifts immediately cease in their lives. They are then left alone, a part of our dark, telestially lit world. Such being the case, how can they possibly expect to receive the protection and direction we all hope we will receive as we move ever closer to the second coming of Christ?

Punishment #2 — Denying the Faith

The second punishment the Lord promises the immoral is that they will "deny the faith." Without the Spirit, people can be so deceived by Satan that the gospel, or certain aspects of it, will no longer appear to be true. For instance, home teaching or holding family prayer will seem ridiculous to an elder who has lost the Spirit through lusting or other sexual abuses. His thoughts as well as his language will begin to be filled with profanities or vulgarities. Church meetings and partaking of the sacrament will seem silly and a waste of time. Breaking the Word of Wisdom will appear more and more attractive. Church service will be ultimately be replaced by athletic events and all sorts of superficial activities. If not checked by sincere and thorough repentance, this spirit of apostasy (for so it is!) will become so powerful that the afflicted person will deny the faith and will no longer be a part of the Church. And this will occur because he no longer has the ability to recognize what is happening to him.

Elder Bruce R. McConkie writes, "The adulterous generation of Christ's day were deaf to the voice of truth, and through their diseased state of mind and heart, sought after signs and preferred empty fables to the message of salvation." (*Mormon Doctrine,* p. 709.) In other words, having lost the Spirit through immorality, these people were deaf to the voice of truth; they could not hear it! So they wandered into darkened and forbidden paths and were lost.

It might easily be argued: "But that doesn't make sense. Being immoral doesn't mean a person becomes stupid in every other area of his or her life. A person's brain still works, doesn't it?"

May we respond to this argument by answering that a wicked person's mind is apparently not as effective as that of a righteous person, especially where understanding gospel subjects is concerned. President Benson has said, "Great nations have fallen when they became morally corrupt, because the sins of immorality left their people scarred and misshapen creatures who were unable to face the challenge of their times." (*The Teachings of Ezra Taft Benson,* p. 279.) To understand the gospel, or even to understand how to live successfully, requires a certain amount of light and truth in a person's mind. But the Lord says, "That wicked one cometh and taketh away light and truth, through disobedience, from the children of men." (D&C 93:39.) When people are disobedient to God, then Satan is allowed to take away what light and truth they have, until finally they are no longer able to understand even basic gospel concepts. Then, being already without the Spirit, they become so foolish that they find themselves denying the very doctrines, the only doctrines, that can bring about their eternal salvation and exaltation. Personally, we would call that sort of behavior very stupid indeed.

Punishment #3 — Fearing

The third punishment is that lustful people "shall fear." Fear is one of the most fascinating aspects of those who lose the Spirit of the Lord, deny the faith, and leave the Church. Such people fear to pray; they fear to face their righteous neighbors or family members; they fear to repent; they even fear for their lives when no one chases them. Mormon calls it "that awful fear of death which fills the breasts of the wicked." (Mormon 6:7.)

According to President Benson, "We live in a world of fear today. Fear seems to be almost everywhere present. But there is no place for fear among the Latter-day Saints, among men and women who keep the commandments, who place their trust in the Almighty, who are not afraid to get down on their knees and pray to our Heavenly Father." (*The Teachings of Ezra Taft Benson,* p. 399.)

Thus fear, which in all its horrible ramifications is a product of Satan's realms, is the final wages of those who choose to involve their minds and bodies with lust and more gross forms of immorality. The Lord declares, "The fearful, and the unbelieving, and all liars, and whosoever loveth and maketh a lie, and the whoremonger, and the sorcerer, shall have their part in that lake which burneth with fire and brimstone, which is the second death." (D&C 63:17.)

Obviously, all three of these promised curses, for curses they are, will dramatically affect our ability to receive and enjoy divine protection during the coming judgments of God. Without the direction of the Spirit, we will wander aimlessly; having denied the faith, we will be unworthy of God's help; and being filled with fear, we will be numbered among those whose hearts will fail them (see D&C 45:26; 88:91) at the sight of the judgments being poured out in the approaching day.

16

Temple Attendance

Recently one of us invited a close friend and his wife to attend a session of the temple with us. He laughed and replied: "No, thanks. I only go once a year whether I need it or not, and my year isn't quite up." Surprised, we pursued the conversation and learned that our friend considered temple attendance a boring waste of time.

"You know how the Prophet is always telling us that he learns something new each time he goes?" our friend asked. "Well, I think that's bunk! In the past fifteen years I have only learned one new thing in the temple, and that is that the men stand up one more time than the women. I'm telling you that going to the temple is a waste of time, and you won't catch me there on a bet. I have too many important things to do."

While our friend's attitude is saddening, thank goodness it is not universal. More and more temples are being com-

---

Some of the material in this chapter has been excerpted from: Blaine and Brenton Yorgason, *Obtaining Priesthood Power* (Orem UT: Keepsake BookCards, 1989).

pleted; more and more Latter-day Saints are becoming regular attenders; and more and more of them are beginning to understand the deep significance of the experience. Nephi, quoting the words of Isaiah, wrote about the excitement that would surround temple attendance in the latter days: "And it shall come to pass in the last days, when the mountain of the Lord's house shall be established in the top of the mountains, and shall be exalted above the hills, and all nations shall flow unto it. And many people shall go and say, Come ye, and let us go up to the mountain of the Lord, to the house of the God of Jacob; and he will teach us of his ways, and we will walk in his paths; for out of Zion shall go forth the law, and the word of the Lord from Jerusalem." (2 Nephi 12:2–3; Isaiah 2:2–3.)

It is a commonly accepted doctrine in the Church that latter-day temples, especially the one in Salt Lake City, Utah, fulfill the words of Nephi and Isaiah. (See *Mormon Doctrine*, p. 781.) Interestingly, both early prophets inform us that the Saints will attend these temples with great anticipation, in order that they might learn the ways of God and how to walk in his paths. Why would they want to do that? In our opinion, it is because the ordinances performed in these temples will be essential to people hoping to obtain divine protection and ultimate exaltation.

Safety through the Endowment

In an interesting and enlightening revelation to Joseph Smith concerning temples, the Lord alludes to future wars in America and tells us the conditions under which we need not fear them. He says: "I show unto you a mystery, a thing which is had in secret chambers, to bring to pass even your destruction in process of time, and ye knew it not; and again, I say unto you that the enemy in secret chambers seeketh your lives. Ye hear of wars in far countries, and ye say that there will soon be great wars in far countries, but ye know not the hearts of men in your own land. I tell you these things because of your prayers; wherefore, treasure up wisdom in your bosoms, lest the wickedness of men reveal these things unto you by their wickedness, in a manner which shall speak in your ears with a voice louder than that which shall shake the earth; but if ye are prepared, ye shall not fear. And that ye might escape the power of the enemy, and be gathered unto me a righteous people without spot and blameless — wherefore, for this cause I gave unto you the commandment that ye should go to the [temple], and there I will give unto you my law; and there you shall be endowed with power from on high." (D&C 38:13, 28–32.)

The Worry over Mysteries

Sadly, many people believe that to even try to understand the temple is to meddle in the mysteries, which, they feel, should be left alone. We're not certain why this is so, especially when we are so frequently told in the scriptures the blessed state of those who understand the mysteries of godliness, and we are told to seek such understanding ourselves. Brother Hugh Nibley writes: "The Book of Mormon contains by far the clearest exposition 'in words of exceeding plainness' of the mysteries, beginning with the meaning of that elusive word itself. The mysteries are not magic or occultism, but any knowledge that men cannot obtain by their own efforts, knowledge to be had only by revelation. The whole Book of Mormon is such a mystery." (*The Prophetic Book of Mormon*, pp. 546–47.)

In the same vein, Joseph Smith said: "I advise all to go on to perfection, and to search deeper and deeper into the mysteries of Godliness." (*Teachings of the Prophet Joseph Smith*, p. 364.) The great prophet Nephi wrote: "He that diligently seeketh shall find; and the mysteries of God shall be unfolded unto them, by the power of the Holy Ghost, as well in these times as in times of old, and as well in times of old as in times to come; wherefore, the course of the Lord is one eternal round." (1 Nephi 10:19.) Alma continued: "He that repenteth and exerciseth faith, and bringeth forth good works, and prayeth continually without ceasing—unto such it is given to know the mysteries of God; yea, unto such it shall be given to reveal things which never have been revealed." (Alma 26:22.) And the Lord concludes: "If thou shalt ask, thou shalt receive revelation upon revelation, knowledge upon knowledge, that thou mayest know the mysteries and peaceable things—that which bringeth joy, that which bringeth life eternal." (D&C 42:61.)

There are at least a dozen additional scriptural references stating the same thing; all Latter-day Saints, if they want to progress spiritually during mortality, must seek to know and understand the mysteries of Godliness. (See Matthew 13:11; Luke 8:10; 1 Nephi 1:1; 2:16; Jacob 4:8; Mosiah 1:5; 2:9; Alma 10:5; 12:9–11; D&C 6:7; 8:11; 63:22–23; 76:5–10.) At least a portion of such understanding comes from within the temple.

An Endowment of Priesthood Keys

Once someone receives the Melchizedek Priesthood, he must obtain the keys or rights to that priesthood. President Ezra Taft Benson states: "Even though the Aaronic Priesthood and Melchizedek Priesthood had been restored to the earth, the Lord urged the Saints to build a temple to receive the keys by which this order of priesthood could be administered on the earth again, 'for there [was] not a place found on earth that he may come to and restore again that which was lost . . . even the fulness of the priesthood' (D&C 124:28). Again, the Prophet Joseph said: 'If a man gets a fullness of the priesthood of God he has to get it in the same way that Jesus Christ obtained it, and that was by keeping all the commandments and obeying all the ordinances of the house of the Lord' (*Teachings of the Prophet Joseph Smith,* p. 308)." (*The Teachings of Ezra Taft Benson,* p. 249.)

These keys were given by Elijah to Joseph Smith and Oliver Cowdery in the Kirtland Temple, and they pertain directly to temple work. Of Elijah's then future visit, Moroni declared to Joseph Smith in 1823: "Behold, I will reveal unto you the priesthood, by the hand of Elijah the prophet, before the coming of the great and dreadful day of the Lord." (D&C 2:1.)

The word *reveal* means "to show" or "to explain." So, Elijah's mission was to give specific temple-oriented keys to priesthood holders so they would know how to use the priesthood they held. The Lord says: "This greater priesthood administereth the gospel and holdeth the key of the mysteries of the kingdom, even the key of the knowledge of God. Therefore, in the ordinances [and where are most of our ordinances found?], the power of godliness is manifest. And without the ordinances thereof, and the authority of the priesthood, the power of godliness is not manifest to men in the flesh; for without this no man can see the face of God, even the Father, and live." (D&C 84:19–22.)

The Purpose of Keys

Occasionally the Lord has revealed spiritual information to his prophets, information that he calls "keys." These keys open spiritual locks and allow spiritual things to begin operating. The Lord revealed to Joseph Smith many keys. Moses held and gave to Joseph the keys to the gathering of Israel (D&C 110:11); Elias gave the keys to the dispensation of the Gospel of Abraham (D&C 110:12); Peter, James, and John restored the keys of the kingdom (D&C 7:7; 27:12–13; 128:20; 81:2). Joseph was given the key to the gift of translation (D&C 6:28), and so forth. There are many scriptural references to keys, but we will discuss only those restored to Joseph Smith and Oliver Cowdery by Elijah. (D&C 110:13–16.) These are called the keys of this dispensation or the keys of the holy priesthood. (D&C 124:34.)

Two Functions of Keys

From what we can learn from the scriptures, as well as from the writings of the modern prophets, keys have two functions, personal and administrative. Regarding administrative keys, President Joseph F. Smith wrote: "The Priesthood in general is the authority given to man to act for God. Every man ordained to any degree of the Priesthood has this authority delegated to him. But it is necessary that every act performed under this authority shall be done at the proper time and place, in the proper way, and after the proper order. The power of directing these labors constitutes the keys of the Priesthood. In their fullness, the keys are held by only one person at a time, the prophet and president of the Church. He may delegate any portion of this power to another, in which case that person holds the keys of that particular labor. Thus, the president of a temple, the president of a stake, the bishop of a ward, the president of a mission, the president of a quorum, each holds the keys of the labors performed in that particular body or locality. He holds the power of directing the official labors performed in the mission or the quorum, or in other words, the keys of that division of the work." (*Gospel Doctrine*, pp. 168–69.)

Since this statement seems clear enough, we will not mention again the use of keys in terms of administration. Instead, we wish to discuss what the Lord seems to say about keys that pertain only to our personal salvation and exaltation.

Revelation of Priesthood

However, it is not possible for us to state precisely what these keys are. Instead, the Lord is the one who must tell us

166

that, for such knowledge is sacred, and it is his alone to impart.

Remember, the priesthood was restored by Peter, James, and John, but it was to be revealed by Elijah the prophet. As we understand it, that means we must gain our understanding of how to use our priesthood with power, as did Joseph, through personal revelation. That is why we referred to these things as part of the mysteries of Godliness. As Brother Hugh Nibley wrote, an understanding of them cannot come from other men but only from God.

Such mysteries are called the "peaceable things of the kingdom" and, according to scripture, are taught by the Holy Ghost. (See D&C 36:2.) In fact, the Lord says: "If thou shalt ask, thou shalt receive revelation upon revelation, knowledge upon knowledge, that thou mayest know the mysteries and peaceable things—that which bringeth joy, that which bringeth life eternal." (D&C 42:61.) But, as Alma explained to Zeezrom: "It is given unto many to know the mysteries of God; nevertheless they are laid under a strict command that they shall not impart only according to the portion of his word which he doth grant unto the children of men, according to the heed and diligence which they give unto him." (Alma 12:9.) And how is the amount of knowledge imparted to be determined? Again Alma answers: "Therefore, he that will harden his heart receiveth the lesser portion of the word . . . until they know nothing concerning the mysteries . . . and he that will not harden his heart, to him is given the greater portion of the word, until it is given unto him to know the mysteries of God until he know them in full." (Alma 12:10–11.)

So, all we can discuss is a little about some of the "whys" and "wherefores" of these keys and perhaps explain why they should one day become important to each of us. Then, when the Holy Ghost inspires us that it is time, and we can no longer rest until we understand these things more fully, we can ask the Lord and obtain all the information about them that we are willing to receive.

We Must Understand the Temple

Until we begin to understand the sacred ordinances of the temple, however, we will never understand the keys of the priesthood. President Benson states: "The temple ceremony was given by a wise Heavenly Father to help us become more Christ-like. The endowment was revealed by revelation and can be understood only by revelation. The instruction is given in symbolic language. The late Apostle John A. Widtsoe taught, 'No man or woman can come out of the temple endowed as he should be, unless he has seen, beyond the symbol, the mighty realities for which the temple stands' ("Temple Worship," an address given in Salt Lake City, 12 October 1920)." (*The Teachings of Ezra Taft Benson*, pp. 250–51.)

And how do we gain that understanding? Joseph Smith said: "The endowment you are so anxious about, you cannot comprehend now, nor could Gabriel explain it to the understanding of your dark minds; but strive to be prepared in your hearts, be faithful in all things, [and] be clean every whit. Let us be faithful and silent, brethren, and if God gives you a manifestation, keep it to yourselves; be watchful and prayerful. . . . Do not watch for iniquity in each other, if you do you will not get an endowment, for God will not bestow it on such. But if we are faithful, and live by every word that proceeds forth from the mouth of God, I will venture to prophesy that we shall get a blessing that will be worth remembering, if we should live as long as John the Revelator." (*Discourses of the Prophet Joseph Smith*, ed. Alma P. Burton [Salt Lake City: Deseret Book Company, 1965], p. 113.)

So, we obtain these blessings, as well as an understanding

of them, through personal righteousness. But here is something for us to consider as we serve and prepare. The word *endow* means "give," and so it is with priesthood power. According to the scriptures, the Lord gives to those who are willing to enter his holy temple worthily, and thereafter keep his commandments, an endowment (or gift) of power, that is, keys to the use of his priesthood.

In the Doctrine and Covenants, the Lord promises the Saints that they will soon "be endowed with power from on high." (D&C 38:32.) Again he says, "I give unto you a commandment that you should build a house, in the which house I design to endow those whom I have chosen with power from on high." (D&C 95:8.) In Nauvoo, the Lord said to the Saints: "Build a house to my name, for the Most High to dwell therein. For there is not a place found on earth that he may come to and restore again that which was lost unto you, or which he hath taken away. For therein are the keys of the holy priesthood ordained, that you may receive honor and glory." (D&C 124:27–28, 34.) And, in a revelation concerning temple work and the sealing powers of the priesthood, Joseph wrote: "Now the great and grand secret of the whole matter, and the summum bonum of the whole subject that is lying before us, consists in obtaining the powers of the holy priesthood. For him to whom these keys are given there is no difficulty in obtaining a knowledge of facts in relation to the salvation of the children of men, both as well for the dead as for the living." (D&C 128:11.) So, we are given priesthood keys when we participate in the ordinances of the temple.

Obtaining Blessings

What sort of spiritual locks do these priesthood keys open for us? Again according to the scriptures, the keys unlock the doors to divine blessings. They are designed so that anyone so endowed may, through temple attendance and mighty prayer, unlock the doors of heaven—go before the Lord and, with confidence, ask for and receive specific blessings, a good many of which are itemized in the scriptures.

Joseph Smith said, "There are certain key words and signs belonging to the priesthood which must be observed in order to obtain blessings." (*Teachings of the Prophet Joseph Smith*, p. 199.) And the Lord says concerning these same keys, "Let my servant William Law also receive the keys by which he may ask and receive blessings." (D&C 124:97.)

And what would some of these blessings be? As quoted above, the keys are to be used to obtain a knowledge of facts in relation to the salvation of the children of men, both the dead as well as the living. (See D&C 128:11.) Joseph Smith added: "You need an endowment, brethren, in order that you may be prepared and able to overcome all things; and those that reject your testimony [afterward] will be damned. The sick will be healed, the lame made to walk, the deaf to hear, and the blind to see, through your instrumentality." (*Discourses of the Prophet Joseph Smith*, p. 113.)

Brigham Young stated, "The Spirit of the Lord and the keys of the priesthood, hold power over all animated beings." (As quoted in Hugh W. Nibley, *Nibley On The Timely and The Timeless* [Provo UT: Brigham Young University Religious Studies Center, 1978], p. 88.) Joseph Smith elaborated on this power over animated beings further when he said: "I preached in the grove on the keys of the kingdom, charity, etc. The keys are certain signs and words by which false spirits and personages may be detected from true, which cannot be revealed to the elders till the temple is completed. The rich can only get them in the temple, the poor may get them on the mountaintop as did Moses. There are signs in heaven, earth and hell; the elders must know them all, to be endowed with power, to finish their work and prevent imposition." (*Discourses of the Prophet Joseph Smith*, p. 116.)

The Mysteries of Godliness

Melchizedek Priesthood keys are also given so that individuals might "have the privilege of receiving the mysteries of the Kingdom of heaven, to have the heavens opened unto them, to commune with the general assembly and church of the Firstborn, and to enjoy the communion and presence of God the Father, and Jesus the mediator of the new covenant." (D&C 107:18–19.) In other words, "this greater priesthood administereth the gospel and holdeth the key of the knowledge of the kingdom, even the key of the knowledge of God." (D&C 84:19.)

To See and Know God

The crowning blessing granted through the priesthood, then, is to see and know personally God the Father and his Beloved Son, Jesus Christ. As Elder Bruce R. McConkie said: "The purpose of the endowment in the house of the Lord is to prepare and sanctify his saints so they will be able to see his face, here and now, as well as to bear the glory of his presence in the eternal worlds." (*The Promised Messiah* [Salt Lake City: Deseret Book Company, 1978], p. 583.)

But if this priesthood promise and potential blessing is ignored or not diligently pursued, then by our own choice the opportunity is taken from us. The scripture states: "This greater priesthood administereth the gospel and holdeth the key of the mysteries of the kingdom, even the key of the knowledge of God. Therefore in the ordinances thereof, the power of Godliness is manifest. And without the ordinances thereof, and the authority of the priesthood, the power of Godliness is not manifest to man in the flesh; for without this no man can see the face of God, even the Father, and live. Now this Moses plainly taught to the children of Israel in the wilderness, and sought diligently to sanctify his people that they might behold the face of God; but they hardened their

171

hearts and could not endure his presence; therefore the Lord in his wrath, for his anger was kindled against them, swore that they should not enter into his rest while in the wilderness, which rest is the fullness of his glory. Therefore he took Moses out of their midst, and the holy priesthood also; and the lesser priesthood continued, which priesthood holdeth the key of the ministering of angels and the preparatory gospel." (D&C 84:19–26.)

Now we ask, how could Moses teach his people so? Why did he think his people could see God? For two reasons, according to the Prophet Joseph. First, because Moses had received the endowment upon the mountain top, had learned its significance, and had, through the use of the priesthood, seen God. (See Moses 1.) And second, because Moses knew that Enoch and other ancient prophets had administered the same endowment to the people they had led, which people had learned the endowment's significance and then gone from grace to grace unto perfection, and so been caught up into the presence of God. (See Moses 6, 7 and *The Words of Joseph Smith,* pp. 142–43.)

How excited and thrilled Moses must have been to teach his people, and how he must have ached when they turned away from all he had taught them, first in fear and finally in idolatry.

Of course, God also ached and turned away, and from what Joseph Smith was taught, God in his righteous wrath took away from the children of Israel the Melchizedek Priesthood portion of the endowment, which enables people to come into the literal presence of God, while mortals, and live.

The children of Israel chose not to be worthy to use the keys of the priesthood that they had been given, and since God must obey all the laws and keep all the promises he has given and made to mankind, he could not allow such unworthy people to progress on into his presence without also taking their lives. Therefore, in actuality, he blessed and preserved the lives of the children of Israel so that they could live and have time to repent, even while they were denying themselves the higher blessings of the priesthood.

These Blessings Are for Everyone

Often we encounter the belief among Church members that such blessings as we have described are only for leaders in the Church, those who, by nature of their callings, devote their lives to service in the kingdom. This belief is incorrect. As Elder Bruce R. McConkie said: "The Lord loves people, not office holders. Every elder is entitled to the same blessings and privileges offered the apostles. . . . The priesthood is greater than any of its offices. . . . All of the elders in the kingdom are expected to live the law as strictly as do the members of the Council of the Twelve, and if they do so live, the same blessings will come to them that flow to apostles and prophets." (*The Promised Messiah*, p. 594.)

Brigham Young said, almost in emphasis to all Latter-day Saints, "Then go on and build the temples of the Lord, that you may receive the endowments in store for you, and possess the keys of the eternal Priesthood, that you may receive every word, sign, and token, and be made acquainted with the laws of angels, and of the kingdom of our Father and our God, and know how to pass from one degree to another, and enter fully into the joy of your Lord." (*Discourses of Brigham Young*, pp. 395–96.)

These Blessings Are for Sisters, Too

Endowed sisters hold the same priesthood blessings and promises of power as do endowed brethren. President Joseph Fielding Smith wrote: "[Joseph Smith] spoke of delivering the keys of the Priesthood to the Church, and said that the faithful members of the Relief Society should receive them with their

173

husbands, that the Saints whose integrity has been tried and proved faithful, might know how to ask the Lord and receive an answer." (*Teachings of the Prophet Joseph Smith*, p. 226.)

Elder James E. Talmage wrote: "In the restored church of Jesus Christ, the holy priesthood is conferred, and an individual bestowal, upon men only, and this in accordance with divine requirement. It is not given to woman to exercise the authority of the priesthood independently; nevertheless, in the sacred endowments associated with the ordinances pertaining to the House of the Lord, woman shares with man the blessings of the priesthood. When the frailties and imperfections of mortality are left behind, in the glorified state of the blessed hereafter, husband and wife will administer in their respective stations, seeing and understanding alike, and cooperating to the full in the government of their family kingdom. Then shall woman be recompensed in rich measure for all the injustice that womanhood has endured in mortality. Then shall woman reign by divine right, a queen in the resplendent realm of her glorified state, even as exalted man shall stand, priest and king unto the most high God. Mortal eye cannot see nor mind comprehend the beauty, glory, and majesty of a righteous woman made perfect in the celestial kingdom of God." (*Young Woman's Journal*, 25:602–3.)

Temple Attendance Imperative

An understanding of these principles should provide ample motivation for all endowed Saints to return to the temples of God at every opportunity, for therein we truly receive priesthood power to bring about our own salvation as well as the salvation of our families, both living and dead.

In conclusion, the endowment we receive in the temple is literally a gift of power from God to us, for therein he gives to each worthy person, male as well as female, the keys of his holy priesthood. (See *Teachings of the Prophet Joseph Smith*,

p. 226.) "For therein [within the temple]," the Lord states, "are the keys of the holy priesthood ordained, that you may receive honor and glory." (D&C 124:27–28, 34.) Once obtained, and once personal worthiness and integrity have been established, each Saint of God can use his or her endowed priesthood keys to obtain knowledge and power sufficient "to overcome all things." (*Discourses of the Prophet Joseph Smith*, p. 113. See also D&C 38:32; 95:8; 128:11; 124:95, 97.) What a glorious promise the Lord has made to those Saints who are worthy of their endowment! Truly will such people be found standing in holy places.

17

Receiving Personal
Revelation

President Benson has told us that if we are to be found standing in holy places, we must be able to receive continual and immediate revelation through personal prayer. We believe this is because only God has the wisdom capable of delivering us from the judgments that are coming.

Joseph Smith taught, "God is the only supreme governor and independent being in whom all fulness and perfection dwell; who is omnipotent, omnipresent, and omniscient; without beginning of days or end of life; and . . . in him every good gift and every good principle dwell." (*Lectures on Faith*, lecture 2, paragraph 2.) "Without the knowledge of all things God would not be able to save any portion of his creatures; for it is by reason of the knowledge which he has of all things, from the beginning to the end, that enables him to give that

Some of the material in this chapter is excerpted from: Blaine and Brenton Yorgason, *Receiving Answers to Prayer* (Orem UT: Keepsake BookCards, 1989).

understanding to his creatures by which they are made partakers of eternal life; and if it were not for the idea existing in the minds of men that God had all knowledge it would be impossible for them to exercise faith in him." (Ibid., lecture 4, paragraph 11.)

From these statements we learn that God is all-powerful (omnipotent), all-present (omnipresent), and all-knowing (omniscient). Mormon declared: "Know ye not that ye are in the hands of God? Know ye not that he hath all power, and at his great command the earth shall be rolled together as a scroll?" (Mormon 5:23.) Several hundred years previous to that statement, King Benjamin said, "Believe . . . that he has all wisdom, and all power, both in heaven and in earth." (Mosiah 4:9.) And as Nephi's brother, Jacob, said concerning God's knowledge: "O how great the holiness of our God! For he knoweth all things, and there is not anything save he knows it." (2 Nephi 9:20.) He is infinite in understanding (Psalm 147:4–5), comprehends all things, and "has all power, all wisdom, and all understanding" (Alma 26:35; D&C 88:41).

Part of God's infinite knowledge is a complete understanding of our difficulties. Even more important, God has a complete knowledge of the best solutions to those same problems or difficulties. Also, God has all power. God's purpose in having all that knowledge and power is "to bring to pass the immortality and eternal life of man." (Moses 1:39.) That purpose is accomplished in part by helping us, through inspiration and guidance, to make correct choices during mortality. If we follow his counsel and walk uprightly, he has the knowledge and power necessary to effect circumstances so that all things will work together for our eternal good, including protection and deliverance from his judgments if protection and deliverance are according to his will. (See D&C 100:15.)

Reasoning further, if our Heavenly Father already knows our problems, as well as the very best solutions to them, and has the power to solve them, then it makes no sense to exclude him while we struggle to solve such problems on our own. In fact, such behavior is foolish in the extreme and is directly contrary to his explicit commandments.

We Are Commanded to Pray

To pray is to talk with God, either vocally or mentally, and he has commanded us to do so at all times. God is a loving Father who is concerned with our lives, and it is his desire that we "keep in touch." Thus, his commandment to pray is an instruction of love. "As soon as we learn the true relationship in which we stand toward God (namely, God is our Father, and we are his children), then at once prayer becomes natural and instinctive on our part (Matthew 7:7–11). Many of the so-called difficulties about prayer arise from forgetting this relationship. Prayer is the act by which the will of the Father and the will of the child are brought into correspondence with each other. The object of prayer is not to change the will of God, but to secure for ourselves and for others blessings that God is already willing to grant, but that are made conditional upon our asking for them. Blessings require some work or effort on our part before we can obtain them. Prayer is a form of work, and is an appointed means for obtaining the highest of all blessings." (Bible Dictionary, pp. 752–53.)

As an angel declared to Adam: "Thou shalt do all that thou doest in the name of the Son, and thou shalt repent and call upon God in the name of the Son forevermore." (Moses 5:8.) In modern as well as ancient scripture, we are commanded emphatically to pray. The Lord says to let every man call upon the name of the Lord (D&C 133:6); he tells us to pray continually that we not be tempted above that which we can bear (Alma 13:28); over and over he tells us to watch and pray always lest we enter into temptation (Matthew 26:41; Mark 13:33; 14:38; Luke 21:36; 22:40, 46; D&C 10:5); and of course through Alma, the Lord commands us that we are to pray about all things and at all times, so that we might be "lifted up at the last day" (Alma 37:35–37). In a remarkable statement to Joseph Smith, the Lord declared: "He that observeth not his prayers before the Lord in the season thereof, let him be had in remembrance before the judge of my people." (D&C 68:33.) Finally, in a grim account that we are certain none of us would like to duplicate, Moroni recorded: "For the space of three hours did the Lord talk with the brother of Jared, and chastened him because he remembered not to call upon the name of the Lord. And the brother of Jared repented of the evil which he had done, and did call upon the name of the Lord." (Ether 2:14–15.) The message we get from this passage is that not praying is evil and retards our spiritual progress.

Praying for Answers

But just praying does not seem to be enough. Apparently we must learn to open a two-way line of communication with heaven; we must be able to pray, ask direct questions, and obtain specific answers. According to President Harold B. Lee: "The fundamental and soul-satisfying step in our eternal quest is to come in a day when each does know, for himself, that God answers his prayers. This will come only after 'our soul hungers,' and after mighty prayer and supplication." (*Conference Report,* April 1969, p. 133.)

Revealed Knowledge Concerning Prayer

When Joseph Smith came forth from the Sacred Grove that spring morning in 1820, he brought with him revealed knowledge about numerous points of doctrine. One of the most significant of these points, for all people, is not only that we should pray, but that God truly hears and answers prayer. It is this aspect of prayer, the obtaining of personal answers or revelation, that President Benson focused on when he explained the meaning of standing in holy places. As Joseph Smith said, "The only way to obtain truth and wisdom, is not to ask it from books, but to go to God in prayer and obtain divine teaching." (*The Words of Joseph Smith,* p. 77.) This is called receiving personal revelation.

Revelation — the Order in Heaven

Again according to Joseph Smith: "All men are liars who say they are of the true Church without the revelations of Jesus Christ and the priesthood of Melchizedek, which is after the order of the Son of God. It is in the order of heavenly things that God should always send [revelations] into the world." (*Discourses of the Prophet Joseph Smith,* p. 52.)

Because there is such order in all heavenly things (see D&C 129:7; 132:8), there must also be order in the process of praying and of obtaining answers to prayer. In heaven there are laws, rules, regulations, order! Upon these laws is Father's heavenly society based. He abides totally by order, and as we come to learn and follow that same order, we draw closer and closer to the society of God, until finally we are one with him. As he so eloquently declared to Joseph Smith nearly a hundred and fifty years ago, "All who will have a blessing at my hands shall abide the law which was appointed for that blessing, and the conditions thereof, as were instituted from before the foundation of the world." (D&C 132:5.)

Thus it will be seen that if we or any other people want to communicate with God through prayer, we have only to abide the eternal laws appointed to prayer, and the conditions thereof, and through the power of the Holy Ghost we will be allowed to communicate. (D&C 121:46.) The first of these laws is the commandment to pray concerning all things.

Topics for Prayer — When to Pray

Some of the best scriptural instructions regarding appropriate topics for prayer, and therefore times to pray, come from Amulek, Alma's missionary companion during his mission to the Zoramites. Interestingly, these scriptural verses not only make clear the law of asking, but they also reveal other eternal laws about prayer. Amulek states: "May God grant unto you, my brethren, that ye may begin to exercise your faith unto repentance, that ye begin to call upon his holy name, that he would have mercy upon you; yea, cry unto him for mercy; for he is mighty to save. Yea, humble yourselves, and continue in prayer unto him. Cry unto him when ye are in your fields, yea, over all your flocks. Cry unto him in your houses, yea, over all your household, both morning, mid-day, and evening. Yea, cry unto him against the power of your enemies. Yea, cry unto him against the devil, who is an enemy to all righteousness. Cry unto him over the crops of your fields, that ye may prosper in them. Cry over the flocks of your fields, that they may increase. But this is not all; ye must pour out your souls in your closets, and your secret places, and in your wilderness. Yea, and when you do not cry unto the Lord, let your hearts be full, drawn out in prayer unto him continually for your welfare, and also for the welfare of those who are around you." (Alma 34:17–27.)

Can any topic be thought of that we should pray about that Amulek didn't cover? Work or a job — Amulek covered it. Business ventures or decisions — covered. Family problems — taken care of. Dating or courtship relationships — he dealt with them. Personal problems — covered. Overcoming large or small temptations — covered. Obtaining forgiveness for sins — covered. Praising God and expressing gratitude for blessings received — covered. Little personal issues that only we know about — covered. Perhaps we might ask if anything can be thought of, after reading Amulek's instructions, that

181

we *shouldn't* pray about. We don't think many things will be thought of.

But, lest it be thought that we are relying too much on the words of one man, let us refresh our memories with the counsel Alma gave to his son, Helaman: "O, remember, my son, and learn wisdom in thy youth; yea, learn in thy youth to keep the commandments of God. Yea, and cry unto God for all thy support; yea, let all thy doings be unto the Lord, and whithersoever thou goest let it be in the Lord; yea, let all thy thoughts be directed unto the Lord; yea, let the affections of thy heart be placed upon the Lord forever. Counsel with the Lord in all thy doings, and he will direct thee for good; yea, when thou liest down at night lie down unto the Lord, that he may watch over you in your sleep; and when thou risest in the morning let thy heart be full of thanks unto God; and if ye do these things, ye shall be lifted up at the last day." (Alma 37:35–37.)

And, if that isn't enough evidence that we are to pray at all times and about all things, the great missionary Ammon, bearing his powerful testimony, declared: "He that repenteth and exerciseth faith, and bringeth forth good works, and prayeth continually without ceasing—unto such it is given to know the mysteries of God; yea, unto such it shall be given to reveal things which never have been revealed; yea, and it shall be given unto such to bring thousands of souls to repentance, even as it has been given us to bring these our brethren to repentance." (Alma 26:22.)

Topics for prayer here? Besides those Alma spoke of, Ammon mentioned three more. We should pray for success in doing missionary work—bringing the light of the gospel to others. Further, we should pray for insight and understanding that we might be great teachers—revealing eternal truths that are normally hidden with God. Finally, we should seek to understand the mysteries of Godliness, the peaceable things that bring joy and life eternal. (See D&C 42:61.) Could we think of greater things to pray about than these?

Finally, perhaps the one topic we ought to pray about more than any other is our own sins. When Nephi encouraged his brethren to pray, it was for a forgiveness of their sins. (1 Nephi 7:21.) And in our day the Lord has said: "I, the Lord, forgive sins unto those who confess their sins before me and ask forgiveness." (D&C 64:7.) In addition, Moroni taught that unless we go before the Lord in prayer, we will not be able to see our weaknesses clearly enough to ever repent of them. (See Ether 12:27.) If we desire to be made clean through the blood of Christ, then constant praying about our sins, which is an important factor in repentance, appears absolutely necessary.

When we consider all these topics, we see that there is no topic we should not be praying about, and no time when we should *not* be praying. That is why we have been instructed to keep a prayer in our hearts at all times. President Ezra Taft Benson says: "We should be alone with our Heavenly Father at least two or three times each day – 'morning, mid-day, and evening,' as the scripture indicates. (Alma 34:21.) In addition, we are told to pray always. (See 2 Nephi 32:9; D&C 88:126.) This means that our hearts should be full, drawn out in prayer unto our Heavenly Father continually. (See Alma 34:27.)" (*Ensign,* February 1990, p. 2.)

Belief Versus Practice

The tragic part of all this is that we can easily say we believe, but when it comes right down to putting these things into practice, it becomes a different story. Many of us find it difficult to pray at all times, over all things. One of us remembers: "A few years ago I approached a good friend about buying an automobile from him. We served together in our ward, we had attended numerous meetings where prayer and in-

spiration and the necessity for both were discussed, and I was certain that we believed the same things. Yet that day, after I had examined the vehicle as carefully as my limited mechanical abilities would allow, and determining that I liked it, he laughed me to scorn when I explained that I wouldn't make a decision regarding the purchase until I had first prayed about it.

" 'Pray about it,' he mocked. 'Don't be so dumb! God doesn't care what kind of a car you buy! Aren't you a big enough man to make up your own mind?'

"When I attempted to explain why I felt it was right to pray about it before I made a commitment, he only laughed harder, and soon all of his employees and a couple of other customers were in on the joke. I finally walked away, sorrowing and aching that I could not find a way to show this dear friend and fellow Latter-day Saint that I was following a correct course. Truly God might not have cared what car I drove; but by asking God I at least gave him the chance to tell me so. As it turned out, in that particular instance Heavenly Father did care—for my sake. I later learned that the man who purchased that car (one of those who laughed at me for praying) had many problems with it. I didn't. Instead I avoided the possibility of unnecessary danger or expense—for the Lord certainly knew all about that particular vehicle and could direct me as soon as I asked! To me such protection seems worthwhile. Finally, by praying about it I guaranteed that God would consecrate my performance (my decision) for the welfare of my soul (see 2 Nephi 32:9), which also seems to me to be a very important guarantee. I'll take as many consecrated performances in this life as I can get."

Satan's Teaching

Nephi, in his farewell address to his people, said, "If ye would hearken unto the Spirit which teacheth a man to pray you would know that ye must pray; for the evil spirit teacheth not a man to pray, but teacheth him that he must not pray." (2 Nephi 32:8.)

How can anyone argue with that? If our friend mocked us for wanting to pray, then, in effect, he was teaching us (and his employees and anyone else who happened to be there) that we shouldn't pray. Whose side does that place him on, then? As Nephi would have asked, of which church is he deciding to be a member? (See 1 Nephi 14:10.) If, as God says, all who are not for Him are against Him (see 2 Nephi 10:16), then the answers to those questions are crystal clear—and frightening.

Reasons to Pray Concerning All Things

Amulek, Alma, and Ammon, in the above quotations, have listed significant reasons why we should pray constantly about all aspects of our lives:

1. Constant prayer invokes what we call "the law of asking." Simply by asking for divine assistance and guidance, we invoke the eternal law that allows God to respond openly to our needs. Jesus said, "Ask, and it shall be given unto you; seek, and ye shall find; knock, and it shall be opened unto you. For everyone that asketh, receiveth; and he that seeketh, findeth; and to him that knocketh, it shall be opened." (3 Nephi 14:7–8.) To obtain any specific blessing from God, we must initiate the process. We ask—he gives. We seek—he helps us find. We knock—he opens unto us. Once we exercise faith sufficient to initiate the action (pray), then by eternal law God is free to respond to our request (answer). Simple, obvious, and true.

2. Constant prayer invokes what we call "the law of consecrated performances." Simply by humbling ourselves enough to address our Heavenly Father before we do something, we invoke the eternal law that allows God to consecrate

185

that particular thing we are doing for our eternal well-being. (2 Nephi 32:9.) Otherwise, God apparently recognizes it as a good deed worthy of some mortal blessings, but no more.

3. Constant prayer establishes clearly whose side we are on in the eternal struggle between right and wrong, between light and darkness, between Christ and Lucifer. (See 2 Nephi 32:8.) Only those who are willing to humble themselves in mighty prayer—"with real intent of heart" (see Moroni 6:9)—can be enlisted on the side of Christ. Truthfully, this should be where we all want to be.

4. Constant prayer allows us to learn of and to understand the mysteries of God. (See Alma 26:22.) These, the peaceable things of the kingdom, are what give us power to return to God's celestial realms (see D&C 42:61) and not to be taken captive by the devil (see Alma 12:9–11).

5. Constant prayer gives us power to be lifted up at the last day. (See Alma 37:35–37.) That means we will have come off conqueror in the war against evil and will be made clean so that we can be lifted up to come with Christ in his glory, to rule and reign with him through all eternity.

6. Constant prayer gives us power to become mighty missionaries, capable of bringing thousands of God's children to a knowledge of the truth. (See Alma 26:32.) This, we feel, is one of the laws of successful missionary work.

7. Constant praying gives us power to become teachers of deep and eternal truths, "revealing things which never have been revealed." (Ibid.)

8. Constant praying allows us to recognize and then obtain a forgiveness for our sins. (See 1 Nephi 7:21; D&C 64:7; Ether 12:27.) It is one of the laws of being made clean.

Progressive Spiritual Ability

Receiving answers to prayer seems to be a growing, or progressive, experience. Joseph Smith said: "A person may profit by noticing the first intimation of the spirit of revelation; for instance, when you feel pure intelligence flowing into you, it may give you sudden strokes of ideas, so that by noticing it, you may find it fulfilled the same day or soon; [that is], those things that were presented unto your minds by the Spirit of God, will come to pass; and thus by learning the Spirit of God and understanding it, you may *grow into the principle of revelation,* until you become perfect in Christ Jesus." (*Teachings of the Prophet Joseph Smith,* p. 151; italics added.)

Isn't that an interesting phrase? "Grow into the principle of revelation." In scriptural confirmation that this is a true principle, we learn: "I, John, saw that [Jesus] received not of the fulness at the first, but received grace for grace; And he received not of the fulness at first, but continued from grace to grace, until he received a fulness; And thus he was called the Son of God, because he received not of the fulness at the first." (D&C 93:12–14.) But then: "He received a fulness of the glory of the Father . . . all power, both in heaven and on earth, and the glory of the Father was with him, for he dwelt in him." (D&C 93:16–17.)

Why are we told that Jesus had to grow into the principle of revelation until he had received the fulness of the Father's power? Christ says: "I give unto you these sayings that you may understand and know how to worship, and know what you worship, that you may come unto the Father in my name, and in due time receive of his fulness. For if you keep my commandments you shall receive of his fulness, and be glorified in me as I am in the Father; therefore, I say unto you, you shall receive grace for grace." (D&C 93:19–20.)

In other words, we are told about Christ's growth so that we can know that Jesus had to do it just as we do: one step at a time. Thus all of us must grow into the principle of revelation until God deems it time to grant us, as he did Christ and the ancient Hebrew Saints, his fulness of knowledge, power, and understanding—a continual stream of personal revelation.

As we have analyzed it, we have come to the conclusion that we all have certain abilities within us that might be called spiritual muscles. And, like physical muscles, these spiritual muscles grow stronger with exercises designed to enhance their growth and ultimate power. And how can we exercise them? By practicing spiritual things. By praying more, by trying harder to keep the commandments, by reading the scriptures more often, by listening to and heeding the words of the prophets, and so forth. In these ways and numerous others we can grow into the principle of personal revelation.

However, most of us have probably been prompted by the Holy Ghost much more often than we might imagine. In fact, we may grow old and die before we finally learn how frequently the Spirit has helped us and guided us in our lives. One day, however, we will learn how often we have been prompted, and while no doubt feeling foolish because of our ignorance, we will yet rejoice in that knowledge.

Receiving Answers

A friend told us that for years he has only known of one way to receive answers to prayer, at least that worked for him; and that was pretty much to do it by default. In other words, he prayed a little bit, then worked like crazy. If things turned out, he would smile and say "thank you," and if they didn't, he would do his best to respond the same way.

We believe that our friend, and all others who approach prayer in that way, is in the beginning stages of spiritual development. Now, we are not saying that this is bad, not at all; these people are where they are spiritually because that is exactly where they should be. Joseph Smith said: "The Lord cannot always be known by the thunder of his voice, by the display of his glory, or by the manifestations of his power, and those that are the most anxious to see these things, are the least prepared to meet them. . . . We would say to the brethren, seek to know God in your closets, call upon him in the fields. Follow the directions of the Book of Mormon, and pray over, and for your families, your cattle, your flocks, your herds, your corn, and all things that you possess; ask the blessing of God upon all your labors, and everything that you engage in. Be virtuous and pure; be men of integrity and truth; keep the commandments of God; and then you will be able more perfectly to understand the difference between right and wrong—between the things of God and the things of men; and your path will be like that of the just, which shineth brighter and brighter unto the perfect day." (*Teachings of the Prophet Joseph Smith*, p. 247.)

Seek Righteousness Rather Than Manifestations

The message we get from that statement is that we must not run faster than we are able nor demand of the Lord things that, in his wisdom, we have thus far been denied. But does that mean it is inappropriate to seek to grow spiritually? Of course not! Remember that Joseph said we are to seek to grow into the principle of revelation, and the Lord told us that we would grow from grace to grace as we kept the commandments. Therefore, we should not seek manifestations but rather righteousness and closeness to the Spirit through obedience and regular repentance—and allow God to handle the manifestations as he sees fit.

A Burning or a Stupor

Still, what does it take to get started? The answer (as always) is in the scriptures. In the book of Ether, Moroni gave us the wonderful account of the brother of Jared and his experience in prayer before the Lord. (Ether 2–3.) As you remember, the Jaredites had built eight barges in which to cross the ocean, but when closed up against the "mountain waves," those barges were inky dark. The brother of Jared asked God about such uncomfortable traveling accommodations, and the Lord responded: "What will ye that I should do that ye may have light in your vessels?" (Ether 2:23.) In other words, the Lord gave the brother of Jared both the responsibility and the opportunity to search out the answer and to come back to the Lord with his best idea for a solution.

How often do we go to the Lord with a problem and ask him to solve it for us? How often do we try to avoid effort or struggle as we pray for spiritual help and direction? Obviously God wants us to put forth some effort on our own, and great answers will not come until we are willing to put forth great effort.

Understanding that principle, the brother of Jared went to work and melted out of the rock sixteen small stones. Apparently these stones were beautifully crafted, and Brother Moriancumr did a beautiful job in crafting them. (Ether 3:1.) So they looked great. But the trouble was, they didn't shine. Nor would they, if left only to the efforts of the brother of Jared. Knowing that, he went again before the Lord, placed the stones on his altar, and humbly asked God to touch them with His finger so they would shine. (Ether 3:4.) In compliance with the request of this man of mighty faith, the Lord did so; and only then did the stones fulfill the brother of Jared's aspirations—giving light to the children of men. (Ether 3:6; 6:3.)

In the same way, once we have done all in our power to solve a problem, and if our solution is appropriate, if we will then in faith lay our solution before the Lord, he will stretch forth his finger and "make it shine" so that our efforts will give light unto the children of men.

In a latter-day confirmation of this principle, the Lord declared to Oliver Cowdery concerning his own receiving of answers: "Behold, you have not understood; you have supposed that I would give it unto you, when you took no thought save it was to ask me. But behold, I say unto you, that you must study it out in your mind; then you must ask me if it be right, and if it is right I will cause that your bosom shall burn within you; therefore, you shall feel that it is right. But if it be not right you shall have no such feelings, but you shall have a stupor of thought that shall cause you to forget the thing which is wrong." (D&C 9:7–9.)

In other words, as we begin our spiritual development, we are to study out our problems within our own minds, make our decisions, and then in prayer present our decisions to the Lord. If, after a certain period of time, we feel good, satisfied, or comforted about our decisions, then we have obtained the Lord's approval. But if, on the other hand, we feel darkness (confused, irritated, frustrated, bothered, or upset), then we will know that the Lord has revealed to us that our decisions are contrary to what he would recommend that we do. In his words, we have been given a stupor of thought.

For some reason, however, too many Latter-day Saints ignore this scriptural promise. Instead, they pray about decisions but then go ahead and make up their own minds without waiting for or obtaining any sort of impression from the Spirit. We suppose they feel that since God didn't reach out and hit them over the head with a baseball bat, the signal was to proceed.

Worthiness, Effort, and Willingness to Listen and Obey

The question might be asked, "Does God have the power to answer every prayer?" The answer, as we have already pointed out, is a resounding yes. Which brings up the next question: "Then why doesn't he always do so?"

191

In our opinion, he doesn't because he can't—not because he lacks power, but because we lack power—power to obtain the answers or blessings we seek. And this lack of power on our part is due only to unworthiness, not to a lack of effort or an unwillingness to listen and obey.

According to the Lord, the only way to accomplish communication with heaven is through the Spirit, the Holy Ghost. (D&C 8:2.) As we have already pointed out, it is the Holy Spirit who will deliver to us the Lord's answers to our prayers. Furthermore, the companionship and ministerings of the Holy Ghost are granted only on condition of meekness and lowliness of heart. (Moroni 8:26.) And, of course, this comes after repentance and a cleansing through baptism and a continuance in keeping the commandments. (4 Nephi 1:1.)

To Joseph Smith the Lord said: "The elders, priests and teachers of this church shall teach the principles of my gospel, which are in the Bible and the Book of Mormon, in the which is the fulness of the gospel. And they shall observe the covenants and church articles to do them, and these shall be their teachings, as they shall be directed by the Spirit. And the Spirit shall be given unto you by the prayer of faith; and if ye receive not the Spirit ye shall not teach." (D&C 42:12–14.)

In terms of our own discussion, we will obtain answers to prayer only when we have the Spirit, and we will have the Spirit only when we are obedient, ourselves, to the things we are taught and know to be truths sent from God, the covenants and Church articles. These we must observe and do! Only then will we have the power to obtain and enjoy the companionship of the Spirit.

Lessons from the Lord's Prayer

Chapter 6 of Matthew, which is the middle portion of the Savior's Sermon on the Mount, is all about prayer. A careful reading of it will show that we must be pure and worthy in mind as well as in deed before we can effectively go before our Heavenly Father in prayer. In that chapter, Christ teaches the following concerning worthiness to receive answers to prayer:

1. We are to keep prayers secret—that is, reverent and humble, and primarily between ourselves and the Lord. (Matthew 6:1–6.)

2. We are instructed to fast righteously—don't moan and groan or boast about our fast to our family, spouse, or others. (Verses 16–18.)

3. We are to keep worldly priorities behind spiritual ones—are we more concerned about clothing, cars, homes, and styles, or about the people we are serving and their needs, both spiritual and temporal? (Verses 19–21.)

4. We are to make sure we do not let our eyes dwell upon evil things—pornography, immodestly dressed people, violence (movies, books, television, soap operas, and so on). (Verses 22–23.) Moroni warned: "Touch not the evil gift, nor the unclean thing." (Moroni 10:39.) In addition, Alma told his son Corianton that if a person "has desired to do evil all the day long even so shall he have his reward of evil when the night cometh." (Alma 41:5.) And finally the Lord says of people who involve themselves with such things, "They sought evil in their hearts, and I, the Lord, withheld my Spirit." (D&C 64:16.)

5. We are to lose ourselves in the work of Christ—and not be unduly consumed with worldly concerns, such as jobs, money, and so on. (Matthew 6:25–34.) Now, we know that this is difficult. But is it impossible? No, not if we have been commanded to do it. We feel that the Lord wants his children to be in a position where they are exercising complete trust in him—in his ability to protect them and to aid them even under seemingly impossible circumstances. Just think of Elijah being fed by the ravens (1 Kings 17:4), or the widow's

cruse of oil and bin of flour never emptying (1 Kings 17:12–16). God has the ability to provide all our needs: food, money, employment, protection, health, spiritual and intellectual growth, and on and on. We simply need to be obedient to the laws upon which our desired blessings are predicated or based, the first of which is to cry unto God in mighty prayer over all things. Then, if they are truly what we need, we shall surely obtain them.

6. If we can't lose ourselves in the work of Christ, then we are not really a servant of Christ but in fact are in the service of Satan. (Matthew 6:24.) Nephi calls this being a member of the church of the devil (1 Nephi 14:10) and records that an angel instructed him that members of the devil's church were characterized by the fact that gold, silver, silks, scarlets, fine-twined linen, precious clothing, immorality, and praise of the world were important to them (1 Nephi 13:7–9), no matter which church they had been baptized into. If we are caught up in serving these idols, whether we be Latter-day Saints or otherwise, then it is easy to understand why we don't have the power to lose ourselves in the work of Christ or to obtain answers to our prayers.

How to Recognize an Answer

Earlier we said that the Holy Ghost influences us far more than we realize. We recognize these incidents only infrequently because we have never learned how to recognize them, the manifestations of the Holy Ghost being so subtle. It is not likely that we will have a visit from Heavenly Father or Jesus Christ, at least without paying the proper prices. Nor is it likely that we will often see angels or receive revelations like the verses we read in the scriptures. As has been stated by others, there is an economy in heaven, an order to things, that apparently dictates always what our spiritual experiences will be. Thus we may, with great faith, depend upon what will happen under specific conditions. And we have been promised that if all things mentioned above are in order, then when we pray, the Lord will respond to those prayers through the workings of the Holy Ghost. (Moroni 10:4–5.)

But remember, we cannot receive such answers unless we listen—in other words, stay on our knees, asking, waiting, asking, listening or feeling, remaining patiently until we feel something. Being in a hurry, or not waiting for an answer, is probably one of the major reasons why more people don't receive answers to their prayers.

Then, too, we are convinced that most prayers are offered without any questions being asked—no specific questions at all! It is vital that we become specific in our requests of the Lord. Just imagine what would have been the result if the light-seeking brother of Jared had gone upon the mountain and prayed only in general terms for health, protection, and so forth. The ocean-going Jaradites would have experienced a long, dark passage. Or suppose that Nephi, even though he wanted to see the vision that his father Lehi had seen, had knelt and simply asked in general terms for a good day. He might certainly have been blessed with a good day, but had he not been specific, millions of us would have surely missed not only the interpretation of Lehi's vision but also the marvelous additional views the Lord granted Nephi. So yes, it is important to be specific in our praises to the Lord and our requests of him as we seek to have our needs fulfilled.

Asking Daily for the Companionship of the Holy Ghost

At the beginning of each personal prayer, just as we do at the beginning of each of our public meetings, wouldn't it be appropriate to ask God, in the name of Christ, to allow the Holy Ghost to come forth and fill our hearts and minds? (See 3 Nephi 19:9, 13; D&C 130:22.) By so doing, the companionship we obtain can help us understand what God wants us to know or do. If all the issues of effort and worthiness are in order, the Holy Spirit will affect our spirits, and we will be very aware of it.

Physical Reactions

Because our spirits are housed in physical bodies, the effect of the Holy Ghost influencing our spirits and minds is almost always accompanied by at least some physical reaction; our bodies feel the workings of the Spirit. When Lehi saw a vision, "he did quake and tremble exceedingly." (1 Nephi 1:6.) Joseph Smith said on one occasion that his "bones [did] quake" (D&C 85:6) when the Spirit was working with him. Also, many accounts exist of Joseph glowing as though a light were within him when the Holy Ghost came upon him. And Philo Dibble, in describing Joseph and Sidney Rigdon receiving what became the 76th section of the Doctrine and Covenants, said that while Joseph glowed and looked serene because he was used to such things, Sidney Rigdon, who was not so accustomed to the physical rigors of spiritual experiences, was left weak and limp as a wet rag. (See *Juvenile Instructor,* May 15, 1892, pp. 303–4.)

The scriptures point out several ways that the Holy Ghost affects our emotions and our physical bodies:

1. A burning in the bosom. (D&C 9:8.) This is a warm, happy feeling that a decision is right. It might also feel a little like difficulty in breathing or a feeling of warmth all over one's body.

2. A quaking frame. (D&C 85:6; 1 Nephi 1:6.) This would be a slight trembling of the body, like a chill or a shiver, except that it isn't cold. This might increase in intensity with more powerful manifestations of the Spirit.

3. A still small voice. (D&C 85:6.) Our minds "hear" a brand new thought or idea that gives us knowledge or direction.

The Spirit also "whispereth through and pierceth all things." (Ibid.) Occasionally this voice even becomes audible to the natural ear.

4. Crying, or weeping, as occurs in almost all gatherings where testimonies are shared. People shouldn't be ashamed of this joyful response to the Spirit or judge others harshly when it occurs, for this is truly one of the most common effects of the Spirit upon a physical body.

5. Enlightened minds or sudden strokes of ideas. (D&C 6:15; D&C 11:13.) As we know, the Holy Ghost is a spirit and so will communicate directly with our own spirit as we receive answers to our prayers. The effect of this Spirit-to-spirit communication is to enlighten our minds. The Lord says: "Thou hast inquired of me, and as often as thou hast inquired thou hast received instructions of my Spirit. If it had not been so, thou wouldst not have come to the place where thou art at this time. Behold, thou knowest that thou hast inquired of me and I did enlighten thy mind; and now I tell thee these things that thou mayest know that thou hast been enlightened by the Spirit of truth; yea, I tell thee, that thou mayest know that there is none else save God that knowest thy thoughts and the intents of thy heart." (D&C 6:14–16.)

6. Peace in the mind and heart. (D&C 6:23.) From our experience, there is no earthly serenity that feels like this does. It can come in the midst of great turmoil and will remove all fear.

7. A constraining or impression not to say or do a specific thing. (4 Nephi 1:48.) This is where we could be prevented from or prompted to avoid doing something that the Lord does not want done. This can be a physical constraint, a verbal constraint, or even a mental constraint. Almost always, however, it comes in response to prayers of faith, offered by ourselves or others, for divine direction, protection, or preservation.

8. A stupor of thought. (D&C 9:9.) This is an understanding that a decision we have made is not in harmony with God's will. This sensation is best described as a sense of darkness or confusion, a feeling of anxiety that something is not working out no matter how hard we might be trying to bring it to pass. A simple prayer of acceptance of divine will brings this awful feeling to an abrupt halt.

9. Comfort from distress or sorrow. (Alma 17:9–10.) If we will only humble ourselves and ask, the Lord says, "blessed are all they that mourn, for they shall be comforted." (3 Nephi 12:4.)

10. An awakening to an understanding of one's sins. (Mosiah 2:38; Ether 12:27.) The Lord declares, "If men come unto me I will show unto them their weakness." (Ether 12:27.) Unless we seek such a revelation of our sins, it will never be possible to see them clearly enough to repent of them.

There are undoubtedly other feelings or physical responses to the presence of the Spirit that we have not mentioned. But we will not all react to the Spirit in exactly the same way, or in the same degree. We are all different, and the Holy Ghost may affect us all differently. But we will be affected, and that is comforting.

As Joseph Smith declared: "The first Comforter or Holy Ghost has no other effect than pure intelligence. It is more powerful in expanding the mind, enlightening the understanding, and storing the intellect with present knowledge, of a man who is of the literal seed of Abraham, than one that is a Gentile, though it may not have half as much visible effect upon the body; for as the Holy Ghost falls upon one of the literal seed of Abraham, it is calm and serene; and his whole soul and body are only exercised by the pure spirit of intelligence; while the effect of the Holy Ghost upon a Gentile, is to purge out the old blood, and make him actually of the seed of Abraham. . . . In such a case, there may be more of a powerful effect upon the body, and visible to the eye, than upon an Israelite, while the Israelite might be far before the Gentile in pure intelligence." (*Teachings of the Prophet Joseph Smith*, p. 150.)

While Joseph seems to be referring to the doctrine of adoption, we wonder if perhaps part of what he meant by his statement concerning the literal seed of Abraham has to do with the principle of revelation that we grow into as we learn to develop spiritually by exercising greater and greater righteousness. Might that be the process through which we become the seed of Abraham? Whether or not this is so, once we become worthy of the companionship of the Holy Ghost, once we are willing to do whatever the Spirit directs us to do, and once we discover how the Holy Ghost affects our own spirits and physical bodies, then it will become much easier for us to kneel down and recognize the counsel and direction that the Lord is giving us. Then we will be receiving personal revelation.

In conclusion, consider Brother Chauncey C. Riddle's personal experience with testimony and revelation. He writes: "I felt I had received some revelation before. However, I saw that random revelation was not sufficient. To be a rock, a bastion of surety, revelation must be something on which one can count and receive in every occasion of real need. I began to seek for it actively. I prayed, I fasted, I lived the gospel as best I knew. I was faithful in my church duties. I tried to live up to every scruple which my conscience enjoined upon me. And dependable revelation did come. Intermittently, haltingly at first, then steadily, over some years it finally came to be a mighty stream of experience. I came to know that at any time of day or night, in any circumstance, for any real need, I could get help. That help came in the form of feelings of encouragement when things seemed hopeless. It came in ideas to unravel puzzles that blocked my accomplishment. It came in priesthood blessings which were fully realized. It came in whisperings of prophecy which were fulfilled. It came in support and even anticipation of what the General Authorities of the Church would say and do in general conference. It came in the gifts of the Spirit, as the wonders of eternity were opened to the eyes of my understanding. That stream of spiritual experience is today for me a river of living water that nourishes my soul in every situation. It is the most important factor of my life. If it were taken away, all that I have and am would be dust and ashes. It is the basis of my love, life, understanding, hope, and progress. My only regret is that though this river is so wonderful, I have not been able to take full advantage of it as yet. My life does not yet conform to all that I know. But now I do know; I do not just believe." ("What a Privilege to Believe!" *Sunstone,* May 1988, p. 10.)

In such a state as Brother Riddle describes, we will have become very powerful tools in the Lord's hands for fulfilling his work. We will also have grown further into the principle of revelation, and we will most certainly be found by the Lord to be standing in holy places.

18

Rearing Spiritually
Unified Families

Recently one of our less-active friends declared: "I won't force my children into baptism. My parents forced me, and I hated it! So, as far as I am concerned, my children don't need to be baptized until they are old enough to make up their own minds."

"But what if they make a wrong choice?" we asked. "What if Satan has made such inroads into their lives by then, because they lacked the protection and influence of the Holy Ghost, that they can't clearly see the truth? What will you do then?"

"It won't happen," our friend replied smugly. "They'll see that I believe in the Church even if I don't do everything exactly right, so they'll believe in it, too."

Well, that is a noble desire, but it is not only unrealistic but also unrighteous.

Some of the material in this chapter has been excerpted from: Blaine and Brenton Yorgason, *To Mothers from the Book of Mormon* (Orem UT: Keepsake BookCards, 1989).

In 1831 the Lord told Joseph Smith: "Inasmuch as parents have children in Zion, or in any of her stakes which are organized, that teach them not to understand the doctrine of repentance, faith in Christ the Son of the living God, and of baptism and the gift of the Holy Ghost by the laying on of the hands, when eight years old, the sin be upon the heads of the parents. And their children shall be baptized for the remission of their sins when eight years old, and receive the laying on of the hands. And they shall also teach their children to pray, and to walk uprightly before the Lord. And the inhabitants of Zion shall also observe the Sabbath day to keep it holy. And the inhabitants of Zion also shall remember their [church callings], inasmuch as they are appointed to labor, in all faithfulness; for the idler shall be had in remembrance before the Lord. Now, I, the Lord, am not well pleased with the inhabitants of Zion, for there are idlers among them; and their children are also growing up in wickedness; they also seek not earnestly the riches of eternity, but their eyes are full of greediness. These things ought not to be, and must be done away from among them." (D&C 68:25–32.)

Without going into the ramifications of the term *Zion*, we feel that this scripture clearly sets forth the Lord's desire that parents in the Church strive earnestly to rear spiritually united families, and to do so from the very beginnings of their children's lives. To ensure that, the Lord gives very specific directions. First, parents are to teach by precept, ensuring that their children have a thorough understanding of the doctrines of:

1. Repentance.

2. Faith in Christ the Son of the living God.

3. Baptism for the remission of sins when eight years of age.

4. The laying on of the hands for the gift of the Holy Ghost at the same time.

5. Prayer.

6. Walking uprightly before the Lord (desiring to keep God's commandments).

Parents are also directed to teach, by example, some additional doctrines. These are:

7. Observing the Sabbath day to keep it holy.

8. Fulfilling their assigned Church labors or callings in all faithfulness, rather than being idle in them.

9. Not being greedy concerning worldly goods but rather seeking earnestly, and at all times, the riches of eternity.

If all of these things are observed faithfully from the time that children are tiny, then parents will not only be spiritual themselves but they will also be enabled to rear spiritual families, families that will have the power to stand in holy places now and remain united eternally hereafter.

First Principles of the Gospel

It will be noted, of course, that the Lord's directive to parents begins with them teaching their children the first principles and ordinances of the gospel. Why? Because the entire spiritual life of every person in the human family must begin and remain sustained by obedience to those first principles and ordinances of the gospel. If we let down in even one of these areas, then the entire process of personal spiritual growth comes to a screeching halt. That is why Joseph Smith called them the *first* principles and ordinances. (See *The Words of Joseph Smith,* pp. 3–4.) They must be complied with first, before anything else of a spiritual nature can transpire. That is also why, if we are to have and enjoy spiritually unified families, we must focus our thinking, as well as the thinking of our children, upon the principles and ordinances that the Lord directs us to learn first. Ultimately, no one can avoid facing this fact.

To help us better understand how these principles are

brought to operate in the lives of ourselves and our children, Joseph Smith stated: "Faith comes by hearing the word of God through the testimony of the servants of God, that testimony is always attended by the Spirit of prophecy and revelation. Repentance is a thing that cannot be trifled with every day. Daily transgression and daily repentance [with no sincere effort to improve] is not that which is pleasing in the sight of God—Baptism is a holy ordinance preparatory to the reception of the Holy Ghost. It is the channel [and] Key by which the Holy Ghost will be administered. The gift of the Holy Ghost by the laying on of hands cannot be received by any other principle than the principle of righteousness." (Ibid.)

What Does Being Spiritual Mean?

What does it really mean to be spiritual? An excellent question, we turned to an excellent teacher for an answer. Brother Hugh Nibley says: "We are everlastingly talking about being 'spiritual'; what does that mean? The highest state of spirituality is to be filled with the spirit of God, the Holy Ghost, which as 'no other effect,' says the Prophet [Joseph], than that of releasing our intelligence, 'expanding the mind, enlightening the understanding, and storing the intellect with present knowledge.' I say 'releasing' because 'intelligence . . . was not created . . . neither indeed can be,' for 'man also was in the beginning with God' (D&C 93:29). Like other latent forces, intelligence is there and waiting to be released. Note the key words in this statement on the high estate of spirituality. [The Holy Ghost] is peculiarly 'powerful in expanding [1] the mind, enlightening [2] the understanding, and storing [3] the intellect with present [4] knowledge, of a man who is the literal seed of Abraham.' And if you do not happen to be that, 'the pure [5] spirit of intelligence,' if one cultivates it, 'will make him actually of the seed of Abraham.' It is [6] 'the

204

spirit of revelation . . . when you feel pure intelligence flowing into you, it will give you sudden strokes of [7] ideas.' It is the merit of the seed of Abraham, with all their stubbornness and backsliding, that above all people they treasure the things of the mind. The first commandment given to the Church in modern times was 'seek not for riches but for wisdom, and behold, the mysteries of God shall be unfolded unto you' (D&C 6:7). It would be hard to imagine a program more repugnant to the present course the world is taking." (*Approaching Zion*, pp. 281–82.)

Spirituality, then, consists of being filled with the Holy Ghost to the extent that we experience:

1. An expanded mind.
2. An enlightened understanding.
3 (and 4). An intellect stored with present knowledge.
5. The spirit of intelligence making us of the seed of Abraham.
6. The spirit of revelation.
7. Pure intelligence in the form of sudden ideas.

Those who can identify with one or more of these seven points are developing in the power of spirituality.

Righteous Parenting Taught in the Book of Mormon

How do we pass the trait of spirituality on to our families? Can we simply assume that it will occcur through osmosis, or do we need to work at it? When Ezra Taft Benson became president of the Church, he did not lose a single opportunity of adjuring the Latter-day Saints to read, to study, and then to live by the precepts and doctrines of the Book of Mormon. Why has he been so emphatic? Perhaps one reason is because he understands, more perfectly than most of us, the singular power, value, completeness, and necessity of that sacred volume of scripture. For truly it does contain the fulness of the gospel of Jesus Christ. Through Joseph Smith, the Lord declared: "[I] gave [Joseph Smith] power from on high, by the means which were before prepared, to translate the Book of Mormon; which contains a record of a fallen people, and the fulness of the gospel of Jesus Christ to the Gentiles, and to the Jews also." (D&C 20:8–9.)

Containing such a fulness, the Book of Mormon addresses all issues pertinent to our salvation. Further, it provides clear direction about righteous, spiritual parenting. With this thought in mind, we examined the Book of Mormon for statements or accounts about motherhood and fatherhood and what the Lord expects of parents in these latter days. We found several, and we feel that these accounts provide an intricate blueprint for parents to use in rearing righteous, spiritual children within the telestial environment of the last days.

Because the issues and lessons learned differ somewhat between fathers and mothers, we will separate them in that order.

Lehi—Father to the Book of Mormon

What we know of Lehi was recorded for us primarily by his sons Nephi and Jacob. Having taught his children in the secular learning of his time, Lehi did not hesitate to discuss with them his spiritual experiences as well. He even went so far as to demand that all of them join with him on the trek in physically obeying the spiritual counsel he had received. It is a credit to his parenting techniques of longsuffering and patience that he was obeyed.

Continuing, Lehi placed confidence in his children when he sent them back to Jerusalem on dangerous missions, even though some of them murmured. By so doing, he treated his grown children as equals, thus doing his best to build their self-esteem. He even went so far as to name valleys and rivers after those who were lacking, in the same attempt to build them up. But his greatest legacy of parenting, in our opinion, was the fact that despite rebellion and gross wickedness on the part of some of his children and children-in-law, Lehi never released himself as their parent and teacher. Even on his deathbed, he insisted on bearing his testimony and bestowing blessings upon all of his posterity.

As the Lord said: "Go, and do thou likewise."

Jacob and His Son Enos

Jacob, the firstborn to Lehi and Sariah in the wilderness, became an incredibly righteous man. In fact, even in his youth he was permitted to receive the Second Comforter, even the personage of Jesus Christ. Knowing what he knew, one can almost feel his anxiety to have his sons and daughters experience the same transcendent things. Thus, his greatest parenting quality must surely have been his patience.

We recognize this as we read the words of his slow-to-respond son, Enos. Enos writes: "I, Enos, knowing my father that he was a just man—for he taught me in his language, and also in the nurture and admonition of the Lord—and blessed be the name of my God for it—and I will tell you of the wrestle which I had before God, before I received a remission of my sins. Behold, I went to hunt beasts in the forests; and the words which I had often heard my father speak concerning eternal life, and the joy of the saints, sunk deep into my heart. And my soul hungered; and I kneeled down before my Maker, and I cried unto him in mighty prayer and supplication for mine own soul." (Enos 1:1–4.)

Therefore, the parenting skill we learn from Jacob is proper and appropriate teaching and bearing of testimony, and then infinite patience while the testimony of those teachings matures to fruition.

King Benjamin and His Sons

King Benjamin had three sons—Mosiah, Helorum, and Helaman. The Book of Mormon indicates that, like Lehi and Jacob before him, King Benjamin taught his sons in the language of his fathers. This he did that they might become men of understanding, and that they might know concerning the prophecies given by the ancients. He also spent a great deal of time explaining the prophecies (the gospel) to them. But in our opinion, King Benjamin's greatest gift of parenting was that he did it by personal example.

To his people, in his final address, King Benjamin declared: "I have been suffered to spend my days in your service, even up to this time, and have not sought gold nor silver nor any manner of riches of you; neither have I suffered that ye should be confined in dungeons, nor that ye should make slaves one of another, nor that ye should murder, or plunder, or steal, or commit adultery; nor even have I suffered that ye should commit any manner of wickedness, and have taught you that ye should keep the commandments of the Lord, in all things which he hath commanded you—and even I, myself, have labored with mine own hands that I might serve you, and that ye should not be laden with taxes, and that there should nothing come upon you which was grievous to be borne—and all of these things which I have spoken, ye yourselves are witnesses this day." (Mosiah 2:12–14.)

The power of a good example is such an unequalled teacher. How, we ask ourselves, could children help but respond positively to such an outstanding testimonial of service and righteousness?

Alma the Elder

As prophet and president of the Church, Alma must have been mortified that one of his sons, even his namesake, had become a volatile, rabble-rousing unbeliever doing his best to disrupt and destroy the Lord's earthly kingdom. We do not know what sorts of conversations Alma and his son had, but we can safely assume that the younger Alma paid little attention to the counsel of his father.

Filled with faith, therefore, Alma pleaded his case before the Lord. Christ, in response to the worthy Alma's fervent pleas, sent an angel to call the younger Alma to repentance. The message for us is that even though all of our efforts to teach and bear testimony to a rebellious child may seem in vain, if we will continually beseech the Lord, he can and will come to our aid. (Mosiah 27:8–32.) From our somewhat limited experience, we have found that faith can intercede and help a child, where his or her faith is wavering. We must never give up on a temporarily blinded child.

King Mosiah and His Four Sons

Alma the Younger's cohorts in apostasy were the four sons of King Mosiah—Ammon, Aaron, Omner, and Himni. Witnesses of the angel who appeared to Alma the Younger, these four brothers desired to show the depth of their repentance by spending the remainder of their lives in missionary service among their previously mortal enemies, the Lamanites.

Faced with the difficult decision of whether or not to allow his sons to embark on such a dangerous and life-consuming assignment, King Mosiah had the faith to go before the Lord and inquire as to what the boys were to do. In reply, the Lord said, "Let them go up [to the Lamanites], for many shall believe on their words, and they shall have eternal life; and I will deliver thy sons out of the hands of the Lamanites." (Mosiah 28:7.)

King Mosiah was obedient to this prompting, and with his testimony ringing in their ears, he sent them on their way. Thus he set an example of obedience to the impressions of the Spirit that we would do well to follow.

Alma the Younger

Perhaps the most extensive quoting of fatherly teachings in the Book of Mormon is attributed to Alma the Younger, who was giving instructions and chastisements to his three sons—Helaman (in Alma 36–37), Shiblon (in Alma 38), and Corianton (in Alma 39–42).

What we find instructive about Alma's lectures to his sons is that they are so individualized. To Helaman, Alma bore his testimony and then counseled him concerning his future assignments and responsibilities. Shiblon, on the other hand, was recipient of his father's praise and kindly instructions. Finally, Corianton, who had broken many of the commandments, was chastised. However, this chastisement was done with gentleness and meekness and was interlaced with much basic instruction in the precepts of the gospel. In other words, Alma dwelt little upon the sins but much upon the instruction of the sinner. Alma took this approach, we feel, because the Spirit had whispered to him that his son had broken the commandments through ignorance; he did not fully understand them.

The message to us, then, besides bearing our testimonies during such teaching moments, is the crucial need to individualize such teaching moments with our children, to instruct them according to their needs as dictated by the impressions of the Holy Spirit—"reproving betimes with sharpness when moved upon by the Holy Ghost; and then showing forth afterward an increase of love." (D&C 121:43.)

Helaman and His 2,060 Stripling Sons

Perhaps the classic example of surrogate fathering, or stepfathering, in the Book of Mormon, is that of Helaman and the young Lamanite warriors who came under his charge. These young men, most of whom were likely teenagers, were the children of a group of righteous Lamanites, who, following their conversion, had covenanted never again to go to war. Therefore, when danger threatened their Nephite neighbors, the young sons of these Lamanites went to war in their parents' stead.

Though the account of their numerous battles and exploits is too lengthy for inclusion here, let it be said that these young men fought against overwhelming odds, on several occasions were most or all severely wounded, and yet were always victorious in their battles. Additionally, all survived.

Because these young men were so willing and obedient and quick to bear testimonies of their own, Helaman began calling them his sons. He taught them at every opportunity, giving them the opportunity to choose their course in war even as they learned to understand his own testimony. But the lesson for us today is Helaman's willingness to lead these young soldiers into battle. According to the scriptural record, he never directed—he always led. He never asked them to go anywhere he was not willing to take them.

Let us add, parenthetically, that our father seems to have mastered this very attribute. On one occasion, as we four sons were returning with him from a fishing trip, Dad said, "Anything you hear me say or see me do, you are free to say and do likewise." From that early day we held our father to that promise, and we soon found that he left us very little margin for deviation.

Dad is now in his mid-seventies, and he and our mother are returned NQSYs, "Not Quite So Young" missionaries. Yesterday he was accepting recommends in the Provo Temple while Mother was attending a couple of sessions; today he and Mother were greeting new missionaries at the Missionary Training Center, and tomorrow he will be fulfilling his calling as a stake high councilor (his sixth calling to this position, since he was released as a bishop in his mid-twenties). In their spare time, he and Mother are involved in the Family-to-Family Book of Mormon program and are companion home teachers to one widow, one divorcée, and two couples. Finally, Dad supports Mother in her calling as the compassionate service leader in their ward Relief Society. How could anyone possibly work much sinning into a schedule like that? Do you see the dilemma that having parents like them presents to a couple of recalcitrant sons like us?

Mormon and His Son Moroni

Perhaps the most poignant father-son relationship in the Book of Mormon was exhibited by the prophet Mormon and his son Moroni, both of whom apparently knew that they and their families were doomed. Living during the days of their society's final destruction, Mormon took the time from his frantic military and literary schedule (he was not only commanding general of all the Nephites but was also the abridger of all the Nephite records) to not only visit when occasion permitted but also to write two lengthy, beautiful letters to his son. In addition, Mormon sent a copy of one of his sermons to Moroni. This sermon, as well as the two letters, have been preserved for us in the Book of Mormon. (Moroni 7–9.)

It is not our intention to encapsulate Mormon's writings but rather to glean the lesson from his interactions with his son that will best help us be better parents. In our opinion, that lesson has to do with simply giving children our time. We are all busy, but we doubt that any of us live under greater time constraints or pressures than did Mormon. Yet still he took the time to keep Moroni informed of the latest events of the war and to teach him the gospel, encourage him in his difficulties, and bear fervent testimony to him of the realities of eternal life. In short, Mormon gave his son quality time. What a great blessing our families will have as we take this same approach in our own child-rearing.

Initial Conclusions

Examining all eight of these examples, then, leads to one conclusion. If we, as fathers in latter-day Israel, are to righteously and successfully fulfill our stewardships of rearing spiritually minded children, we must first and foremost obtain the Holy Spirit ourselves, and then with the power of that Spirit bear fervent testimony to our children regularly. Then, in our daily lives, we can (1) trust our children and never abdicate our role as father (Lehi); (2) exercise patience while our children mature in their understanding of the gospel (Jacob); (3) set a clear-cut example of how we want our children to live (King Benjamin); (4) turn to the Lord in perfect faith when all else seems to fail (Alma the Elder); (5) willingly obey the directives of the Lord in rearing our families (King Mosiah); (6) prayerfully give each child individualized instructions (Alma the Younger); (7) always lead our children rather than simply giving orders (Helaman); and finally, (8) make a conscious and constant effort to spend quality time with our children (Mormon). If these things are done with due diligence, we honestly believe that we, as fathers, will have moved significantly toward fulfilling successful stewardships as we rear spiritually unified families.

Now, let us discuss the lessons the Book of Mormon presents concerning mothering.

Sariah, Lehi's Wife

First we read of Sariah, a good and virtuous woman who, at least for a time, lacked the power of testimony to teach her children the things of eternity—until she repented of her doubting and murmuring and regained the companionship of the Holy Spirit. Then she began bearing testimony. (1 Nephi 1–5.) We wonder if her weakness might be at least part of the reason why Laman and Lemuel did not ultimately partake of the fruit of the tree of life, as did her other children.

We think that this account of Sariah may have been given to us as a warning. No matter our lofty positions, no matter our spiritual strengths, if we do not obtain the Holy Spirit and then use it constantly, we will experience pain, suffering, and failure.

There is another warning here that we would like to add. Through the years we have seen our wives "worry" about our collective sixteen children. This is an important part of the strong mothering instinct, and, as brothers, we have often expressed our gratitude in marrying such unusually conscientious women. However, in our travels we have seen instances where women have taken this worrying to an extreme. When this happens, their fretting becomes a wall that keeps the Holy Spirit from being able to penetrate, in his role as the Comforter, to give them a sense of peace that all is well with their children. We hope that in sharing Sariah's account, all of us will more fervently seek peace from the Spirit of the Lord, especially in times of trial, so that we won't let undue worrying bring us to the point of despair, as it did to Sariah.

Mary, the Mother of Christ

Next we learn of Mary, the mother of Jesus, the supreme example of motherhood in all recorded history. The qualities recorded about the mother of Christ are as follows: (1) she was a virgin (1 Nephi 11:13, 15); (2) she was fair (just and decent) (ibid.); (3) she was white (pure and spotless) (ibid.); (4) she was beautiful (divine and God-like) (ibid.); (5) she was precious (priceless and cherished) (Alma 7:10); and (6) she was chosen (ibid.).

Virtue Is Necessary

Since Isaiah also declared from revelation that the mother of Jesus was to be a virgin (Isaiah 8:8; 2 Nephi 17:14), as did Matthew and Luke (Matthew 1:23; Luke 1:27), this quality was listed more than any other for Mary. Thus virtue and moral cleanliness seem to be first and foremost the qualities that God would have us understand and emulate as fathers and as mothers.

The Holy Spirit Gave Mary Power

Because Mary was virtuous "above all other virgins" (1 Nephi 11:15), she was enabled to become the mother of the Son of God after the manner of the flesh. According to Alma, it was because of the constant companionship of the Holy Ghost that Mary was given power to fulfill her singularly spectacular mission of motherhood. (Alma 7:10.)

Virtue Necessary in Obtaining the Holy Ghost

Virtue is essential if one is to have the companionship of the Holy Ghost. "Let virtue garnish thy thoughts unceasingly," the Lord declares, and then "the Holy Ghost shall be thy constant companion." (D&C 121:45–46.) On the other hand, "if a man looketh on a women to lust after her, or if any shall commit adultery in their hearts, they shall not have the Spirit." (D&C 63:16.) Thus, if we are going to have the companionship and guidance of the Holy Ghost to help us rear spiritual offspring, we must be virtuous and pure.

Emphasizing this, President Benson states, "A reason for virtue — which includes personal chastity, clean thoughts and practices, and integrity — is that we must have the Spirit and power of God in our lives to do God's work." (*The Teachings of Ezra Taft Benson*, p. 278.) And what could more be called God's work than the righteous rearing of our children? The Prophet also declares: "No sin is causing the loss of the Spirit of the Lord among our people more today than sexual promiscuity. It is causing our people to stumble, damning their growth, darkening their spiritual powers, and making them subject to other sins." (Ibid., p. 279.)

Mothers of Helaman's 2,060 Stripling Warriors

Last we read of the host of mothers of the 2,060 stripling warriors, who also obtained the companionship of the Holy Ghost sufficiently that they could teach their children with power from on high. With that divine power, they taught through example and testimony with such effectiveness that what must have been a great majority of their sons, in the heat of terrible battle, exercised strict obedience, trusted the Lord, and showed such remarkable faith that, to a man, their lives were preserved in righteousness while all around them others perished. What a tribute to these righteous mothers!

And what qualities made these young men so outstanding? Their faith; their strictness in obedience, not only to God, but to man; their courage; and their continual trust in God. And where had they received these qualities? Again, from the testimonies of their mothers! Helaman explicitly points out that fact three separate times, and he implies it twice more. He writes, "They never had fought, yet they did not fear death; and they did think more upon the liberty of their fathers than they did upon their own lives; yea, they had been taught by their mothers, that if they did not doubt, God would deliver them. And they rehearsed unto me the words of their mothers, saying: We do not doubt our mothers knew it." (Alma 56:47–48.)

Second Conclusions

It appears that the Lord really wants us to understand the message of the Book of Mormon for mothers in the latter days. Along with what we have pointed out concerning fathers, our children will prosper in righteousness and our families will be united spiritually only so fast as mothers in Zion practice virtue. Only then will these mothers be able to rely upon the Spirit. With that Spirit they must then bear constant and fervent testimony to their children, in word as well as deed, of the truthfulness of the gospel of Jesus Christ. Thus, they will be empowered to rear their families in an environment of spiritual unity.

On the other hand, to whatever degree members of the Church are without virtue, sexual or otherwise, so also are they without the power and companionship of the Holy Ghost. Thus they cannot bear testimony to their children with power, nor can they discern their children's eternal needs. Left thus alone, such parents cannot rear their fair sons and daughters in righteousness, and there is the distinct possibility that either here or in eternity their families will be dismantled.

Such children as are converted, however, with the witness of their mothers and fathers burning in their hearts by the Holy Ghost's power, no matter the terrible scenes of sin and evil and blood and carnage to which they might be subjected between now and the second coming of the Lord, will ultimately stand in holy places. And they will ever after, in this life as well as the next, be followers of the Great Jehovah, the Lord Jesus Christ.

But What If?

A legitimate concern that might be raised here is that many good parents in the Church today have reared one or more children who choose to live unrighteously. We imagine that some mothers among the people of Helaman also experienced at least a partial "fallout." By this we mean that some of the friends and associates of the 2,060 stripling warriors probably chose to ignore the blessings of the gospel and to embrace the wicked but tempting "lifestyles of the rich and famous."

True it is that no family is an island. We cannot completely isolate our children from Satan's ploys any more than our Heavenly Parents could isolate us from them before we were placed on the earth. All of us are entitled to our agency. Nor is it possible for any of us to live totally free of sin or mistakes. We are mortal. Therefore, it is possible that, even though we provide a righteous home and environment for our children, one or more of them will fall victim to Satan's snares.

Responding to Commandment-Breakers — with Hope

When we encounter commandment-breaking in a family member near and dear to us, perhaps we could do as Lehi and Alma did—persevere. Why? Because we are never released from being that person's family, their eternal support group. We should then do as the remainder of our Book of Mormon examples have done: continue to love unconditionally, continue to exercise patience, continue to bear pure testimony whenever the Spirit directs, and continue to pray and exercise faith in the fallen one's behalf. Thus we can do much to insulate our children from potential disaster, as well as to bring them back if such a disaster has occurred.

But remember—if each of us would simply dedicate our lives to repenting and becoming justified and then sanctified, as we have been commanded to do, then surely we would see a major shift upward in the level of righteousness and strength of testimony among our families. According to the Prophet Joseph Smith, "When a seal is put upon the father and mother [the fulness of the Priesthood], it secures their posterity so that 'if they have not transgressed' they cannot be lost but will be saved by virtue of the covenant of their [parents]." (*The Words of Joseph Smith*, p. 242. The phrase "if they have not transgressed" is part of the text of these remarks, found on page 241.)

Since the fulness of the priesthood can come to a couple only after great repenting and righteousness, as well as after a long period of refinement, then it can be seen what great impact for good such repenting and righteousness would have upon the posterity of such a couple. And if all of us would become such worthy couples, then it can be imagined what a righteous society we would present to the Lord.

From Latter-day Brethren

To complement the parenting instructions given in the Book of Mormon, the Lord has given a great deal of inspiration and revelation to our latter-day apostles and prophets. And always the theme is the same—keeping the commandments, including the directions given by the Lord about the righteous exercise of authority in the home (D&C 121:41–44) will produce spiritually strong, eternally unified families, which families the Lord loves and accepts as his own. President Ezra Taft Benson declares: "The Church of Jesus Christ of Latter-day Saints views the family as the most important organization in time and all eternity. The Church teaches that everything should center in and around the family. It stresses that the preservation of family life in time and eternity takes precedence above all other interests; it venerates parental and filial love and duty." (*The Teachings of Ezra Taft Benson,* p. 489.)

Becoming even more precise and specific, President Benson continues: "Successful families have love and respect for each family member. Family members know they are loved and appreciated. Children feel they are loved by their parents. Thus, they are secure and self-assured. Strong families cultivate an attribute of effective communication. They talk out their problems, make plans together, and cooperate toward common objectives. Family home evening and family councils are practiced and used as effective tools toward this end. Fathers and mothers in strong families stay close to their children. They talk. Some fathers formally interview each child, others do so informally, and others take occasion to regularly spend time alone with each child. Every family has problems and challenges. But successful families try to work together toward solutions instead of resorting to criticism and contention. They pray for each other, discuss, and give encouragement. Occasionally these families fast together in support of one of the family members. Strong families support each other. Successful families do things together: family projects, work, vacations, recreation, and reunions." (*The Teachings of Ezra Taft Benson,* p. 490.)

And why does the Lord encourage us to strengthen our families in this manner? Elder Bruce R. McConkie wrote: "Life both here and hereafter is very personal and real. We know what the associations of life are in this sphere and what they will be for the faithful in the realms ahead. Godly and upright living in both realms centers in the family unit. There is no more sweet or tender or loving relationship known on earth than that which should exist between a man and his wife. And they twain should have like feelings for their children and descendants and for their parents and progenitors. With this in mind, we quote the inspired word that says: 'And that same sociality which exists among us here will exist among us there, only it will be coupled with eternal glory, which glory we do not now enjoy.' (D&C 130:2.)" (*The Millennial Messiah,* pp. 706–7.)

Spirituality Should Be Our Focus

Above all else, however, the Lord has counseled us, through his prophets, to create and maintain a spiritual atmosphere in our homes. As very young boys, we lost our mother in an automobile accident. From that difficult moment forward, however, we were never allowed to forget that her spirit was eternal. Furthermore, we were taught, through parental sharing of sacred, spiritual experiences, that she remained very involved as our mother. A year after our mother's untimely death, Dad was married again—this time to our aunt, our mother's younger sister. She, perhaps more than anyone else, was responsible for focusing our acceptance of things spiritual. From that day to this, spirituality and the reality of unseen direction from the other side of the veil has been our family theme. We will always be grateful and indebted to our three parents for this spiritual focus.

In a like manner, all Latter-day Saint parents need to focus the thinking of their children upon things of the Spirit. President Benson says, "The most important teachings in the home are spiritual." (*The Teachings of Ezra Taft Benson*, p. 501.) Also: "We encourage parents to teach their children fundamental spiritual principles that will instill faith in God." (Ibid., p. 498.) And finally: "Remember, the family is one of God's greatest fortresses against the evils of our day. Help keep your family strong and close and worthy of our Father in Heaven's blessings. As you do, you will receive faith and strength which will bless your lives forever." (Ibid., p. 492.)

Surely if we will follow these directives, quietly but with great constancy, we and our families will be spiritually unified, and we will be found standing together in holy places when the Lord comes.

3

Belonging to the Family of Jesus Christ

CHAPTER

19

The Agency of Man

Having now discussed not only what is coming but also what we can do about it, let us briefly consider the ability that enables each of us to make such choices at all. This ability, of course, is called agency.

Agency is the ability and freedom to choose good or evil. It is not free, and in fact nowhere in all the scriptures is the phrase "free agency" ever mentioned. The Lord calls it "agency," and according to one of the General Authorities who visited one of our stake conferences two or three years ago, so should we.

Agency is an eternal principle and in fact was the cause of Lucifer's rebellion against God, for he "sought to destroy the agency of man." (Moses 4:3.) President Ezra Taft Benson declares: "Freedom of choice is a God-given eternal principle. The great plan of liberty is the plan of the gospel. There is no coercion about it; no force, no intimidation. A man is free

Some of the material in this chapter is excerpted from: Blaine and Brenton Yorgason, *Agency, Spiritual Progression, and the Mighty Change* (Orem UT: Keepsake BookCards, 1989).

to accept the gospel or reject it. He may accept it and then refuse to live it, or he may accept it and live it fully. But God will never force us to live the gospel. He will use persuasion through His servants. He will call us and He will direct us and He will persuade us and encourage us and He will bless us when we respond, but He will never force the human mind." (*The Teachings of Ezra Taft Benson,* p. 82.) And Joseph Smith said: "Those who resist the Spirit of God, are liable to be led into temptation, and then the association of heaven is withdrawn from those who refuse to be made partakers of such great glory—God would not exert any compulsory means and the devil could not." (*The Words of Joseph Smith,* p. 72.)

So, agency, the great eternal guarantee of the right to make choices, is with us today. However, for agency to exist, four great principles must also be in force.

1. Laws must exist that can be either obeyed or disobeyed.

2. Opposites must exist—good and evil, virtue and vice, right and wrong, pulling us one way or the other.

3. We must have a knowledge of good and evil.

4. An unfettered power of choice must prevail.

As Lehi said: "Men are free according to the flesh, and all things are given them which are expedient unto man. And they are free to choose liberty and eternal life, through the great mediation of all men, or to choose captivity and death, according to the power of the devil; for he seeketh that all men might be miserable like unto himself." (2 Nephi 2:26–30.)

Who Am I?

This information about agency becomes pertinent when we realize that we who are members of Christ's church must come to grips not only with the law of agency but also with ourselves. Who are we? Whom do we wish to become? Whom do we wish to serve? How hard are we willing to work? How obedient to the requirements of our callings are we willing to be? How obedient to the commandments of God are we willing to be? What sorts of things are we willing to think about? There are only two rules that govern thinking in this life. The first is that we can think of only one thing at a time — when we think of one thing all other things drop into the background; and the second is that, except when we are asleep, we must keep thinking. But the choice, the agency to think of what we wish, is ours! Thus the question: What sorts of things are we willing to think about?

Every active Latter-day Saint, at some point or other, must answer, with honesty, these questions. The labor becomes too difficult, too intense, too demanding, to simply slide by. We must finally determine who we are and why we are members of this Church and kingdom. Then we must decide whether to move forward in the kingdom and accept the consequences, or to drop out and suffer the same. We must decide! Any attempt to evade the decision is a decision after all — a decision to drop out.

As Brother Hugh Nibley puts it: "Every day of our lives we have to make a choice, a choice that will show where our real interests and desires lie. From the very beginning of the world the choice was provided as a test for each of us during this time of probation. Satan is allowed to try and tempt us in his way, and God is allowed in his: as Moroni puts it, 'The devil . . . inviteth and enticeth to sin, and to do that which is evil continually. But behold, that which is of God inviteth and enticeth to do good continually' (Moroni 7:12–13). It is going on all the time, the ancient doctrine of the Two Ways. The point is that we cannot choose both ways. They go in opposite directions — man simply cannot serve both God and mammon, the Lord said, and mammon is simply the Hebrew word (both ancient and modern) for dealing in money. So the first commandment given to the Church was 'Seek not for riches but for wisdom' (D&C 6:7)—making it perfectly clear that they are mutually exclusive." (*Approaching Zion*, pp. 125–26.)

Nephi's brother Jacob made the choice between these two opposite ways even plainer when he cautioned, "Remember, to be carnally-minded is death, and to be spiritually-minded is life eternal." (2 Nephi 9:39.) Truly it is an impossibility for any of us to have the best of both worlds. The instant we try, we have lost.

Setting Up Stakes

Thus we see how serious and lifelong this matter of agency and making correct choices becomes. In fact, as Jacob pointed out, it goes even beyond mortal labors. Joseph Smith taught that we all have agency to go as far as we want toward the celestial kingdom and Godhood, but that most, including the angels, would "set up stakes" or personal limitations and say, "I cannot (or will not) go any further." (*The Words of Joseph Smith*, pp. 244–47, 256.) Nor would they, because they have so decided.

By making choices about the issues raised in parts 1 and 2 of this volume, as well as numerous others not mentioned but surely just as important, we will either "set up stakes" and so stop ourselves, or we will make continual progression. We will either become powerful advocates in the kingdom, or we will not. We will either become obedient servants of God, or we will not. We will either be found standing in holy places, or we will not. The choice, the agency to decide, is ours, and ours alone.

Light and Truth

In the 93rd section of the Doctrine and Covenants, the Lord talks at great depth about spirit and truth. He says: "Ye were also in the beginning with the Father; that which is Spirit, even the Spirit of truth; and truth is knowledge of things as they are, and as they were, and as they are to come; and whatsoever is more or less than this is the spirit of that wicked one who was a liar from the beginning. The Spirit of truth is of God. . . . And no man receiveth a fulness unless he keepeth his commandments. He that keepeth his commandments receiveth truth and light, until he is glorified in truth and knoweth all things. . . . All truth is independent in that sphere in which God has placed it, to act for itself, as all intelligence also; otherwise there is no existence. Behold, here is the agency of man, and here is the condemnation of man, because that which was from the beginning is plainly manifest unto them, and they receive not the light. And every man whose spirit receiveth not the light is under condemnation. For man is spirit. The elements are eternal, and spirit and element, inseparably connected, receive a fulness of joy; and when separated, man cannot receive a fulness of joy. The elements are the tabernacle of God; yea, man is the tabernacle of God, even temples; and whatsoever temple is defiled, God shall destroy that temple. The glory of God is intelligence, or in other words, light and truth. Light and truth forsake the evil one. Every spirit of man was innocent in the beginning; and God having redeemed man from the fall, men became again, in their infant state, innocent before God. And that wicked one cometh and taketh away light and truth, through disobedience, from the children of men, and because of the tradition of their fathers. But I have commanded you to bring up your children in light and truth." (D&C 93:23–25, 27–28, 30–36, 38–40.)

This is a lengthy and doctrinally intense scripture. But from what we understand, it is also perhaps the most comprehensive statement the Lord has ever given us concerning the agency and accountability portion of the plan of salvation. Let us explain.

We learn from this section that our premortal spirits were composed of matter that the Lord calls a Spirit of truth (verse 23) and knowledge (verse 24), which, when combined with light, becomes intelligence or the glory of God (verse 36). This truth, or spirit, had independence or agency from the beginning, to act for itself by making correct choices (verse 30). Satan, a liar from the beginning, sought to add to or take away from our spirit selves by convincing us that our God-given knowledge was false, thus taking away our ability to act for ourselves with wisdom (verse 25). Obviously, he was completely successful with a third of us. These did not keep their first estate.

As the rest of us enter mortality, our second estate, through the redemption from the fall wrought by Christ we are granted once again innocence before God (verse 38). But Satan, still trying to entice us into making foolish choices, has been given the power, under two conditions, to take from us light and truth, or to diminish our spirit selves. Those conditions are disobedience and acceptance of the false traditions of our fathers (verse 39).

However, if we will but choose to begin keeping God's commandments once again as we did premortally, we are promised that spirit matter, once again called truth and light, will be granted back to us in increasing amounts (verse 28) until we have received a fulness of it (verse 27)!

In other words, by increasing our ability, through practice, to keep the commandments, we can counter and totally destroy Satan's ability to take away our light and truth. If this is done throughout our lives (enduring to the end, the Lord calls it), we are promised that we will be glorified in truth, as God is, and will then know all things (verse 28).

The Agency and Condemnation of Man

All of this amounts to the agency or condemnation of man (verse 31). Our agency if we choose to make a diligent attempt to keep the commandments; our condemnation if we choose otherwise (verse 32). Thus we are accountable. And this accountability exists because the elements of our spirits — light, truth, and accurate knowledge — naturally cleave to each other in an inseparable manner (verse 33), and in the same inseparable manner to all eternal light and truth outside of ourselves. However, if we choose not to receive this light and truth that instinctively comes to us, but to let Satan separate light and truth from us, then we are under condemnation (verse 32). And because we have allowed Satan to separate a portion of our own light and truth (spirit) from us, we cannot receive a fulness of joy (verse 34).

Therefore, so that Satan will have less power over our children, we are commanded to bring them up in light and truth (verse 40).

Putting aside all thoughts of ourselves, it is no wonder that our missionary efforts are so important. We have been called to declare to an entire generation that the traditions of their fathers are incorrect, and that because of that, Satan is taking away from them huge portions of their light and truth. Without that light and truth, they can never have a fulness of joy. Further, the only way for them to get out of the mess they are in is to learn the commandments of God, as revealed in the restored gospel, and then live them to the best of their abilities. More and more we begin to see how important our mission in mortality is, in terms of the eternal salvation of the other inhabitants of this world.

We can also see, in terms of our own agency, how eternally important it is, not only to ourselves but to perhaps millions of others who will become our descendants; not only because we desire protection during the coming judgments but because we truly desire to be standing in holy places, that we train ourselves to make the right choices as we learn to cherish and keep the commandments of God.

20

Joining the Family of Christ

Now that we have described not only the judgments and chastisements of God but the arduous path required to avoid them, the setting has been established for introducing this most relevant theme of belonging to the family of Christ.

As Elder Bruce R. McConkie has said: "Few doctrines are better known by members of the true church than the doctrine of preexistence. We are well aware that all men are the children of God, the offspring of the Father, his sons and his daughters. We know that we were all born in his courts as spirit beings, long before the foundations of this earth were laid, and that the Lord Jehovah was in fact the Firstborn Son. What is not so well known is that nearly all the passages of scripture, both ancient and modern, which speak of God as our Father and of men on earth being the sons of God, have

---

Some of the material in this chapter has been excerpted from: Blaine and Brenton Yorgason, *Agency, Spiritual Progression, and the Mighty Change* (Orem UT: Keepsake BookCards, 1989).

no reference to our birth in preexistence as the children of Elohim, but teach rather that Jehovah is to be our Father and we are to become his children." (*The Promised Messiah,* pp. 351–52.)

Progressive Relationships with God and Christ

If our knowledge was limited to the fact that we should choose right instead of wrong, it is likely that we would all be very frustrated. We would feel a great burden, but we would also lack clear understanding of the direction to go in order to have that burden lifted. However, the Lord has not left us in such darkness. In fact, he revealed to Joseph Smith over the course of several years that there were progressive levels in our relationship with God and Christ, levels that we could chart and aim for if we truly wanted to return to dwell as he dwells, in celestial glory. The Lord did this by allowing Joseph to advance through each level on his own, thus learning of their sequential importance.

Let us add, parenthetically, that Joseph Smith experienced two separate types of progression. First, he progressed in his priesthood calling, that is, in his role as prophet, seer, and revelator—as president of the Church. Secondly, he progressed spiritually on a personal level.

Elder Angel Abrea, speaking in a recent multiregional conference, listed the following scriptures, which outline Joseph's growth in power as a prophet:

D&C 28:6–7: The Lord declares that the prophet is at the head of the Church.

D&C 35:18: The Prophet holds the keys of the mysteries of heaven—if he abides in the Lord. If he chooses to vary, another will be planted in his stead.

D&C 43:3–4: None other is appointed to receive revelation and commandments but the prophet. Again, though, if he varies, the gift will be taken from him.

D&C 64:5: Joseph holds the keys of the mysteries of heaven, and they will not be taken from him while he lives—if he obeys God's ordinances.

D&C 90:3: The keys of the kingdom will not be taken from Joseph in this world nor in the world to come.

D&C 112:15: God is with Joseph, and the keys will not be taken from him until the Lord comes.

D&C 132:49: God is with Joseph unto the end of the world and through all eternity—his exaltation is sealed upon him.

D&C 136:37–39: God called upon Joseph to bring forth His work. Joseph was faithful, and the Lord took him unto Himself, his death being needful to seal his testimony with his blood—that he might be honored and the wicked condemned. (Multiregional Conference, American Fork and Provo, Utah North Regions, Sunday, February 25, 1990; from notes taken by the authors.)

As can be seen, Joseph progressed slowly over several years. As he grew in power in his role as prophet, the Lord not only sealed upon Joseph the keys of the kingdom but also sealed upon him his eternal exaltation.

In terms of personal growth, the Lord publicly acknowledges Joseph as his servant 101 times in the Doctrine and Covenants, beginning with D&C 1:17, when he refers to the Prophet as "my servant Joseph Smith, Jun." After Joseph had been the prophet of an organized church for three years, and thirteen years after he had first seen the Father and the Son, Christ acknowledged him as his *son*. (D&C 90:1.) It is interesting that only three months after this, on May 6, 1833, the Savior called Joseph his friend (D&C 93:45), though for the Lord's sake, Joseph remained a servant of the people (D&C 93:46). Finally, a full decade later, on July 12, 1843, the Lord sealed upon Joseph his exaltation, thus pronouncing him a joint-heir with Christ to all that the Father has to offer through time and all eternity. (Romans 8:17.) Thus we see that Joseph progressed through four separate levels of relationships with the Savior.

In addition to these four levels that we have just identified, we are aware of three additional but lower levels that ought to be included briefly in this discussion. Beginning at the lowest level that we know of, or the level farthest removed from God, these are:

1. Enemies to God. (James 4:4; Mosiah 2:27.) These people resist all enticements from the Holy Spirit within their own lives and do all within their power to halt or thwart the work of God within the lives of those around them.

2. Strangers and foreigners. (Ephesians 2:19.) While not actively campaigning against God and his work, these people have no knowledge of him. Neither is it common for them to think much of him, unless something (such as contact with a Latter-day Saint, the missionaries, the Book of Mormon, and so on) motivates them to kindle a burning desire to find out about God.

3. Fellowcitizens with the saints. (Ephesians 2:19.) These people are members of the Lord's earthly church but for one reason or another are not actively involved in building the kingdom of God. This may simply be because of their youthfulness, either in age or in Church membership, but it may also be because they don't want to be involved or to extend themselves as fully "active" members.

4. Servants or handmaidens of God. (D&C 76:12; D&C 93:46.) Like Joseph Smith, these people are actively involved, through various callings, assignments, and personally generated efforts, in building the kingdom of God on the earth.

5. Sons or daughters of Jesus Christ. (Mosiah 5:7; Ether 3:14; Moroni 7:19.) These people have experienced the magnificent baptism of the Holy Ghost and, being dramatically changed in the inner man, have been adopted into the family

of Jesus Christ. Therefore, they have literally become his sons and his daughters.

6. Friends of Jesus Christ. (D&C 93:45; D&C 84:77; James 2:23.) These people, members of Christ's earthly family, have continued to press forward in righteousness until through the Holy Spirit, they have been declared by Christ as his friends.

7. Joint-heirs with Jesus Christ. (Romans 8:17.) Having overcome all, these people have their exaltation assured while still in mortality and so have become joint-heirs with Christ in receiving all the blessings the Father can bestow upon them.

Enemies, Strangers and Foreigners, and Fellow-citizens

While it would be interesting to examine the nature and experiences of "enemies" to Christ, such as Korihor in the Book of Mormon, or to discuss the numerous people who fall under the category of "strangers and foreigners" to Christ, this would not serve the purpose of this volume. In terms of "fellowcitizens with the saints," Latter-day Saints are familiar enough with themselves that we do not feel a need to expand upon this category.

Let us therefore move to the fourth category or level, the first of the levels of relationships in which the Lord placed Joseph Smith—that of "servant of Christ."

Servant or Handmaiden

When we were set apart for our first Church calling, we advanced or progressed from the "fellowcitizen" status to the "servant or handmaiden" status in our relationship with God and Jesus Christ. Having fulfilled the laws of obedience to the first principles and ordinances of the gospel, we were granted the right of advancing spiritually to this closer relationship with the Lord, where we actually became a partner with him in building the kingdom of God here upon the earth. Such are his servants.

Being Damned or Stopped

While all who are granted the wondrous blessing of becoming servants of God should remain so throughout their lives, at least in terms of rendering service to the kingdom and their fellow-beings, sadly, many Latter-day Saints choose to remain at this spiritual level. While partaking of the sealing ordinance in the temple and thus setting the stage for far greater blessings for themselves and for their families, they choose, by the way they live, to remain spiritually dormant or immature. They have obtained the gift of the Holy Ghost but rarely the fruits of that gift. These people choose never to pay the price required to move on, and they are never quite certain of their status or position before the Lord. In other words, though they might serve diligently all their lives and receive blessings for such service, they have effectively "set up stakes" for themselves. Using their agency they have stopped, or damned, themselves from further mortal progression.

Forging Ahead

But we *can* move forward. Joseph Smith taught: "After a person has faith in Christ, repents of his sins, and is baptized for the remission of his sins and receives the Holy Ghost, (by the laying on of hands), which is the first Comforter, then let him continue to humble himself before God, hungering and thirsting after righteousness, and living by every word of God, and the Lord will soon say unto him, Son, thou shalt be exalted. When the Lord has thoroughly proved him, and finds that the man is determined to serve him at all hazards, then the man will find his calling and election made sure, and it will be his privilege to receive the other Comforter, which the Lord hath promised the Saints, as is recorded in the testimony of St. John, in the 14th chapter, from the 12th to the 27th verses." (*Teachings of the Prophet Joseph Smith*, p. 150.)

As we will note, the Prophet covers quickly most of the above list. Let us point out the three requisites Joseph says are requirements for any degree of spiritual growth. They are (1) continuing humility, (2) hungering and thirsting after righteousness, and (3) living by every word of God.

Being specific, if we choose not to fulfil our callings, if we declare ourselves too busy to do our home teaching, if we don't like to be "forced" to do our visiting teaching, if we are too busy to go to the temple regularly, or to study the scriptures daily, by ourselves and with our families, or to hold morning and evening prayer together, are we hungering or thirsting after righteousness? Are we continuing in humility? Are we living by every word of God that our prophets and apostles have declared unto us? If we choose to fill our minds with the satanically inspired noise that some call music, the filth of pornography, the callous profanity and immorality of soap operas and prime-time TV, or the drivel of so much of our reading material, are we truly hungering and thirsting after righteousness?

Of course we aren't, and so again we have "set up stakes" and damned ourselves from further spiritual growth or progression.

Being Born of the Spirit—a Mighty Change

But if we choose to forge ahead by doing as Joseph outlined, then being called as "sons or daughters of Jesus Christ" is the next logical step. For that designation to be made, however, a mighty change of heart is required—we must be born of the Spirit. And, as the great King Benjamin explained, this can only be brought about by total repentance and sincere dedication to the will, and work, of God. (Mosiah 2–6.) Technically, the way for this to happen is provided through baptism and the reception of the gift of the Holy Ghost. Thus, this mighty change should occur on that occasion. But for most of us it does not work that way, especially if our baptism came when we were children. But beginning that day, the educational process does begin, and it continues until we have reached the maturity to decide which way we want to go.

If we decide we want to follow Christ, such a decision means that our daily actions must be pointed constantly toward building the kingdom; it means the words we speak should be edifying and Christ-like; and it means that our thoughts must, of our own choice again, be pure and wholesome.

"What things then should we think about?" questions Hugh Nibley. "Here the Prophet is very helpful. In the first place, that question itself is what we should think about. We won't get very far on our way until we have faced up to it. But as soon as we start very seriously thinking about that, we find ourselves covered with confusion, overwhelmed by our feelings of guilt and inadequacy—in other words, repenting for our past delinquency. In this condition, we call upon the Lord for aid, and he hears us. We begin to know what the Prophet Joseph meant about the constant searching, steadily storing our minds with knowledge and information—the more we get of it, the better we are able to judge the proper priorities as we feel our way forward, as we become increasingly alert to the promptings of the Spirit which become ever more clear and more frequent, following the guidance of the Holy Ghost: and as we go forward, we learn to cope with the hostile world with which our way is sure to bring us into collision. . . . That calls for sacrifice, but what of that? Eternal life is not cheaply bought." (*Approaching Zion,* p. 78.)

When we are willing to pay this price, when we truly desire a closer walk with God, after diligent prayer and an earnest enough anxiety to know our own sins that we are willing to pray about them (see Ether 12:27, D&C 66:3), we begin to feel:

1. A godly sorrow for all sin. (2 Corinthians 7:10.)

2. An unending desire to repent and to be made clean. (Alma 29:4.)

3. An understanding that this cleanliness cannot be self-induced. (1 Corinthians 15:3; Alma 5:27.)

4. A fixed determination to purify ourselves until such cleanliness has been granted. (Alma 5:21; D&C 121:45.)

5. A profound willingness to live so that such pain and sorrow as is being experienced will never come upon us again. (Acts 17:30; 2 Nephi 9:23; 3 Nephi 11:32; D&C 133:16.)

6. An understanding that all sins, even favorite little previously protected ones, are a source of great pain to the Savior. (Matthew 5:19; Alma 45:16.)

7. A recognition that it was we ourselves, who, by our own bad choices, drove the nails that day on Golgotha. (Hebrews 6:6.)

8. A willingness to apologize to Christ for choosing to wound him. (Mosiah 26:29–30.)

9. An unending anxiety to cry forth the plea that Christ, through the spilling of his precious blood, will remove the burden of pain from us, thereby allowing us to be finally and forever free of our guilt. (Mosiah 27:24–26; Alma 36:13–21; 38:8.)

10. A burning desire to sing the song of redeeming love. (Alma 5:26.)

Do these emotions sound familiar? We certainly hope they do, for every mature Latter-day Saint, every human being, in fact, should experience them. (Mosiah 27:25.) As Lehi explained to his son Jacob, when we personally push forward with these desires, our hearts become broken and our spirits become contrite, and we are finally in a position where Jesus Christ, the Lord God omnipotent, can answer the ends of the law in our behalf. (See 2 Nephi 2:7.)

And that is where we all should be. President Benson's plea to every one of us is, "May we be convinced that Jesus is the Christ, choose to follow Him, be changed for Him, captained by Him, consumed in Him, and born again." (*The Teachings of Ezra Taft Benson*, p. 13.) Then he adds: "When you choose to follow Christ, you choose to be changed. 'No man,' said President David O. McKay, 'can sincerely resolve to apply to his daily life the teachings of Jesus of Nazareth without sensing a change in his own nature. The phrase *born again* has a deeper significance than many people attach to it. This changed feeling may be indescribable, but it is real.' Our Lord told Nicodemus that 'except a man be born again, he cannot see the kingdom of God' (John 3:3). Of these words President Spencer W. Kimball said, 'This is the simple total answer to the weightiest of all questions. . . . To gain eternal life there must be a rebirth, a transformation.' . . . Christ called for an entire revolution of Nicodemus's 'inner man.' His manner of thinking, feeling and acting with reference to spiritual things would have to undergo a fundamental and permanent change." (Ibid., pp. 77–78.)

Alma said: "The Lord said unto me: Marvel not that all mankind, yea, men and women, all nations, kindreds, tongues, and people, must be born again; yea, born of God, changed from their carnal and fallen state, to a state of righteousness, being redeemed of God, becoming his sons and his daughters; and thus they become new creatures; and unless they do this, they can in nowise inherit the kingdom of God." (Mosiah 27:25–26.) Such people have "no more disposition to do evil, but to do good continually." (Mosiah 5:2, 7.) As Alma frankly asked: "Have ye spiritually been born of

God? Have ye received his image in your countenances? Have ye experienced this mighty change in your hearts?" (Alma 5:14.)

Our Sins Will Be Taken from Us

If we cannot yet answer these questions affirmatively, but if we will nevertheless be willing to persist in this quest for internal peace and a knowledge that we have been made clean every whit through the blood of Christ, and do it for as many days, weeks, months, or years as the Lord requires of us, then we are promised that God will finally grant our petitions. We will then have truly repented of our sins. We will have been miraculously and in an instant, as it were, relieved of our burdens through the unbelievable power and burning of the Holy Ghost. All guilt will have been swept away in an incredible lifting experience and rush of the Holy Ghost. (See Mosiah 27:24–26; Alma 36:12–21.) We will then have been born of the Spirit. (John 3:7.) We will have experienced the baptism of fire (Matthew 3:11; 2 Nephi 31:13–14) or the remission of sins by fire and the Holy Ghost (2 Nephi 31:17). We will be privileged to enjoy the companionship of the Holy Ghost more and more frequently until his companionship becomes constant. (D&C 121:46.) Finally, we will have experienced the mighty change. (Mosiah 5:2; Alma 5:12–14.)

Have We Experienced the Mighty Change?

The best answer we can give to the question "Have I had the mighty change?" is, if we need to ask, then it would seem logical that we have not experienced it. Virtually every person we know who has paid the price and has experienced the mighty change knows full well of the experience. The process and the event are too profound, too soul-stretching, too incredible not to know about. Besides, the peace that comes with the experience of knowing where we stand with God, of realizing that the blood of Christ has made us clean of all in our past, is so all-powerful and all-consuming that it cannot be misunderstood or forgotten. Thus, we know by experiencing it. And once we have, it is not easily forgotten.

President Brigham Young once asked, "How shall [you] know [if the Mighty Change] has occurred?" He then answered his own question: "By the Spirit that shall come unto you through obedience, which will make you feel like little children, and cause you to delight in doing good, to love your Father in Heaven and the society of the righteous. Have you malice and wrath, then? No, it is taken from you, and you feel like the child in its mother's lap. You will feel kind to your children, to your parents and neighbors, and to all around you; you will feel a glow, as of fire, burning within you; and if you open your mouths to talk you will declare ideas which you did not formerly think of; they will flow into your mind, even such as you have not thought of in years. The Scriptures will be opened to you, and you will see how clear and reasonable everything is which this or that Elder teaches you. Your hearts will be comforted, you can lie down and sleep in peace, and wake up with feelings as pleasant as the breezes of summer. This is a witness to you." (*Discourses of Brigham Young*, p. 331.)

Alma's Quiz

For those who still wonder, the Prophet Alma the Younger has provided a quiz. Further, the quiz is also designed for those who have experienced the mighty change, that they might know if they have slipped backward. Alma's questions are:

1. Have ye spiritually been born of God?
2. Have ye received his image in your countenances?
3. Have ye experienced this mighty change in your hearts?

4. Do ye exercise faith in the redemption of him who created you?

5. Do ye look forward with an eye of faith, and view this mortal body, raised in immortality, and this corruption, raised in incorruption, to stand before God to be judged according to the deeds which have been done in the mortal body?

6. Can you imagine that ye hear the voice of the Lord, saying unto you, in that day: Come unto me ye blessed, for behold, your works have been the works of righteousness upon the face of the earth?

7. Or do ye imagine to yourselves that ye can lie unto the Lord in that day, and say—Lord, our works have been righteous works upon the face of the earth—and that he will save you?

8. Or otherwise, can ye imagine yourselves brought before the tribunal of God with your souls filled with guilt and remorse, having a remembrance of all your guilt, yea, a perfect remembrance of all your wickedness, yea, a remembrance that ye have set at defiance the commandments of God?

9. Can ye look to God at that day with a pure heart and clean hands?

10. Can ye look up, having the image of God engraven upon your countenances? (A repeated question, obviously very important.)

11. Can ye think of being saved when you have yielded yourselves to become subjects to the devil? (See Alma 5:14–21.)

Alma then answers many of his own questions, pointing out how we will feel when we "shall stand before the bar of God." He asks: "[How will you feel,] having your garments stained with blood and all manner of filthiness. Behold, what will these things testify against you? . . . That ye are murderers, yea, and also that ye are guilty of all manner of wickedness. . . . Do ye suppose that such an one can have a place to sit down in the kingdom of God?" (Alma 5:21–25.) No, he again answers himself, for such people have now become children of the devil.

And then his questions begin for those who have once experienced the mighty change but who may have regressed or fallen from this state.

1. If ye have experienced a change of heart, can ye feel so now?

2. If ye have felt to sing the song of redeeming love, can ye feel so now?

3. Have ye walked, keeping yourself blameless before God?

4. Could ye say, if ye were called to die at this time, within yourselves, that ye have been sufficiently humble?

5. Could ye say that your garments have been cleansed and made white through the blood of Christ, who [has come] to redeem his people from their sins?

6. Are ye stripped of pride?

7. [Are ye] stripped of envy?

8. Do ye make a mockery of your brother, or heap upon him persecutions? (See Alma 5:26–30.)

And then again, Alma launches into a plea to members of the Church that they hurry and repent (Alma 5:31–36), that Christ will receive them into his royal family. "O ye workers of iniquity," he says to Latter-day Saints who have not repented fully of their favorite sins and so cannot respond positively to his questions, "ye that are puffed up in the vain things of the world, ye that have professed to have known the ways of righteousness nevertheless have gone astray, as sheep having no shepherd, notwithstanding a shepherd hath called after you and is still calling after you, but ye will not hearken unto his voice . . . because the devil is your shepherd, and ye are of his fold." (Alma 5:37–42.)

If we aren't in the Lord's flock because we have not pressed forward diligently in seeking the things of the Spirit, then we are in the devil's herd. As we have pointed out so often in this volume, the issue of agency or choice makes things pretty much black and white. As Nephi said (may we remind you again?), there are save two churches only, Christ's and Satan's. (1 Nephi 14:10.) By our choices or agency, we determine which one we have joined. That is why we, as brothers, feel so strongly that we should not only know about but also *do* the things discussed in this book.

No Shortcuts

But remember, for all who do not strive spiritually until this mighty change is granted, spiritual and eternal progression must be stopped. As the Lord declared, that is the agency and the condemnation of man. No laws can be skipped over, nor are there shortcuts. People who attempt to find shortcuts remain spiritually stagnant, living, earning blessings and rewards for goodness performed or vice-versa, but not achieving the higher spiritual potential that is reached by those who are more willing to pay the price. Thus they are damned.

"Can't the Spirit hurry things up?" it has been asked. As Hugh Nibley writes: "No—there is no place for the cram course or quickie, or above all the superficial survey course or quick trips to the Holy Land, where the gospel is concerned: [Joseph Smith said]: 'We consider that God has created man with a mind capable of instruction, and a faculty which may be enlarged in proportion to the heed and diligence given to the light communicated from heaven to the intellect; . . . but no man ever arrived in a moment: he must have been instructed . . . by proper degrees' (TPJS, p. 51). 'The things of God are of deep import; and time, and experience, and careful and ponderous and solemn thoughts can only find them out. Thy mind, O man! if thou wilt lead a soul unto salvation, must stretch as high as the utmost heavens' (TPJS, p. 137).

No shortcuts or easy lessons here! Note well that the Prophet makes no distinction between things of the spirit and things of the intellect." (*Approaching Zion*, p. 72.)

So whatever else we do, we must go at this carefully, thoughtfully, and diligently.

A New Family

If we persist in the direction we have been given by the prophets, however, earnestly repenting of our sins and striving to keep God's commandments, then surely our sins will be removed through the precious blood of Christ, and we will experience the Mighty Change. And because this Mighty Change will have been wrought upon our heart by the power of God, we will also begin to take upon our countenance the image of Christ. (Alma 5:14.) As a host of prophets declare, this occurs because we have been adopted into the family of our Savior. We will quite literally be called by God as a son or daughter of Jesus Christ, and, just as literally, Jesus Christ will become our father. Thus our spirit will begin to look like Jesus Christ, and others will be able to see the change in us.

It is difficult to imagine the honor of being allowed to trace one's genealogical lineage back to Jesus Christ. Yet in eternity, so it will be. If we continue to repent and choose righteousness, we will, worlds without end, be a member of that royal church and family.

Called as Sons and Daughters of Christ

Concerning this calling into the family of Christ, King Benjamin said to his people, "Ye shall be called the children of Christ, his sons and his daughters; for behold, this day he hath spiritually begotten you; for ye say that your hearts are changed through faith on his name; therefore ye are born of him and have become his sons and his daughters." (Mosiah 5:7.)

King Benjamin then made an interesting promise. He said that people who strive for righteousness until they become sons and daughters of Christ will be found on the right hand of God (as is Christ) and shall be called by the name of Christ, thus becoming joint heirs with Him in eternity. This is granted them because they have been "steadfast and immovable, always abounding in good works, that Christ, the Lord God omnipotent, may seal [them] his, that [they] may be brought to heaven, that [they] may have everlasting salvation and eternal life." (Mosiah 5:15.)

This doctrine of being called as children of Christ through a personal covenant and mighty works is expounded upon by other prophets as well. Moses said: "[Adam] heard a voice out of heaven, saying: Thou art baptized with fire, and with the Holy Ghost. This is the record of the Father, and the Son, from henceforth and forever; and thou art after the order of him who was without beginning of days or end of years, from all eternity to all eternity. Behold, thou art one in me, a son of God; and thus may all become my [Jesus Christ's] sons." (Moses 6:66–68.)

Moroni said, "I beseech of you . . . that ye should search diligently in the light of Christ that ye may know good from evil; and if ye will lay hold upon every good thing, and condemn it not, ye certainly will be a child of Christ." (Moroni 7:19.)

To the wicked King Noah, Abinadi declared that through obedience to the words of the prophets, men and women would become Christ's seed, or children. He declared: "When [Christ's] soul has been made an offering for sin he shall see his seed. And now what say ye? And who shall be his seed? Behold I say unto you, that whosoever has heard the words of the prophets, yea, all the holy prophets who have prophesied concerning the coming of the Lord—I say unto you, that all those who have hearkened unto their words, and believed that the Lord would redeem his people, and have looked forward to that day for a remission of their sins, I say unto you, that these are his seed, or they are the heirs of the kingdom of God. For these are they whose sins he has borne; these are they for whom he has died, to redeem them from their transgressions. And now, are they not his seed?" (Mosiah 15:10–12.)

In an interesting sequel to this thought of seeds, the resurrected Lord declared to the Nephites that only the humble and righteous (the seed of Christ) would be allowed to sprout and have eternal roots and branches, which obviously has reference to dwelling with eternal families (3 Nephi 25:1–2), which is called a "continuation of the seeds forever and ever." (D&C 132:19.)

Finally, in his introductory remarks to the brother of Jared, Jesus Christ declared: "Behold, I am he who was prepared from the foundation of the world to redeem my people. Behold, I am Jesus Christ. I am the Father and the Son. In me shall all mankind have life, and that eternally, even they who shall believe on my name; and they shall become my sons and my daughters." (Ether 3:14.)

Elder Bruce R. McConkie said: "In setting forth that all men must be born again to gain salvation, we have seen that this means they must be 'born of God, changed from their carnal and fallen state, to a state of righteousness, being redeemed of God, becoming his sons and daughters.' (Mosiah 27:25.) Whose sons and whose daughters do we become when we are born again? Who is our new Father? The answer is, Christ is our Father; we become his children by adoption; he makes us members of his family." (*The Promised Messiah*, pp. 351–52.) Elder McConkie also said: "Those who are born again not only live a new life, but they also have a new father. Their new life is one of righteousness, and their new father is God. They become the sons of God; or, more particularly, they become the sons and daughters of Jesus Christ. They bear, ever thereafter, the name of their new parent; that is, they take upon themselves the name of Christ and become Christians, not only in word but in very deed. They become by adoption the seed or offspring of Christ, the children in his family, the members of his household, which is the perfect household of perfect faith. . . .

"John tells us that the Lord Jesus, who came in time's meridian unto his own, was rejected by them. 'But as many as received him,' as their Messiah and Savior, 'to them gave he power to become the sons of God, even to them that believe on his name.' (John 1:12.) Speaking of that same meridian day, the same Lord said in our day: 'To as many as received me, gave I power to become my sons.' Be it noted that true believers are not automatically born to a newness of life by the mere fact of belief alone. That belief and that acceptance of the Savior gives them power to become the sons of God. And in our day the divine word continues: 'Even so will I give unto as many as will receive me, power to become my sons.' And how are those who receive the Lord identified? By way of answer, he tells us: 'Verily, verily, I say unto you, he that receiveth my gospel receiveth me; and he that receiveth not my gospel receiveth not me.' (D&C 39:4–5.) Those who have accepted the fulness of the everlasting gospel as it has come again in our day through the instrumentality of Joseph Smith have power to become the sons of God; those who reject this heaven-sent message of salvation reject that Lord whose message it is and remain outside the Lord's family. . . .

"Thus it is that the saints are born of Christ because they have been born of the Spirit; they are alive in Christ because they enjoy the companionship of the Spirit, and they are members of his family because they are clean as he is clean. 'And under this head ye are made free' — being in Christ, they are free from the bondage of sin— 'and there is no other head [other than Christ our Head] whereby ye can be made free.' Only those who accept Christ and receive the Spirit can free themselves from the sins of the world. 'There is no other name given whereby salvation cometh; therefore, I would that ye should take upon you the name of Christ, all you that have entered into the covenant with God that ye should be obedient unto the end of your lives.' (Mosiah 5:7–8.) (*A New Witness for the Articles of Faith* [Salt Lake City: Deseret Book Company, 1988], pp. 284–85.)

Blessings of Membership in Christ's Royal Family

As a member of Christ's family, we (who set up *no* stakes or limitations for ourselves by choosing to sin and remain in sin by not repenting) will be given permission and power to move forward spiritually. We will be able to go on and obtain all the blessings mentioned by the Prophet Joseph Smith and become sons and daughters of Christ, as well as friends of Christ. At that time, we will have become worthy of having our ordinances (temple and otherwise) sealed upon us by the Holy Spirit of Promise (D&C 132:7–8), and finally we will be joint heirs with Christ, to inherit with him all that the Father has promised throughout all eternity. This is the law of eternal progression.

Justification

Actually, there are two parts to this progression, Christ's part and our part. According to the scriptures, the Savior's part of our eternal progression has to do with what is called justification. On the day the Church was organized, Joseph Smith declared, "Justification through the grace of our Lord and Savior Jesus Christ is just and true." (D&C 20:30.) To Moses the Lord said, "By the water ye keep the commandment; by the Spirit ye are justified, and by the blood ye are sanctified." (Moses 6:60.) And to Joseph Smith the Lord said: "All kingdoms have a law given. . . . And unto every kingdom is given a law; and unto every law there are certain bounds also and conditions. All beings who abide not those conditions are not justified." (D&C 88:36, 38–39.) Justification and its necessity are also spoken of at great length by the Apostle Paul and other New Testament writers, who all declare that it is a gift from Christ, for those who exercise faith in him. (Luke 18:14; Acts 13:39; Romans 2:13; 4:16; 5:1, 9; 8:30; Galatians 2:16–17; 3:24–29.)

Justification is part of the law of justice. In that law the Lord says that for every obedience to law there is a blessing, while for every disobedience there is a punishment. (D&C 130:20–21.) In other words, we receive joy from obedience, misery from disobedience. So, we should always be obedient to all God's laws, for then the law of justice would demand that we have pure joy. The trouble with this, however, is that none of us keeps all the laws of God perfectly. That is why Lehi taught that "by the law no flesh is justified." (2 Nephi 2:5.) In other words, because of the law of justice we are all in a world of hurt, at least in terms of eternal progression. On our own merits we will never make it, will never know true joy, because we have experienced our own personal fall from premortal and mortal purity!

But does that mean we should all give up in despair? Lehi says: "Redemption [from our personal sins] cometh in and through the Holy Messiah." (2 Nephi 2:6.) Simply put, we are condemned by the law but redeemed by the Messiah, Jesus Christ, "who is full of grace and truth." (Ibid.) These, grace and truth, are the ingredients that give Christ the enabling power to become our Redeemer. And who enjoys this great redemption brought about by Christ's enabling power? Only those "who have a broken heart and a contrite spirit;

and unto none else can the ends of the law be answered."
(2 Nephi 2:7.) In other words, only those who have brought
forth true repentance through faith and godly sorrow are
justified by Christ's sacrifice and atonement.

Jesus says, "Listen to him who is the advocate with the
Father, who is pleading your cause before him—saying: Father, behold the sufferings and death of him who did no sin,
in whom thou wast well pleased; behold the blood of thy Son
which was shed, the blood of him whom thou gavest that
thyself might be glorified; wherefore, Father, spare these my
brethren that believe on my name, that they may come unto
me and have everlasting life." (D&C 45:3–5.)

Those who go through godly sorrow until their sins have
been forgiven them are acquitted of their sinful natures.
Though prone to mortal weaknesses, these people (who are
now called as sons or daughters of Christ) no longer sin
intentionally, and God justifies them despite their weaknesses
and allows them almost instant repentance and forgiveness.
Of course, such people ask for forgiveness instantly, too, and
they do all within their power to avoid making the same
mistakes again. Thus they are justified and are allowed to
progress onward toward sanctification and, ultimately, perfection, all of it through Jesus Christ. (D&C 129:3, 6.)

To summarize, we could say that justification means that
the Holy Ghost justifies our acts because we have exercised
faith in Christ unto repentance and are striving with all our
hearts to live righteously. Then this gift of Christ's is granted
to us.

Pressing Forward with Steadfastness

The process of sanctification or eternal progression comes
after justification. Nephi explained that repentance and a remission of our sins "by fire and by the Holy Ghost" take us
through the gate and place us on the "strait and narrow path

which leads to eternal life." (2 Nephi 31:17–18.) Still, as LDS scholar Larry E. Dahl writes: "This is a sobering thought! With what it takes to get to that point, one might wish that it were near the end of the path to eternal life, rather than the very beginning. But Nephi's point is clear: 'And then are ye in this strait and narrow path which leads to eternal life; yea, ye have entered in by the gate.' (Ibid.) Nephi then asks and answers the next obvious question: 'And now, my beloved brethren, after ye have gotten into this strait and narrow path, I would ask if all is done? Behold, I say unto you, Nay; for ye have not come thus far save it were by the word of Christ with unshaken faith in him, relying wholly upon the merits of him who is mighty to save. Wherefore . . . ' (2 Nephi 31:19–20). And then he goes on to tell us what else we must do. The essence of this . . . seems to be that the credit for our getting through the gate and onto the strait and narrow path belongs to Christ, not us, but that now we must rely appropriately upon our own merit, and not depend 'wholly' upon the merit of Christ. We must demonstrate that our change of heart is permanent, that our commitment to obey is stronger than the enticements of the world and the devil, and we must do this day after day, year after year, through good times and bad." ("The Doctrine of Christ," *The Book of Mormon: Second Nephi, the Doctrinal Structure* [Provo UT: Brigham Young University Religious Studies Center, 1989], pp. 368–69.)

Therefore, according to Nephi (2 Nephi 31:20), we must "press forward with a steadfastness in Christ"; we must have "a perfect brightness of hope," which is a whole lot of desire coupled with full expectation of receiving eternal salvation for ourselves and for others, which hope begins to develop after the mighty change; and we must "feast upon the word of Christ," not a nibble or a snack but a savory banquet of feasting "from the scriptures and the inspired words of the

Lord's servants, [as well as by] receiving personal revelation." (*Second Nephi, the Doctrinal Structure,* p. 371.) In other words, we must have a hearty appetite—hungering and thirsting after righteousness and in every way filling our own platter!

But for Those Who Won't

Once again, let's see what happens to those who do not meet the basic requirement of having a broken heart and a contrite spirit. Christ's redemption becomes inoperative for those who are hard of heart and proud of spirit and who refuse to accept redemptive ordinances. Because they are of such natures, Christ does not make intercession in their behalf, and this is clearly explained in modern revelation: "Surely every man must repent or suffer. . . . Therefore I command you to repent—repent, lest I smite you by the rod of my mouth, and by my wrath, and by my anger, and your sufferings be sore—how sore you know not. . . . For behold, I, God, have suffered these things for all, that they might not suffer if they would repent; but if they would not repent they must suffer even as I." (D&C 19:4, 15–17.) "Either way," as LDS scholar Gerald Lund writes, "by Christ's suffering or the individual's, justice is paid. The price is paid by suffering. For the humble and obedient, the price was paid by the atoning sacrifice of the Messiah; for the rest it must be paid by themselves." (Gerald N. Lund, "The Fall of Man and His Redemption," *The Book of Mormon: Second Nephi, The Doctrinal Structure,* p. 99.)

Sanctification

It surprised us to learn that there are 220 references in our computer scripture file to the word *sanctify* and its derivatives—an indication that the topic must be very important to the Lord. Why would that be so? We think because becoming sanctified is the first great personal reward granted to those who have become justified and who have then gone to work for the Lord.

As we said, where justification comes strictly through Christ's great efforts rather than our own ("for we know that it is by grace that we are saved, after all that we can do" [2 Nephi 25:23]), sanctification is also granted us through his sacrifice and by the power of the Holy Ghost, but based upon our own efforts. Bruce R. McConkie wrote: "To the saints the continual cry of the gospel is: Sanctify yourselves. (D&C 39:18; 43:9, 11, 16; 133:4; Lev. 11:14; 1 Peter 1:15.) This is accomplished by obedience to the 'law of Christ' (D&C 88:21, 34–35), and is possible because of His atoning sacrifice. (D&C 76:41.)" (*Mormon Doctrine,* p. 675.)

According to Brigham Young: "Sanctification . . . consists in overcoming every sin and bringing all into subjection to the law of Christ. God has placed in us a pure spirit; when this reigns predominant . . . and triumphs over the flesh and rules and governs and controls as the Lord controls the heavens and the earth, this I call the blessing of sanctification." (*Journal of Discourses,* 10:173.) Such Saints have become "pure and spotless before God," being unable to "look upon sin save it were with abhorrence." (Alma 13:11–12.)

President Spencer W. Kimball stated that the attitude basic to sanctification "is that the former transgressor must have reached a 'point of no return' to sin wherein there is not merely a renunciation but also a deep abhorrence of the sin — where the sin becomes most distasteful to him and where the desire or urge to sin is cleared out of his life." (*The Miracle of Forgiveness* [Salt Lake City: Bookcraft, 1969], pp. 354–55.)

Stated simply, then, sanctification is the process of becoming, through true and constant repentance and a love of that which is good, pure and spotless before God through the power of the sanctifier, who is the Holy Ghost.

Once we are part of the family of Jesus Christ, and once we have been justified and sanctified, then our eternal progression is allowed to proceed still further, and we will be drawing ever nearer to God.

21

Seven Steps to Exaltation

The scriptures indicate that there are seven steps we each must take before we can gain exaltation. All of these are to be accomplished during this life, though of course Alma points out that this life lasts from birth until the resurrection. (See Alma 12:24.) Therefore, we have that length of time to accomplish these things. But if we do not accomplish each of these steps sometime during that period, then we can never expect to dwell with God as exalted beings.

These seven steps, these eternally significant events, are:

1. Being born.
2. Being baptized.
3. Receiving the endowment.
4. Entering into the new and everlasting covenant of marriage.
5. Being called as a son or daughter of Christ.

Some of the material in this chapter has been excerpted from: Blaine and Brenton Yorgason, *Agency, Spiritual Progression, and the Mighty Change* (Orem UT: Keepsake BookCards, 1989).

6. Being elected to membership in Christ's eternal church, the General Assembly and Church of the Firstborn.

7. Having this last mentioned calling and election made sure through revelation and the holy priesthood of God.

Being Born

As we can see, God gave us the first step of birth as a reward for keeping our first estate, which diligence we are not allowed to remember. In this process, according to Spencer W. Kimball, we are granted the privilege of obtaining physical bodies, "which become the permanent tabernacle of our spirits through the eternities." (*The Teaching of Spencer W. Kimball,* p. 31). It is this combination of spirit and physical body, resurrected and made eternal through the atonement of Christ, that allows us to seek after a fulness of joy, or to become as God. Joseph Smith said, "We came to this earth that we might have a body and present it pure before God in the celestial kingdom. The great principle of happiness [or Godhood] consists in having a body." (*Teaching of the Prophet Joseph Smith,* p. 181.) And, "No person can have salvation except through a tabernacle." (Ibid., p. 297.)

Being Baptized

The second step, that of being baptized for a remission of sins, and as a token that we are entering into Christ's Church, is the first step required for entrance into the celestial kingdom. Joseph Smith states, "A man may be saved, after the judgment, in the terrestrial kingdom, or in the telestial kingdom, but he can never see the celestial kingdom of God, without being born of water and the Spirit." (*Teachings of the Prophet Joseph Smith,* p. 12.)

Being Endowed

The third step, that of receiving our individual endowments in the holy temple, we have discussed at length in chapter 16 of this volume. But as an additional thought, the endowment is the next step, after baptism, if we are to secure a place with the Church of the Firstborn in the celestial kingdom. As Joseph Smith said, "I spent the day in the upper part of the story, . . . instructing [the brethren] in the principles and order of the Priesthood, attending to washings, anointings, endowments and the communication of keys . . . and all those plans and principles by which anyone is enabled to secure the fullness of those blessings which have been prepared for the Church of the Firstborn, and come up and abide in the presence of the Eloheim in the eternal worlds." (*Teachings of the Prophet Joseph Smith,* p. 237.)

Being Married Eternally

The fourth step, the joining with an eternal companion in the new and everlasting covenant of marriage, is the first of these seven steps in which two people must join together in order to obtain the blessing. Again, the Prophet Joseph Smith said: "Except a man and his wife enter into an everlasting covenant and be married for eternity, while in this probation, by the power and authority of the Holy Priesthood, they will cease to increase when they die; that is, they will not have any children after the resurrection. But those who are married by the power and authority of the priesthood in this life, and continue without committing sin against the Holy Ghost, will continue to increase and have children in the celestial glory." (*Teachings of the Prophet Joseph Smith,* pp. 300–301.)

We must be very careful, as we read Joseph's words, to remember that "this life" refers not to the period between birth and death but to the time between birth and the resurrection. (See Alma 40.) This becomes very important when we realize that for many righteous Latter-day Saints, marriage may not occur during mortality. Thus, temple work has been ordained of God that the ordinance may be performed, in mortality and by proxy, for those to whom the opportunity of marriage has been denied but who in the spirit world have selected a companion and are now ready for it.

As President Ezra Taft Benson has stated, "Young women, you are not required to lower your standards to get a husband. Keep yourselves attractive, maintain high standards, place yourselves in a position to meet worthy men, and be engaged in constructive work. Then, if you are married later than sooner—if you even have to wait until the next life to get a choice man—God will make up the difference to you. Time is numbered only to man. God has your eternal perspective in mind." (*The Teachings of Ezra Taft Benson,* p. 532.) We assume that this injunction applies to brethren who are denied the opportunity of marriage as well.

Being Called to the Family of Christ

Since we have already discussed at length the fifth step, that of being called as a son or daughter of Christ, let's move on briefly to the sixth step, the election. This, of course, means being elected to the General Assembly and Church of the Firstborn, Christ's eternal church. (See Hebrews 12:22–24.)

Being Elected

The Lord explains what it means to receive this election: "Whoso is faithful unto the obtaining of these two priesthoods of which I have spoken, and the magnifying their calling, are sanctified by the Spirit unto the renewing of their bodies. They become the sons of Moses and of Aaron and the seed of Abraham, and the church and kingdom, and the elect of God. And also all they who receive this priesthood receive me, saith the Lord; For he that receiveth my servants receiveth me; And he that receiveth me receiveth my Father; And he that receiveth my Father receiveth my Father's kingdom; therefore all that my Father hath shall be given unto him

262

[joint heirship]. And this is according to the oath and covenant which belongeth to the Priesthood." (D&C 84:33–39.)

Of course the scripture goes on, giving promises and warnings to all priesthood holders. But the basic idea is that we are to be true and faithful in our callings from the Lord. If we are, the Holy Ghost sanctifies, or purifies, us so that our bodies are renewed as bodies of light rather than bodies of darkness. (See D&C 50:24; 88:24.) After this, we are in a position to receive even greater light and knowledge than before (ibid.; see also D&C 88:67), the personal revelation that Nephi said we are to feast upon as the words of Christ. It is under such conditions that Christ declares us to be his friends as well as his sons and daughters. As Christ declared: "Ye are my friends, if ye do whatsoever I command you. Henceforth I call you not servants; for the servant knoweth not what his lord doeth: but I have called you friends; for all things that I have heard of my Father I have made known unto you." (John 15:14–15.)

Next, as friends of Christ, we are worthy to be elected or adopted into the family and lineage of the prophets Moses, Aaron, and Abraham, which is also the family of Christ, and to use our temple endowment with more power. And of course this great and royal family of Christ's is actually the church and kingdom and the elect of God, Christ's General Assembly and Church of the Firstborn. As Christ declared through Joseph Smith: "And all those who are begotten through me [Christ's children or family] are partakers of the glory of the [Father], and are the church of the Firstborn." (D&C 93:22. See also Hebrews 12:23; D&C 76:54, 67, 71, 94, 102; 78:21; 88:5; 107:19.)

We use the word *election* and wonder what it means and how it will be accomplished. We will attempt to answer this with another question. How are members accepted into a new position here in the earthly church? Their names are presented by one in authority, and then the members sustain them (or do not sustain them) by the raising of the right hand; by an election.

By the same token, it is our understanding that when we, through our diligent faith, repentance, and godly sorrow, are called to membership in Christ's eternal family and church, then we must also be elected or sustained in a like manner. Our names will undoubtedly be presented by Christ (the one in authority, who has declared us to be his family and friends) to his church, and by their vote, or election, those who are already part of that august and glorified group, the General Assembly and Church of the Firstborn, will accept or reject our membership and position with them. If they sustain us by the raising of their right hands, we will have been elected.

As the Lord declared to Joseph Smith's wife, Emma: "Hearken unto the voice of the Lord your God, while I speak unto you, Emma Smith, my daughter; for verily I say unto you, all those who receive my gospel are sons and daughters in my kingdom. . . . Behold, thy sins are forgiven thee, and thou art an elect lady, whom I have called." (D&C 25:1, 3.)

Simply stated, we are called as sons or daughters of Christ and then elected or sustained to the position of membership in his family, which is also his eternal church.

Calling and Election Made Sure

But even yet there remains a great deal to do, for apparently this calling and election are provisional. The Apostle Peter wrote: "Give diligence to make your calling and election sure: for if ye do these things, ye shall never fall," and "We have also a more sure word of prophecy; whereunto ye do well that ye take heed." (2 Peter 1:10, 19.) Speaking frequently on this same topic, Joseph Smith said: "There is some grand secret here, and keys to unlock the subject. Notwithstanding the apostle [Peter] exhorts them to add to their faith virtue, knowledge, temperance, etc., yet he exhorts them to make their calling and election sure. . . . They then would want that more sure word of prophecy, that they were sealed in the heavens and had the promise of eternal life in the kingdom of God. Then, having this promise sealed unto them, it was an anchor to the soul, sure and steadfast." (*Teachings of the Prophet Joseph Smith,* p. 298.) On another occasion he declared: "Let [a person] continue to humble himself before God, hungering and thirsting after righteousness, and living by every word of God, and the Lord will soon say to him, Son, thou shalt be exalted. When the Lord has thoroughly proved him, and finds that the man is determined to serve him at all hazards, then the man will find his calling and election made sure, and it will be his privilege to receive the other comforter, which the Lord hath promised the Saints." (Ibid., p. 150.)

And what are Peter and Joseph Smith talking about? They are saying that we must make our callings as sons or daughters of Christ, as well as our election to membership in the General Assembly and Church of the Firstborn, a sure thing, through what is called the more sure word of prophecy. In other words, we are to seek a divine guarantee that our calling and election will be eternally valid.

The Lord says: "The more sure word of prophecy means a man's knowing that he is sealed up unto eternal life, by revelation and the spirit of prophecy, through the power of the Holy Priesthood." (D&C 131:5.)

Joseph concluded: "I would exhort you to go on and continue to call upon God until you make your calling and election sure for yourselves by obtaining this more sure word of prophecy, [but you must] wait patiently for the promise until you obtain it." (*The Words of Joseph Smith,* p. 202.)

Further, it is at this stage of our spiritual progression that we are given full power to use our endowment, the keys of the holy priesthood. As Brigham Young declared: "The ordinances of the house of God are expressly for the Church of the Firstborn." (*Discourses of Brigham Young,* p. 397.) What motivation that should give us as Latter-day Saints, as we strive for the further light and knowledge that the Lord has promised the faithful!

Joint-Heirs with Christ

Once our calling and election have been made sure, then we are given the privilege of being made joint-heirs with Jesus Christ to all that the Father has. As Elder Bruce R. McConkie stated: "It is perfectly clear that faithful saints become the sons and daughters of Jesus Christ by adoption. But there is more than this to the doctrine of becoming sons of God. Those who so obtain are adopted also into the family of Elohim. They become his adopted sons so that they can receive, inherit, and possess along with his natural Son. . . .

"Now here is a wondrous presumption, one that neither Paul nor any sane man would dare make, unless its verity burst upon him by the spirit of revelation. It is a case of a man making himself a God. It is a plain statement that mortal man shall inherit equally with Christ. It is the promise: 'All that my Father hath shall be given unto him.' (D&C 84:38.) The reasoning is perfect. The Father had a Son, a natural Son, his own literal Seed, the Offspring of his body. This Son is his heir. As an heir he inherits all things from his Father — all power, all might, all dominion, the world, the universe, kingship, eternal exaltation, all things. But our revelations speak of men being exalted also and of their ascending the throne of eternal power. How is it done? Paul has explained it perfectly. They are adopted into the family of the Father. They become joint-heirs with his natural Son, 'For it became him, for whom are all things, and by whom are all things, in bringing many sons unto glory, to make the captain of their salvation perfect.' (Heb. 2:10.) . . .

266

"As to the infinite scope of the laws of adoption and sonship, the voice from heaven spoke also to Joseph Smith and Sidney Rigdon, bearing testimony that the Lamb of God is the Only Begotten of the Father, and saying: 'That by him, and through him, and of him, the worlds are and were created, and the inhabitants thereof are begotten sons and daughters unto God.' (D&C 76:21–24.) This means that through the infinite and eternal atonement, those who are true and faithful among all the endless creations of Christ are adopted into the family of the Father as heirs, as joint-heirs, who will with him receive, inherit, and possess all that the Father hath." (*The Promised Messiah*, pp. 354–57.)

The Second Comforter

Once this has happened, and we have become joint-heirs with Christ to all that the Father has, then we will be granted the privilege of associating with the Gods themselves, even while yet in mortality. As Joseph Smith said, "Then the man will find his calling and his election made sure, then it will be his privilege to receive the other comforter, which the Lord hath promised the Saints, as is recorded in the testimony of St. John, in the 14th chapter, from the 12th to the 27th verses." (*Teachings of the Prophet Joseph Smith*, p. 150.)

Joseph then quoted many of these verses and concluded: "Now what is this other comforter? It is no more nor less than the Lord Jesus Christ Himself; and this is the sum and substance of the whole matter; that when any man obtains this last Comforter, he will have the presence of Jesus to attend him, or appear unto him from time to time, and even He will manifest the Father to him, and they will take up their abode with him, and the visions of the heavens will be opened unto him, and the Lord will teach him face to face, and he may have a perfect knowledge of the mysteries of the Kingdom of God; and this is the state and place the ancient Saints arrived at when they had such glorious visions—Isaiah, Ezekiel, John upon the Isle of Patmos, St. Paul in the three heavens, and all the Saints who held communion with the general assembly and Church of the Firstborn." (Ibid., pp. 150–51.) Wondrous promises, borne out through numerous scriptural references. (See JST, Exodus 33:11, 20; Matthew 5:8; 1 John 3:2–3; 3 Nephi 12:8; Ether 3:19–20; Moses 1:2, 11; D&C 50:40–45; 67:10–14; 76:114–18; 84:19, 25; 88:68–75; 93:1; 97:15–17; 101:37–38; 107:19; 130:3.) But it must all begin with crying unto the Lord until we have obtained a forgiveness of our sins and a mighty change of heart. It must begin with sincerely desiring to stand in holy places, being not moved until the day of the Lord's coming.

We Are Not to Be Discouraged

We know that all we have discussed can be greatly discouraging, especially when we remember that we are so imperfect and filled with weaknesses. We can look at these lofty spiritual goals and throw our hands into the air in despair, certain that we will never make it. Both of us feel that way regularly. But allowing such an attitude to remain with us would be a mistake, for these goals are within our reach. We may need to develop great patience with our own imperfections, but we can receive the blessings the Lord desires to give us. That is why he sent us here. As the Lord says, we must "continue in patience until [we] are perfected." (D&C 67:13.)

It is likely, however, that most of us are doing much better than we think. Elder Bruce R. McConkie stated: "I'd like to append to them the fact—and this is a true gospel verity—that everyone in the Church who is on the straight and narrow path, who is striving and struggling and desiring to do what is right, though far from perfect in this life; if he passes out of this life while he's on the straight and narrow, he's going to go on to an eternal reward in his Father's kingdom.

"You don't need to get a complex or get a feeling that you have to be perfect to be saved. You don't. There's only been one perfect person, and that's the Lord Jesus, but in order to be saved in the Kingdom of God and in order to pass the test of mortality, what you have to do is get on the straight and narrow path—thus charting a course leading to eternal life—and then, being on that path, pass out of this life in full fellowship. I'm not saying that you don't have to keep the commandments. I'm saying you don't have to be perfect to be saved. The way it operates is this: you get on the path that's named the 'straight and narrow.' You do it by entering the gate of repentance and baptism. The straight and narrow path leads from the gate of repentance and baptism, a very great distance, to a reward that's called eternal life. If you're on that path and pressing forward, and you die, you'll never get off the path. There is no such thing as falling off the straight and narrow path in the life to come, and the reason is that this life is the time that is given to men to prepare for eternity. Now is the time and the day of your salvation, so if you're working zealously in this life—though you haven't fully overcome the world and you haven't done all you hoped you might do—you're still going to be saved. You don't have to do what Jacob said, 'Go beyond the mark.' You don't have to live a life that's truer than true. You don't have to have an excessive zeal that becomes fanatical and unbalancing. What you have to do is stay in the mainstream of the Church and live as upright and decent people in the Church—keeping the commandments, paying your tithing, serving in the organizations of the Church, loving the Lord, staying on the straight and narrow path. If you're on that path when death comes—because this is the time and day appointed, this is the probationary estate—you'll never fall off from it, and, for all practical purposes, your calling and election is made sure." ("The Probationary Test of Mortality," address given at the University of Utah, January 10, 1982, p. 11.)

Praises to God

In conclusion, may we take a moment to express some personal feelings we share concerning our Savior, the Lord Jesus Christ, and the gospel he has provided for us. We are the first to acknowledge our own incredible ignorance when it comes to the things of eternity. Still, we are trying to learn, and as we do so, the power and magnitude and glory of Christ's gospel continue to grow beyond our comprehension. Truly has our Savior shown us the path we must tread to be delivered in the coming day. Truly has his atonement provided us with the ability to become clean, that we might be found worthy of divine protection. No wonder the poets wrote, "I Stand All Amazed" and "How Great Thou Art!" Whenever we think of the magnitude of that gift; whenever we cast our minds back to that glorious moment of peace and knowledge and understanding that came into our own lives, then we, too, are compelled to sing the praises of Almighty God!

"Hear, O ye heavens," we exclaim, with words that are the prophet's and yet we hope are also becoming ours, "and give ear, O earth, and rejoice ye inhabitants thereof, for the Lord is God, and beside him there is no Savior. Great is his wisdom, marvelous are his ways, and the extent of his doings none can find out. His purposes fail not, neither are there any who can stay his hand. From eternity to eternity he is the same, and his years never fail. For thus saith the Lord—I, the Lord, am merciful and gracious unto those who fear me, and delight to honor those who serve me in righteousness and in truth unto the end. Great shall be their reward and eternal shall be their glory. And to them will I reveal all mysteries, yea, even all the hidden mysteries of my kingdom from days of old, and for ages to come, will I make known unto them the good pleasure of my will concerning all things pertaining to my kingdom. Yea, even the wonders of eternity shall they know, and things to come will I show them, even the things of many generations. And their wisdom shall be great, and their understanding reach to heaven; and before them the wisdom of the wise shall perish, and the understanding of the prudent shall come to naught. For by my Spirit will I enlighten them, and by my power will I make known unto them the secret acts of my will—yea, even those things which eye hath not seen, nor ear heard, nor yet entered into the heart of man." (D&C 76:1–10.)

Father, we exclaim in hushed and reverent tones, praise be to thy holy name! Praise and honor and glory be unto thee forever. Blessed be the name of thy Son, even Jehovah, the Redeemer, God of heaven and earth, spiritual father of all those who seek him earnestly and do not faint! Please grant us the power to stand in holy places at all times and under all conditions. Please grant us the privilege of belonging to thy holy family, even the family of thy Beloved Son, Jesus Christ.

As Nephi once said, in words that are beginning to ring so clearly to the ears of our understanding, "Rejoice, O my heart, and cry unto the Lord, and say: O Lord, I will praise thee forever; yea, my soul will rejoice in thee, my God and the rock of my salvation. Behold, my voice shall forever ascend up unto thee, my rock and mine everlasting God." (2 Nephi 4:30, 35.)

Index

Abraham, seed of, 199
Abrea, Angel, 234–35
Agency: exercising, to avoid Satan's influence, 99–100; children possess, 217–18; definition of, 225; is eternal principle, 225–26; conditions of existence of, 226; limits to, we ourselves impose, 228, 238; creates accountability, 231
Alcohol: profits involved in, 135; wide promotion of, 138; deaths and other costs related to, 142–43
Alma the Elder, 208–9
Alma the Younger, 210, 244–46
America: war in, 23, 31, 40; promises of, contingent upon righteousness, 36–37, 38; as land of desolation, 40–54
American Academy of Pediatrics, drug study prepared by, 141–42
Anger: God's wrath differentiated from, 7
Apostasy, individual: signs of, 85;

resulting from sexual promiscuity, 157–59
Asking, law of, 185

Baptism, 260
Benjamin, King, 208
Bennett, William H., 152–53
Benson, Ezra Taft: on preservation of U.S. constitution, 35; on urgency of moving forward Book of Mormon, 60; on standing in holy places, 71–72; on sin of pride, 93; on Lord's preparing his prophets, 110; on food storage, 115; on avoiding debt, 118–21; on using agency to be obedient, 125; on dangers of harmful substances, 138; on controlling thoughts, 144; on avoiding pornographic materials, 144; on offensiveness of rock music, 146; on self-indulgence, 148; on mothers staying home, 149; on Word of Wisdom, 150, 151; on covenant of

273

Sariah, 213–14

Satan: leads people by flaxen cords, 93–94, 125; literal reality of, 95–96; ambition of, 96; laughter of, 96–97; varying tactics of, 97–98; avoiding influence of, 98–100; campaigns of, promoting illicit sex, 154; takes away light and truth, 230–31

Second Comforter, 267–68

Second coming of Christ, signs to precede, 5

Secret combinations: Book of Mormon warns of, 132–34; illicit drugs as product of, 134–36

Self-indulgence, 130–31; mental, 144–46; patterns of, taught to children, 148–49

Servants or handmaidens of God, 236, 237–38

Sexual promiscuity: as form of greed, 103; Satan's concern with promoting, 154; Latter-day Saints succumbing to, 154–55; misunderstanding seriousness of, 156; Spirit lost as consequence of, 157; leads to denial of faith, 157–59; fear resulting from, 159–60

Sexual purity: covenants regarding, 155

Signs of the times: natural disasters, 3–4; war, 4; prophecies detailing, 5–6; act as both chastisements and wrath, 17–18; to begin with God's own house, 19–20; outlined by Brigham Young, 28–29

Smith, Emma, 264

Smith, George Albert, on war, 31

Smith, Joseph: prophecies of, on war, 26–28, 40–41; on U.S. constitution hanging by thread, 31–32; on Saints in Rocky Mountains, 67–68; gaining

witness of, as prophet, 75; on spirit of prophecy, 76; on having power over Satan, 99–100; on bounds of wicked spirits, 100; on detecting false personages, 101; on purity, 155; on searching into mysteries of godliness, 163; keys given to, 165–66; on preparing to understand endowment, 168; on priesthood keys, 169, 170; on need for endowment, 170, 261; on God's infinite knowledge, 176–77; on obtaining truth through revelation, 179–80; on growing into principle of revelation, 186–87; on prayer and obedience leading to understanding, 188–89; glowed under influence of Holy Ghost, 196; on influence of Holy Ghost on seed of Abraham, 198–99; on first principles of gospel, 204; on sealing of families, 218; on temptation and agency, 226; progression of, 234–35; on calling and election made sure, 238–39, 265; on having physical body, 260; on baptism, 260; on eternal marriage, 261; on more sure word of prophecy, 265; on Second Comforter, 267–68

Smith, Joseph F.: on judgments of God, 20; on priesthood keys, 166

Smith, Joseph Fielding: on refuge of Zion, 68; on being faithful to covenants, 73; on spiritual versus secular education, 79–80; on priesthood blessings promised to sisters, 173–74

Sons and daughters of Jesus Christ, 236–37, 248–52; blessings available to, 252; justification of, 252–54; sanctification of, 256–58

Spirituality: definition of, 204–5;

279

281

Books by Blaine M. and/or Brenton G. Yorgason

Spiritual Survival in the Last Days
The Warm Spirit
Here Stands a Man
Into the Rainbow
Roger and Sybil Ferguson Biography
  (private printing)
Sacred Intimacy
Little Known Evidences of the Book of
  Mormon
Decision Point
Pardners: Three Stories on Friendship
In Search of Steenie Bergman
  (Soderberg Series #5)
KING — The Life of Jerome Palmer King
  (private printing)
The Greatest Quest
Seven Days For Ruby (Soderberg
  Series #4)
Dirty Socks and Shining Armor — A Tale
  from Camelot
The Eleven Dollar Surgery
Becoming
Bfpstk and the Smile Song (out of print)
The Shadow Taker
Tales from the Book of Mormon
Brother Brigham's Gold (Soderberg
  Series #3)
Ride the Laughing Wind
The Miracle
The Thanksgiving Promise
Chester, I Love You (Soderberg
  Series #2)
Double Exposure
Seeker of the Gentle Heart
The Krystal Promise
A Town Called Charity, and Other
  Stories about Decisions

The Bishop's Horse Race (Soderberg
  Series #1)
And Should We Die
Windwalker (movie version — out of
  print)
The Windwalker
Others
Charlie's Monument
From First Date to Chosen Mate
Tall Timber (out of print)
Miracles and the Latter-day Teenager
  (out of print)
From Two to One
From This Day Forth
Creating a Celestial Marriage
  (textbook — out of print)
Marriage and Family Stewardships
  (textbook)

"Gospel Power Series"

1: Binding the Lord
2: The Sword of Testimony
3: Receiving Answers to Prayer
4: How to Repent
5: Satan and His Host
6: Obtaining Priesthood Power
7: The Problem with Immorality
8: Agency, Spiritual Progression,
  and the Mighty Change
9: Seeking Wealth
10: A Gift of Dogfood
11: To Mothers, from the Book of
  Mormon
12: Cory and the Horned Toad

and more . . .